Children's Anxiety

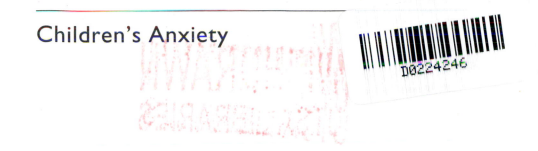

Children's Anxiety: A Contextual Approach provides an introduction to anxiety in children and teenagers, emphasising the importance of understanding the life circumstances of young people. The book provides an up-to-date account of research on the developmental, familial and social context of child anxiety, along with nine vibrant and detailed case studies illustrating the ways in which young people can be helped to deal with serious and complex anxiety problems.

In order to begin to understand complex anxiety within children's life circumstances Part 1 of the book provides the reader with a developmental framework for thinking about children's anxiety. Part 2 then presents nine in-depth case studies, organised not by the type or nature of anxiety but by the context within which problematic anxiety can occur. Part 3 acts a summary of the key points emerging from the clinical case studies.

This book will be essential reading for those working and training in the specialist field of child mental health, as well as community and hospital professionals working with children and young people, including teachers, doctors, social workers and nurses.

Peter Appleton is a chartered clinical psychologist in Cambridge, and Honorary Consultant Clinical Psychologist at the Bedfordshire and Luton Mental Health and Social Care Partnership NHS Trust.

Contributors: Peter Appleton, Helen Bell, Mandy Bryon, Andrew Edge, Ayla Humphrey, Clare Jackson, Miriam Richardson, David Trickey, Clare White.

In this outstanding volume Peter Appleton and his colleagues show that to understand and treat a child's anxiety, it is essential to take account of the social context within which it occurs – whether it be war, domestic violence, child abuse, out-of-home placement, parental separation, parental mental health problems or childhood disability. This book presents a developmental and systemic framework for conceptualizing children's anxieties, and a fascinating series of complex case studies written by experienced clinicians. *Children's Anxiety* will be of interest to all mental health professionals who provide clinical services to young people in clinical and educational settings.

Alan Carr, PhD, Professor Clinical Psychology,
University College Dublin, Ireland

This book provides a refreshing approach towards understanding the development and maintenance of anxiety in children, with chapters organized around individuals rather than types of disorder. Nine chapters, each by an expert clinician, present case studies emphasizing developmental context and set within a range of theoretical and clinical orientations. The volume forms a coherent whole, with three comprehensive introductory chapters and a final chapter of unifying conclusions. An excellent, thought-provoking book, for research workers as well as clinicians, and indeed anyone interested in the psychology of anxiety.

Joan Stevenson-Hinde, Sc.D., Emeritus Senior Research Fellow,
University of Cambridge

Congratulations to Peter Appleton for writing, editing, and gathering state of the art, in-depth information about contextual issues in the area of childhood anxiety disorders. This book is an excellent resource for both clinicians and academics. The variety of chapters across a broad range of childhood anxiety disorders advances our knowledge not only about 'what to do' but 'how to do it', and the important consideration of family doctors as well as preventative strategies. I strongly recommend the use of this book in postgraduate clinical training courses as well as a very useful tool for clinicians across mental health disciplines.

Paula Barrett, PhD, Professor of Education, University of Queensland

Children's Anxiety

A contextual approach

Edited by Peter Appleton

Routledge
Taylor & Francis Group

LONDON AND NEW YORK

First published 2008 by Routledge
27 Church Road, Hove, East Sussex BN3 2FA

Simultaneously published in the USA and Canada
by Routledge
270 Madison Avenue, New York, NY 10016

Routledge is an imprint of the Taylor & Francis Group, an Informa business

Typeset in Times by Garfield Morgan, Swansea, West Glamorgan
Printed and bound in Great Britain by TJ International Ltd, Padstow, Cornwall
Paperback cover design by Sandra Heath

British Library Cataloguing in Publication Data
A catalogue record for this book is available from the British Library

Library of Congress Cataloging-in-Publication Data
Children's anxiety : a contextual approach / edited by Peter Appleton.
      p. ; cm.
   Includes bibliographical references and index.
   ISBN 978-0-415-41248-3 (hardback) – ISBN 978-0-415-45944-0 (pbk.)
   1. Anxiety in children. 2. Anxiety in adolescence. I. Appleton, Peter (Peter
Leonard), 1948-
   [DNLM: 1. Anxiety Disorders. 2. Adolescent. 3. Child. WM 172 C536
2008]
   RJ506.A58C49 2008
   618.92'8522–dc22

                                                                2007036601

ISBN 978-0-415-41248-3 (hbk)
ISBN 978-0-415-45944-0 (pbk)

To Hilary, Catherine and Edward,
and to the memory of my parents

The lifelong adventure of gathering meaning from experience is in the service of two overriding motivations: to make sense and to make relationships. At the outset of postnatal life, the latter – relations with others, critically with a mother figure – is most important, but sense making is equally built into the human cognitive structure, and the two proceed in tandem.

(Nelson, 2007, p. 14)

Contents

List of boxes, figures and table

Notes on contributors

Dr Peter Appleton is a chartered clinical psychologist in Cambridge, and Honorary Consultant Clinical Psychologist at the Bedford NHS Child and Adolescent Mental Health Service (CAMHS). He read psychology at Durham, trained in clinical psychology at Glasgow, and gained his PhD at Liverpool University Department of Public Health. He has worked as a children's clinical psychologist in Oxford, Norwich, North Wales (where he was Senior Lecturer in Clinical Psychology, University of Wales, Bangor), Cambridge (where he was Affiliated Lecturer in the Department of Psychiatry, University of Cambridge) and Bedford. He has a special interest in community aspects of children's mental health – designing and leading one of the first dedicated primary care child mental health services in the UK, and contributing to early developments of multi-agency care coordination for children with disabilities. He has published on primary care CAMHS, child disability, and smoking cessation in pregnancy.

Dr Helen Bell is a clinical psychologist with further postgraduate training in psychotherapy with people with learning disabilities. She works in the specialist CAMH services in Cambridge with children/young people and their families with a wide range of mental health difficulties. She is now solely based within the Cambridge specialist multi-disciplinary team for children/young people with learning disabilities and their families. Her main areas of interest are psychotherapeutic approaches to working with children with learning disabilities, and infant mental health.

Dr Mandy Bryon is a Consultant Clinical Psychologist and Joint Head of the Paediatric Psychology Service at Great Ormond Street Hospital for Children, London, UK. She lectures extensively within the UK on psychosocial aspects of childhood illness. Mandy is a regular advisor to the BBC on factual programmes on child behaviour. She co-founded and co-chairs the UK Psychosocial Professionals in Cystic Fibrosis Group. Mandy has presented to international audiences at cystic fibrosis conferences in Europe and North America and was an invited international guest speaker to the Australian and New Zealand Cystic Fibrosis conference in August 2001. She has published on sibling relationships, adherence to treatment, transition to adult services, consultation in paediatric psychology, eating disorders in cystic fibrosis, introduction of oral feeding in tube-fed children and dying, death and bereavement.

Andrew Edge is dual qualified both as a Systemic and Family Psychotherapist and a Play Therapist. Currently Andrew works as a Systemic and Family Psychotherapist for the Children Looked After Service, a targeted team within Bedfordshire and Luton Mental Health and Social Care Partnership NHS Trust and has recently completed his MA in Play Therapy at the University of York. Andrew has previously been employed as a therapist at a community based Family Centre, a countywide Childhood Sexual Abuse Project, and a national Therapeutic Fostering Agency, before taking up his current position.

Dr Ayla Humphrey is a consultant clinical psychologist and Head of Child Psychology in the NHS CAMHS, Cambridge and an Affiliated Lecturer in the Section of Developmental Psychiatry, Department of Psychiatry, University of Cambridge. She specialises in working with children who have autism spectrum disorders, Tuberous Sclerosis, and specific learning disorders. She is a world expert in the early development of infants with Tuberous Sclerosis on which she has published extensively. She sits on the Medical Advisory Committee for the Tuberous Sclerosis Association and has contributed to British Psychological Society position papers on autism spectrum disorders. She earned her PhD at Columbia University, New York, and completed postdoctoral training at Albert Einstein College of Medicine and the Tavistock Centre, London, UK.

Dr Clare Jackson completed her Doctorate in Clinical Psychology in 2003 at Oxford University. She then worked in a CAMH service in Cambridgeshire, before taking up her current post as a clinical psychologist at Great Ormond Street Hospital.

Miriam Richardson holds an MSc in Systemic Psychotherapy and a Diploma in Systemic Teaching, Training and Supervision, both obtained through the KCC Foundation. She currently works as Lead Clinician for the Children Looked After Service with Bedfordshire and Luton Mental Health and Social Care Partnership NHS Trust CAMHS. She is a tutor with the KCC Foundation MSc/Postgraduate Diploma in Systemic Therapy at the University of Bedfordshire, and undertakes independent work within adult mental health services, plus supervision and consultation to individuals and organisations.

David Trickey is the Lead Consultant Clinical Psychologist in the Paediatric Psychology Department, Leicestershire Partnership NHS Trust at

Leicester Royal Infirmary. He has specialised in traumatised and bereaved children and families since 2000. He is often consulted immediately following a traumatic event and asked to inform the crisis response by police, social services, and education. He also offers teaching and training to other professionals and supervises research.

Dr Clare White completed her clinical psychology training at Cambridge University and the University of East Anglia. She has worked in CAMH services in Cambridgeshire since 1995 and is currently a Consultant Clinical Psychologist in Fenland, Cambridgeshire.

Preface

The purpose of this book is to provide an introduction to the subject of severe and complex anxiety in children and adolescents. The main body of the book (Part 2, Chapters 4 to 12) consists of case studies of young people and their families. The case studies are *not* organised by the type or nature of the anxiety, but by the nature of the life-context within which the young person's psychological difficulties are taking place: experiencing refugee status after previous trauma; a change of foster family for a looked-after child; prevention of problematic anxiety following a traumatic accident; anxiety and aggressive behaviour at home and school, with a history of domestic violence; anxiety in two young people with Asperger's Disorder; anxiety in a young person with learning disabilities; health anxiety in the context of parental mental health problems; panic disorder in the context of parental separation and stepfamily transition; gaining autonomy in late adolescence, following abuse and peer victimisation.

In order to begin to understand complex anxiety within children's life circumstances Part 1 of the book provides a *developmental* framework for thinking about children's anxiety (Chapter 1), a brief account of children's anxiety disorders (Chapter 2), and an introduction to community-based professional help for children with severe and complex anxiety (Chapter 3).

Most research on anxiety has tended to focus on the medical and psychological nature of anxiety itself, rather than on its life-context. Much of this research has been very productive, and we have new psychological and medical treatments that work – for some children. This book will not downplay these major achievements, which bring real hope for children struggling with severe anxiety (for instance: cognitive behaviour therapy [CBT] can be extremely successful in helping some young people overcome severe anxiety disorders). But what is *missing* in some of this clinical research is an understanding and appreciation of individual children and young people growing up in stressful and adverse circumstances – over considerable lengths of time. Our discussion of the relevant literature does therefore emphasise research that has attempted to look at *multiple* risks – and resilience. In the case study chapters we illustrate how the child's immediate life-context exerts a profound influence on how treatment or prevention of anxiety goes forward.

The range of theoretical orientations utilised by the authors of the clinical case chapters includes psychodynamic, cognitive, attachment, and family systemic/social constructionist approaches. In Part 1 I have tried to incorporate a number of different theoretical approaches to children's *development*, keeping in mind Katherine Nelson's notion of children's (and adults') 'two overriding motivations: to make sense and to make relationships' (Nelson, 2007, p. 14). In general the core literature on children's anxiety focuses well on information-processing and 'making sense', but seems to have a long-standing problem with including fully our rich understanding of children's attachment relationships. The relevance of attachment relationships to our understanding of children's anxiety is therefore given due space.

A conclusion (Part 3, Chapter 13) summarises key points emerging from the clinical case studies.

The emphasis of our book is on the *psychology* of anxiety, in developmental context.

Acknowledgements

I am extremely grateful to Emilia Dowling for her detailed and supportive encouragement, especially during the early stages of the development of the idea of this book. I am also very grateful to David Trickey for his close reading and comments on several sections of the book, and to Miriam Richardson for her discussions on theory. Many thanks to Jenny Doe, Lorraine Jewell, Jennifer Walker, Phil Chadwick, Uttom Chowdhury, Gani, and all members of the North Bedfordshire Specialist CAMHS team for their magnificent support, including our regular child anxiety special interest group. I am grateful to Jennifer Walker and an anonymous reviewer for constructive criticism of an earlier unpublished draft of Chapter 7. Hilary Appleton provided continuous encouragement and support, and detailed commentary on several chapters. Catherine Appleton provided advice at key times. I am grateful to the editorial team at Routledge for all their help. Finally I am grateful to the children, young people and families whose stories inspired all the chapters.

Part I

Chapter 1

A developmental framework for understanding children's anxiety

Peter Appleton

> In point of fact, evidence suggests that in an overwhelming proportion of cases the eventualities a child fears can be understood wholly, or at least in part, in terms of his actual experiences.
>
> (Bowlby, 1973, p. 272)

We start with four brief examples of complex anxiety, in particular life-contexts:

1

In October 1998, 400 young people were enjoying a discotheque in an old warehouse in Göteborg, Sweden. At midnight a fire erupted and swept through the building, leaving 63 dead. Two hundred and thirteen teenagers were physically injured. The majority of survivors had witnessed terrifying scenes. At 18-month follow-up, 25 per cent of the survivors were experiencing diagnosable levels of post-traumatic stress disorder (PTSD) – flashbacks, nightmares, intense distress at memories or reminders of the event, efforts to avoid thoughts and activities that might remind one of the event, hypervigilance, and difficulties in concentration. Schoolwork had been badly affected, with a high rate of school drop-out, and for those attending, difficulties in concentration, and lower grades (Broberg et al., 2005).

The majority of the young people attending the disco were from immigrant families. Many of the families had war-related experiences from their countries of origin. For those adolescents born outside Sweden, the rate of PTSD was 31 per cent, compared with 17 per cent for those born in Sweden. Immediately after the fire there were strong feelings that the public services had not done everything they could to provide help, and find out what had happened. The authorities responded by providing a special support organisation, which continued its work for three years. Many adolescents found it immensely difficult to request help.

2

Children who have seen their parents repeatedly being violent to each other will usually experience severe anxiety. Very young children can show clear signs of post-traumatic stress, following the witnessing of domestic violence (Scheeringa et al., 1995; Scheeringa et al., 2005). Flashbacks occur as repetitive and trauma-re-enacting play. If children themselves are hit repeatedly, or sexually abused, or exposed to significant emotional maltreatment or neglect, anxiety, depression, and behavioural difficulties may occur (Cicchetti, 2004; Maughan and Cicchetti, 2002).

Some children who have been repeatedly abused may go into foster care. Sadly, many children then find themselves unable to form secure attachments to a foster carer. A succession of foster homes may then ensue. The original anxiety associated with abuse (and with close relationships) is compounded by anxiety about when the next move might be. Agencies may not have the resources to provide therapeutic help for the child, or indeed to support the foster parents. This may increase the chance of additional moves for the child.

3

Social anxiety disorder (or social phobia) is a condition in which the young person fears negative evaluation or rejection by others, or humiliation in front of others (Albano and Hayward, 2004). The perception that negative evaluation by others is likely, and may have serious consequences, is amplified by intense self-consciousness. Exposure to the feared social situation provokes anxiety and may provoke panic. Worry about these specific situations interferes with day-to-day life, and active avoidance of particular social situations is usual. In severe cases the young person may not be able to acknowledge the difficulties, may have lost contact with friends, and may have withdrawn from school. Depression is frequently associated with social anxiety disorder.

Although shyness is a risk factor for social anxiety, it is only 'minimally or quite important' in explaining the development of the problem (Albano and Hayward, 2004, p. 204). In one prospective study, other risk factors include parental divorce, early puberty in girls, and ethnic minority status. Retrospective studies have thrown up a very wide range of family and social risk factors, many suggesting that parents may 'overprotect' the child, not supporting him or her in learning to approach new and difficult situations. Some parents, in these circumstances, may themselves have experienced trauma as a child, and may feel that they are protecting their child from undue distress. Some socially anxious children are bullied and rejected by classmates, confirming the child's expectation that he or she will be humiliated. Schools vary in their capacity to address the complex issues that arise for children with anxiety disorders, and for children who are bullied.

4

Children with intellectual (or learning) disabilities are more likely to develop emotional and behavioural difficulties (including problematic anxiety) than those without intellectual disabilities. Part of the multifold explanation for this association is the greater number and range of adverse life events experienced by children with intellectual disabilities. In particular, children with intellectual disabilities are more likely than children without intellectual disabilities to experience parental separation, parents being in trouble with the police, serious illness requiring hospitalisation, and death of a close friend (Hatton and Emerson, 2004). The specific life events of parental separation, parents having problems with the police, death of a close friend, parental financial crisis, serious childhood illness, and break-up of an adolescent's steady relationship, are all associated with higher prevalence of emotional disorders in children with intellectual disabilities (Hatton and Emerson, 2004). In addition, the cumulative effects of a series of adverse life events on children's psychological difficulties seem to be more pronounced in children with intellectual disabilities.

In each of the four examples above, anxiety, fear, and other psychological difficulties exist as part of a complex background and time-line of previous, current, and possible future contextual factors. These factors clearly need to be borne in mind when trying to understand the nature of the child's anxiety. In Sweden the young peoples' PTSD symptoms had to be understood in the context of their family's previous war-related experience, and the immensely complex current concerns of the immigrant communities about the fire and its aftermath. For children who have witnessed domestic violence, or have been abused within the family, there is likely to have been a history of traumatic relationship difficulties before the abuse, and there are likely to be further separations and losses for the child, some of which will be difficult to comprehend, and will therefore raise further anxiety. For specific anxiety disorders, such as social anxiety disorder, there may be additional psychological difficulties (such as depression), and there may be family and/or school contextual issues, all of which need careful account in understanding the anxiety. And for children with developmental disorders, we need to understand both the nature of the specific developmental disorder, and the child's family and social circumstances.

Anxiety and child development

In this first chapter I will lay out a framework of thinking about children's anxiety, in its developmental and life-context.

When a developmental approach is applied to our thinking about children's anxiety, 10 key themes emerge (see Box 1.1). Each of these themes will be explored in turn.

Box 1.1 A developmental framework for children's anxiety

1 No single causative factor: children's problematic anxiety is the outcome of a number of factors coming together, over time.
2 Development-in-context: the individual child developing in his or her family, a network of shared relationships, neighbourhood, school, and culture.
3 Risk and resilience.
4 Anxiety and fear as 'early warning systems' or 'defence systems' during the long period of children's development.
5 The central part attachment relationships play in the child's sense of security and safety, and their experience of anxiety.
6 Parents, carers, and families: protecting children, and providing encouragement to explore and problem-solve.
7 The key role of peers and friends in understanding children's anxiety and confidence.
8 The developing self and anxiety.
9 The concept of pathways – the individual child's 'trajectory' through his or her development.
10 Pathways to change, and turning points.

No single cause

A key message from the developmental anxiety literature is that no *single* factor in a child's background, or genetic history, causes him or her to experience problematic levels of anxiety (Sameroff, 2006; Vasey and Dadds, 2001). It is always useful to assume that there are several factors, and that these factors have interacted during the child's development.

Patrick Bateson and Paul Martin offer a cooking analogy:

> The processes involved in behavioural and psychological development have certain metaphorical similarities to cooking. Both the raw ingredients and the manner in which they are combined are important. Timing also matters. In the cooking analogy, the raw ingredients represent the many genetic and environmental influences, while cooking represents the biological and psychological processes of development. Nobody expects to find all the separate ingredients represented as discrete, identifiable components in a soufflé. Similarly, nobody should expect to find a simple correspondence between a particular gene (or a particular experience) and particular aspects of an individual's behaviour or personality.
>
> (Bateson and Martin, 1999, p. 9)

For those of us working with children and their psychological difficulties there are at least three reasons why the multiple cause account of anxiety is important. First it seems to be true! Second, it allows children and their parents not to feel that there is one original cause (e.g. mum's depression, or dad's genes, or a single trauma). And third, parents and children are themselves right in the middle of this process of 'cooking' (as are professionals, and anyone else who might be helping or hindering the child's development), so families can begin to think constructively about a *range* of ways of overcoming anxiety.

Arnold Sameroff, citing work by Michael Rutter, summarises this key point as follows:

> The two greatest intervention myths he [i.e. Rutter, 1982] identified were: (1) that there are single causes for disorders, and (2) that these causes can be eliminated by treating the individual child and ignoring the social context.
>
> (Sameroff, 2006, p. 54)

Development-in-context

In beginning to understand an individual child's experience of problematic anxiety we will be taking careful account of several factors, nested within each other, 'like a Russian doll' (Bronfenbrenner, 1979).

First, the nature of the anxiety itself, together with any other specific psychological difficulties, like depression or conduct problems.

Second, the individual child or young person 'as a whole'. This is the immediate and unique context of the problematic anxiety. Anxiety cannot be assessed and understood, and cannot be 'treated', without appreciating the individuality of the child. His or her individuality is signalled by gender, age, ethnicity, religion, interests and activities, goals and plans, personality, developmental difficulties (e.g. pervasive developmental difficulties such as autism), life history.

Third, the individual child's relationships with parents, other family members, and others who are important to the child.

Fourth, 'linked lives'. The child's life is lived 'interdependently within networks of shared relationships' (Schoon, 2006, p. 31), for instance between family at home and teachers and peers at school. These complex relationships are managed by all parties, e.g. the child, parents, and teachers. In addition all parties are themselves situated within wider contexts of influence – the parents' work patterns and culture, the child's peer cultures, and the school and educational policy setting. Several clinical chapters (especially Chapters 4, 5, 6, 7, 12) deal directly with the relevance of linked lives to interventions.

Fifth, neighbourhoods are a 'cradle' of risk and resilience for young people. Risks associated with urban poverty, such as local drug misuse, violence, and low levels of resources, are well-known contributors to children's vulnerability to (and maintenance of) anxiety and other psychological problems. Schools, which may be part of the child's local neighbourhood, and are such a fundamental part of a child's experience, can be a major source of protection and opportunity for children, but can also act as risk contexts.

Sixth, the wider cultural context impacts on all of the levels we have outlined.

Finally, it is important to remember that a child's 'social address' – social class, family size, one or two parent family – obscures the detailed understanding of children's actual lives (Bronfenbrenner, 1992). Actual lives occur in specific and describable contexts.

A longitudinal study conducted in New Zealand (Fergusson and Horwood, 2003) showed that, with increasing adversity (socioeconomic adversity, parental change and conflict, child abuse, parental alcohol problems or criminality), there were corresponding increases in rates of anxiety disorder (and other psychological difficulties). This finding is in line with many other studies – Sameroff summarises these findings as follows:

> As children often experience many risks and recurring stressors, focusing on a single risk factor does not address the reality of most children's lives. To increase specificity, it is necessary to take a broader perspective when examining the factors that may be targeted for intervention efforts. Multiple settings and multiple systems must be examined simultaneously because risk factors tend to cluster in the same individuals. Conversely, indices of successful adaptation also tend to cluster.
>
> (Sameroff et al., 2003, p. 367)

In an important study (Phillips et al., 2005), in which children were followed up from birth, several *early* childhood family stressors were found specifically to predict teenage anxiety disorders. Frequency of maternal partner change, maternal partner criminality, and higher relative number of adversities, predicted anxiety disorder, but not depression, in teenagers. When the teenagers with anxiety disorders were compared with 'controls' (i.e. not depressed or anxious), those who were anxious were more likely to have had mothers who (1) changed partner before the child was age 5; (2) were not satisfied with their marriage before and after the child's birth; (3) had experienced prenatal and postnatal stressors, and: (4) had a partner involved with the police.

Further work on this dataset (Espejo et al., 2007) suggested that young people with greater exposure to adversity in childhood, and experience of an anxiety disorder, subsequently showed increased risk of depression.

Risk and resilience

> It has been argued that the downward pathologising gaze of welfare professions may compound the problems of their clients and undermine their capabilities and resilience.
>
> (Schoon, 2006, p. 161)

Professionals are aware that families asking for help with a child's psychological problem will frequently also be struggling with a number of specific stresses, e.g. domestic violence, or continuing to negotiate the consequences of a parental separation and divorce, or adult mental health problems, or problems with neighbours, or racial discrimination, or school difficulties, or a chronically ill family member, or housing and financial stress. For many families there are *multiple* contextual difficulties, clustering together at a point in the life of the family.

However, it is important to balance this so-called *deficit* model of childhood problems with an awareness of *resilience* processes which enable some children to emerge strengthened, or at least less disadvantaged than might have been expected, from families with multiple contextual difficulties (Luthar, 2003; Rutter, 1987). Strengths which may help the individual child overcome adversity include individual characteristics (e.g. doing well at school, or doing well in a preferred activity outside school), family factors (e.g. a parent, grandparent, or family friend who has an especially supportive relationship with the child), and wider social context qualities (e.g. a supportive school, or a move to a less stressful neighbourhood). Resilience therefore is not a trait, or a specific feature of an individual (although this is often the way it is described), but rather refers to processes during development which open up opportunities and lead to successes. We shall see how important this concept is in a number of the case studies, where the intervention for anxiety was woven in with a careful assessment of the strengths within the child's complex social world.

Anxiety and fear as 'early warning systems', or 'defence systems', during the long period of children's development

Fear and anxiety are concerned with detection of threat. The threat may be real and immediate – for instance a house fire, or an approaching poisonous snake. Or it might be suggested or implied by events – for instance TV descriptions of bomb attacks on civilian targets in one's own country. Or it might be provoked by memories, thoughts or reminders of fear-inducing events – for instance memories of a traumatic event.

The 'fight or flight' concept of *fear* is well known: nature has designed extremely efficient, rapid responses to dangerous situations: fright can lead to flight, attack, or freezing. These defences against danger involve the body and the mind: heart rate increases, breathing speeds up, muscles are placed on high alert, and attention becomes tightly focused on the source of the threat and on avenues for retreat. Action has to be simple, and is controlled by parts of the brain which evolved over millenia during which protection from predators was a primary survival theme. There is usually no time to think. Fear emerges in very young children, where 'escape' frequently implies active and urgent seeking for the primary attachment figure.

Anxiety is closely related to fear, but psychologists have found it useful to distinguish the two (Barlow, 2002; Gray and McNaughton, 2000; Rachman, 2004). Anxiety implies *potential* threat, rather than immediate threat. It is characterised by wariness, watchfulness, inhibition, apparent conflict between approach and avoidance, 'risk assessment', searching memory for examples of similar situations, and 'hypervigilance'. Barlow calls this state 'anxious apprehension'. Gray refers to it as 'behavioural inhibition'. Studies of behavioural inhibition in children have begun with infants aged 6 to 9 months, usually in the form of a wary reaction to strangers (Kagan and Snidman, 2004). Anxious apprehension is part of most children's and adults' experience, particularly at certain stressful periods of life, during key life events.

Fear and anxiety are not only concerned with the detection of threat – they are also concerned with the assessment of safety or security. For children and adolescents this will in many instances involve a question of the availability or accessibility of a parent or parent figure as a source of safety, and as a resource for the development of confidence in exploration, problem-solving, and dealing with novelty and stress-inducing events.

During the experience of fear and anxiety, attention becomes highly focused on the source of threat, potential source of threat, and on access to safety. The 'narrowing' of attention may be visual, with intent looking. Or it might be auditory – listening so carefully that the slightest sound might be interpreted as signifying the source of threat. It might also be 'internal'. A physical sensation can be a source of threat – for instance if a child is afraid of developing a migraine (perhaps because a family member has migraines), then the slightest headache sensation might cause the child to focus attention on mild variations in sensations in the head region.

Narrowing of attention leads to relative neglect of other stimuli. For a child in school who may be worried about an ill parent at home, and preoccupied with thoughts of home, attending to school lessons will be psychologically difficult.

Focusing on a perceived threat for any length of time, and the planning and deployment of avoidance tactics, is tiring and draining, leaving a child or teenager irritable and unable to concentrate properly on anything except the source of threat, and avoidance strategies. One of the key characteristics of problematic anxiety is this wearing down of the person's resources, as more and more 'psychological energy' is drawn into the management of anxiety.

Avoidance

Avoidance (of anxiety and fear) has many aspects. First, there is active avoidance of *situations* that the young person expects will cause fear, anxiety, or stress. For the child who has been frightened at school (or feels stressed at home, and feels unable to deal with the additional psychological demands of school) then avoidance of attending may be a first line of defence. For the teenager who has experienced a formal panic attack on a school bus, then avoidance of travelling on the bus, and perhaps any public transport, is an understandable response.

Second, avoidance of anxiety-provoking thoughts or information (as distinct from situations) may be an equally important feature of problematic anxiety (Mogg and Bradley, 2004). If a young person has been waking with nightmares, it is understandable that they might not want to go to sleep. Or, more immediately, if a young person with social anxiety meets a new person, or has to deal with a particularly challenging situation, attention may be directed *away* from the other person (external threat cues), and instead focused on themselves.

Third, avoidance of memories is a key part of PTSD (Stallard and Smith, 2007). Memories of the distressing event are, by definition, anxiety-provoking. Young people with PTSD work hard to prevent themselves gaining access to the distressing memories.

Fourth, safety-seeking behaviours provide short-term relief from anticipated anxiety or fear, and are regarded as a *major* type of avoidance. Safety-seeking behaviours, or to be accurate 'within-situation safety-seeking behaviours' (Harvey et al., 2004), range from physical avoidance techniques such as sitting down just before an anticipated panic attack, to repeated social reassurance-seeking. Examples of safety-seeking-based reassurance-seeking by a child to a parent include: requesting information about cooking details by a child with health anxieties; requests for information about detailed travel arrangements by a child with generalised anxiety or panic; refusals to go out of the house without mum by a child with separation anxiety disorder. In his introductory book on anxiety, Rachman talks about 'the search for safety', a phrase highly descriptive of very anxious children and young people who have become preoccupied and overly focused on specific sources of threat (Rachman, 2004).

Safety-seeking behaviours, in certain contexts, are of course also a natural coping response by people of all ages, but particularly children and young people. Safety and security, during the long period of immaturity, are part of the normative developmental experience, providing both nurturance and preparation for dealing with stressful experiences (see Chapter 13).

Avoidance, including non-productive safety-seeking behaviour, occurs in all problematic anxiety, and anxiety disorders. Some young people, after a number of years of suffering with problematic anxiety, adopt a highly restricted lifestyle, staying at home, and restricting their activities at home. Fortunately there are effective therapies to help young people and their families who find themselves in this situation (see Chapters 2 and 3).

Developmental vulnerability to anxiety

Some children are more prone to anxiety from an early age. It has been shown that about 15 per cent of children are more prone to show anxiety, restraint, reticence, and withdrawal in response to novelty and unfamiliarity – and that this developmental characteristic – known as behavioural inhibition to the unfamiliar (BI) – tends to be a consistent personality feature (Kagan and Snidman, 2004; Klein and Pine, 2002). There is evidence that BI is a risk factor for anxiety disorders, although the degree of risk varies from culture to culture, depending on the value placed by the culture on inhibited versus outgoing styles of personality (Kagan and Snidman, 2004).

BI refers to the tendency to show high reactivity, fearfulness and anxious apprehension in the presence of new situations, and with unfamiliar people and places. High BI toddlers will tend to cling to their mothers in unfamiliar situations, refuse to approach new toys, and find mixing with peers initially daunting. Slightly older children will be quiet, tend not to smile, and will not initiate conversations. These children will be more likely to be solitary, at least initially, in social groups. High BI is moderately stable during childhood, and is moderately heritable (Hirshfeld-Becker et al., 2004).

High reactivity to new situations makes any transition, for instance to a new school, especially difficult for these children. It is not just the new *social* demands, but also the sheer newness of novel situations that concerns children with high BI. These are not children who will dive into new situations, to see what will happen. Instead, a strategy of careful and quiet observation will be used.

Socially, children with high BI tend to be more sensitive to punishment and criticism (Gray and McNaughton, 2000), whether from family, or teachers, or peers. Attentive parents will soon discover that gentle discipline is more effective with these children (compared with a sibling with a more outgoing personality [Kochanska et al., 2007]). High BI children will tend to be observant and sharp-eyed about parental wishes and preferences.

There is some evidence that high BI may predispose *some* children specifically to social anxiety disorder, in which the young person is extremely concerned about potential negative evaluation by other people (Kagan and Snidman, 2004). This condition usually starts in adolescence. As Jerome Kagan points out, most high BI children find a niche that protects them from frequent contact with new people, or people about whom they might have specific concerns. But for some children, a combination of other risk factors, taken together with a history of BI (which will usually include *less* experience of dealing with routine social negotiations and conflict) may lead to problematic levels of social anxiety.

There are a number of other important aspects of BI to keep in mind:

1   Most functional levels of BI have benefits as well as costs. The benefits include readiness to learn social rules, and restraint from impulsive responding (Rothbart and Putnam, 2002).
2   BI is an aspect of an individual child's functioning, but it has a 'continuous interplay' (Stevenson-Hinde, 2005) during development with parenting sensitivity and attachment relationship experiences – there is evidence that both insecure attachment *and* high BI are risk factors for problematic anxiety (Shamir-Essakow et al., 2005).
3   High BI children draw out different types of responses from parents, depending on both the gender of the child (high BI may be more acceptable in girls than in boys – at least in Western cultures), the parents' previous experiences (parents who themselves have a history of anxiety disorder may tend to be critical of a high BI son or daughter), and the cultural setting (high BI was found to be associated with warm and accepting attitudes in China, in contrast to more negative attitudes in a Canadian comparison group [Chen et al., 1998; Stevenson-Hinde, 2005]).

Problematic anxiety as 'high alert'

In Chapter 2 I will describe anxiety disorders, each of which has elements of fear, anxiety, and avoidance. For instance, PTSD includes fear responses to the original trauma, fear responses to trauma memories, anxiety about situations that might act as reminders of the trauma, and a range of avoidance behaviours and thoughts to 'deal' with the anxiety and fear. Generalised Anxiety Disorder is characterised by anxious and persistent worry about numerous areas of day-to-day life – the future, school demands, health, going out with friends, safety of family and friends, and so on.

Box 1.2 Problematic anxiety as 'high alert'

Problematic anxiety may be thought of as 'high alert' in two senses:

1   The child is experiencing high levels of anxiety and/or fear, which for children and young people may be profoundly emotionally distressing. The child may not be able to envisage any solution to the anxiety, and some children may feel that there is no one to turn to.
2   It is a signal to parents, and to those caring for the child, that there is a problem in the child's life circumstances which requires some protective and problem-solving attention.

Problematic levels of anxiety, i.e. levels of anxiety which impair the child's ability to function normally in day-to-day life may be thought of as 'high alert' in two different ways (see Box 1.2).

The central part attachment relationships play in the child's sense of security and safety, and their experience of anxiety

> In recent years, I have increasingly emphasised the importance of the attachment figure as providing the primary solution to situations of fear for human infants.
>
> (Main, 1999a, p. 853)

As we have said, anxiety and fear are defence systems. But for the child (and for the young of many species) flight or fight will not always be effective in the face of threat, especially from a predator. For the young what counts is access to an available, protective, adult who will provide an immediate 'solution' to perceived threat. Attachment theory is based on the core idea that the *primary function* of attachment relationships is to protect the young from undue risk, including predatory attack. The child's attachment relationships provide him or her with protection, during the long period of human immaturity (Bowlby, 1969).

The attachment relationship *also* provides the child with what has come to be known as a *secure base*, from which he or she can explore the environment, and play, in relative safety and security. It was Mary Ainsworth, while observing 2- to 14-month-old children in Uganda in the 1950s, who first described the development of *use of the mother as a secure base for exploration*. Secure base behaviours were seen alongside other early attachment behaviours such as differential smiling, differential crying, crying when mother leaves, following, burying the face in mother, clinging, lifting arms in greeting, and clapping hands in greeting (Ainsworth, 1967; Main, 1999b). Attachment theorists such as Everett Waters, and Klaus and Karin Grossman, believe that the secure base/exploration aspects of attachment relationships are equally as important as the emergency protection functions (Grossman et al., 1999; Waters and Cummings, 2000). This is indeed in line with John Bowlby's original approach to attachment, emphasising that secure relationships with a caregiver give the child confidence to explore, solve problems, mix with peers, and feel increasingly safe in unfamiliar settings (Bowlby, 1973).

Both aspects of attachment theory, i.e. the child's access to emergency protection (under conditions of fear and anxiety), and the child's confidence in exploration and play (via secure relationships with parents or parent figures), provide rich insights into the experience of children showing problematic anxiety, or anxiety disorders. Attachment theory is therefore a key part of our developmental framework.

Secure attachment

Following initial work with John Bowlby, Mary Ainsworth started to describe individual differences in the quality and nature of infants' attachment relationships with their mothers. Toddlers who cried little, except on separation (or if hurt, or ill), and seemed content in the presence of mother, and were able to use her as a secure base for exploring, were called *secure*.

Box 1.3 The Ainsworth Strange Situation

Attachment classification of young children is based on the behaviour of the toddler (12 to 20 months old) in the 'strange situation' (Ainsworth et al., 1971). This is a 20-minute research laboratory procedure investigating the balance of attachment and exploratory behaviour under conditions of moderate stress. There are eight mini-episodes, presented in fixed order, in which the child is faced with an unfamiliar environment, and then also a stranger. The stranger is present first with the child and parent together – then the parent leaves the child with the stranger. Classification is based on the behaviour of the child to the caregiver during two reunions, in the context of preceding mini-episodes. The child's attachment relationship is categorised, using detailed coding criteria, as secure, ambivalent/resistant, or avoidant. An additional category, disorganised, is now also used (Main and Solomon, 1990).

'Secure' 12-month-old infants were those who were seen to check back with the caregiver as they explored new toys; upon separation (in a lab-based 'strange situation' – see Box 1.3), secure infants would indeed be distressed, and play might become impoverished; upon reunion with the mother, the secure infant would greet her, immediately seek proximity, and would be *readily comforted*; most would then return to play. The stress of the strange situation was handled well by both child and mother – the 'threat' of separation had led to resolution, and return to active secure base behaviour. Follow-up research (Sroufe et al., 2005) with children who show secure attachment behaviour in infancy (comparing outcomes with those who showed *insecure* behaviour – see below) has shown that secure attachment relationships tend to be maintained throughout development, predict greater social competence with peers, and greater confidence and persistence in solving cognitive problems. Secure attachments in infancy also predict more open and emotionally congruent dialogues with their mothers at age 4.5 and 7.5 (Oppenheim et al., 2007). A secure attachment relationship is therefore regarded as a major resilience factor during childhood.

Secure attachment behaviour to a parent is not inherited (Stevenson-Hinde, 2005). The development of secure attachment to a specific parent is associated with very particular aspects of that parent's thinking and behaviour in relation to the individual child. Ainsworth showed many years ago that parental warmth was *not* the key factor (Ainsworth, 1967; Main, 1999b). Parental sensitivity (defined as seeing things from the baby's point of view, being tuned-in to the baby's signals, correctly interpreting the child's communications, and responding appropriately; *not* rejecting, interfering, or ignoring [Ainsworth et al., 1971]) was found to be associated with secure attachment. Recent research has shown that key aspects of parental sensitivity are the adult's ability to acknowledge the child's individual experience, to show flexibility of thinking about the child, and, interestingly, to talk openly, coherently, and calmly about *their own* developmental history (Bretherton and Mulholland, 1999; Fonagy and Target, 2005; Main, 1999a; Slade, 2005).

Parents' own secure attachment, as adults, is associated with their capacity to provide sensitive parenting, and predicts the infant's strange situation response to the parent (Hesse, 1999; Main, 1996).

Peter Fonagy and Mary Target summarise the intergenerational link as follows:

> Secure attachment history of the mother permits and enhances her capacity to explore her own mind and liberates and promotes a similar enquiring stance towards the mental state of the new human being who has just joined her social world.
>
> (Fonagy and Target, 2005, p. 337)

Of course not all infants have parents with a secure or resolved attachment history. Two sorts of strategy have been shown to be normal responses by infants and young children to uncertainty about the availability of a parent, under stressful conditions: ambivalent/resistant attachment, and avoidant attachment.

Ambivalent/resistant attachment

In the Ainsworth 'strange situation' (and in real-life novel or challenging situations) some 12-month-olds first tend not to explore, despite the initial presence of the mother (see Box 1.3). These infants are vigilant and wary, and unable readily to use the parent as a secure base. Close contact is actively maintained with the parent, even before separation – as if the situation already constitutes a 'threat'. On separation these infants are less able to be calmed by a stranger, and on reunion with the parent are not easily calmed. An ambivalent pattern of seeking contact, then rejecting it angrily, is seen. This pattern is found in about 7 to 15 per cent of community samples in Western studies (Cassidy and Berlin, 1994), and has been shown to be associated with relatively low availability of mother, compared with secure infants. There is some evidence that mothers of these infants tend to 'interfere' with the child's exploration. This results in what Cassidy and Berlin call 'a particular form of exploratory incompetence . . . fearful and inhibited in exploration with both toys and peers . . . in no case have insecure/ambivalent children shown greater exploratory competence than other children' (Cassidy and Berlin, 1994, pp. 979–980).

Parents of infants who tended to use ambivalent strategies have been found to be less tuned in to moment-to-moment interactions with an infant, and less predictable, than parents of securely attached children. In discussions about their own developmental histories, these parents seem 'preoccupied' with particular experiences, seem angry, or fearful and overwhelmed (Main, 1996). We shall return to these observations when we discuss taking a history from parents of anxious children.

In summary, this strategy involves increased dependence on the attachment figure, and reduced exploratory competence in new or challenging situations. One research study has shown that ambivalent attachment is a specific risk factor (amongst other factors) for anxiety disorders in later childhood and adolescence (Warren et al., 1997).

Avoidant attachment

A second normally-occurring insecure strategy in the Ainsworth 'strange situation' test is referred to as 'avoidant' (see Box 1.3). These 12-month-old infants *do* explore, but with less reference (e.g. less frequent smiling, and less sharing of toys) to mother than secure infants (Weinfield et al., 1999). At separation the infant is less likely to be distressed, continuing with exploration. At reunion, the avoidant infant does not greet, and tends to ignore, turn away, or move past the caregiver. Mary Main notes that these infants use 'restriction of attention' under this level of stressor, 'attending virtually inflexibly to the toys', and sometimes to the stranger (Main et al., 2005). It is important to note that in the home environment, some 'avoidant' infants show high anxiety when the mother leaves the room, suggesting that in the higher stress situation of the lab there is a *suppression* of the child's usual hypervigilance and anxiety (Main et al., 2005). Suppression of anxiety (under conditions of significant challenge) is further supported by studies of the avoidant child's physiological state during the strange situation – one study showed that heart rate showed an increase at separation, and remained elevated long into the reunion session, despite outward appearance of being unaffected (study by Sroufe and Waters, cited by Fox and Card, 1999, p. 231).

Mothers of avoidant infants tend to give positive, but unsupported, descriptions of their own parents, with very little specific memory of events, sometimes dismissing the importance of relationships (Main, 1996). They may be actively rejecting of infant proximity-seeking at home.

To recap so far, both the ambivalent and the avoidant strategies for dealing with the threat of brief separation in a strange environment, demonstrate particular forms of anxiety and defence, in early infancy. Ambivalent behaviour includes wary, conflictful, anxious apprehension, capitalising on the presence of the mother as protection from perceived threat.

But the avoidant pattern introduces something else – at home these children are anxious when mum leaves the room, but in the additional stress of a research lab (and possibly on, for instance, the first trip to day-care?) another form of defence comes into play – organised avoidance, and *turning away from the mother*. Bowlby first noticed the avoidance of a mother by the child, on reunion, when he was studying longer term (war-time) separations, and regarded it as representing a strategy 'beyond protest' i.e. beyond separation anxiety, when protest had failed, and when a form of detachment had begun (Bowlby, 1973). Ainsworth also regarded avoidance of the mother (after brief separation) as beyond protest, as a form of detachment behaviour, and as a part of the behavioural repertoire of children who have experienced some degree of maternal rejection of bids for comfort, when distressed (Ainsworth et al., 1971). As a strategy it involved a shift of attention (albeit unconscious) away from the mother, and an inhibition of attachment-related distress behaviours such as crying, proximity-seeking, and anger. Avoidant responses 'downplay' attachment and emotional responses, 'deactivating' attachment behaviours, and controlling negative emotions.

Disorganised attachment

Secure, ambivalent and avoidant responses to brief separations, in the 'strange situation', are regarded as organised, systematic strategies individual children have found, for managing attachment-oriented emotional and behavioural challenges. But some infants show more complex and unpredictable responses in the 'strange situation' – freezing, stilling and slowed movements; contradictory behaviours, e.g. proximity-seeking then avoidance; interrupted movements; strong fear or apprehension upon return of parent (Main and Solomon, 1990; Solomon and George, 1999). Observation of these behaviours has led to the development of a fourth category of attachment – disorganised/disoriented. This attachment pattern is found more frequently in studies of children whose parents are experiencing mental health problems, or have experienced unresolved trauma, and/or in cases where the child has been abused. Main and Solomon describe one 12-month-old's response to the mother coming back into the room:

The infant went at once to her mother at the door, arms up for contact in a full, strong, "secure" reunion response. She was identified as disorganised, however, when she turned away from the door with a confused, puzzled expression, advanced a few steps into the room, and stood with a dazed look staring straight ahead. This was an abused infant, who, on the basis of her strong, immediate proximity-seeking behaviour, had been classified as secure within the traditional system.

(Main and Solomon, 1990, p. 140)

Main and Solomon's interpretation of the apprehension seen in these behaviours is that anxiety about, or fear of, an attachment figure (as distinct from other fear-inducing objects or situations), leads to *disorganisation* of behaviour, because the child wishes both to approach and to withdraw. Fear of the parent activates the attachment system, and the child seeks proximity; however, the proximity-seeking increases the child's anxiety.

About 14 per cent of Western middle-class infants, and 24 per cent of low-socioeconomic-status infants, show disorganised attachment, whereas 70 per cent of maltreated infants show disorganised attachment (Main et al., 2005). Evidence suggests that, whether a child has been abused, or whether he or she has experienced other forms of parental emotional unavailability (chronic hostility, role reversal, regular withdrawal of affection) the trauma involved in these experiences tends to result in a disorganised attachment relationship with that caregiver (Lyons-Ruth et al., 2005). Recent research suggests that parents of disorganised infants may have experienced unresolved trauma, and/or tend to devalue attachment figures from their own family of origin (while also strongly identifying with them), think of themselves as 'bad', experience high levels of fearful emotion, and tend to 'laugh off' painful experiences (Lyons-Ruth et al., 2005).

For children, coping with these very early exposures to unresolved high levels of fear and anxiety (associated with an attachment figure) presents extraordinary challenges. A young child is not in a position to consider what to do, or where to go. We can, as adults, perhaps only begin to understand how young children survive these experiences. One solution is to 'take control'. By age 6 *some* children who showed disorganised attachment as infants have developed strategies to control interactions with the caregiver – either coercively, bossing and humiliating the parent, or using a caregiving approach, being overly cheerful. The solution, though, is only at a 'behavioural' level. Cognitively and emotionally these children show mental representations of fear, confusion, chaos, and disorganisation – evident in their play, and sometimes in conversational responses (Teti, 1999).

In research using doll-play and story-stems involving experimenter-provided themes of separation and reunion, controlling children may portray both the self and caregivers as both frightening and unpredictable, or frightened and helpless. These representations contrast with those of children classified as secure, avoidant or ambivalent. Other controlling children show markedly inhibited play. Some of the children showing catastrophic depictions in their play and stories say that *they surprised themselves with the direction the story took*, but had seemed driven by another part of themselves to portray events in this particular way. Some children show a mix of highly 'constricted' and 'flooded' material. One 6-year-old's play narrative was as follows:

> 'And see, and then, you know what happens? Their whole house blows up. See . . . They get destroyed and not even their bones are left. Nobody can even get their bones. Look. I'm jumping on a rock. Ahhh! Guess what? The hills are alive, the hills are shakin' and shakin'. Because the hills are alive. Ohhh! I fall smack off a hill. And got blowed up in an explosion. And then the rocks tumbled down and smashed everyone. And they all died.'
>
> (Solomon and George, 1999, p. 17)

As we have said, these children show controlling behaviour, either rejecting or humiliating the mother, or cheering-up or reassuring the mother. A number of longitudinal and cross-sectional studies have shown that children showing this apparently organised controlling behaviour, tend to have a history of attachment disorganisation.

Attachment, anxiety, and anxiety disorders

The attachment literature shows that anxiety and fear are part of the experience of children in the first two years of life. Studies of attachment processes during childhood and adolescence provide a rich source of information about the development of 'strategies' for dealing with fear and anxiety, and how these strategies are linked to the child's experience of close relationships (Warren and Sroufe, 2004).

Research on how precisely the child's attachment relationship experiences might be linked to anxiety disorders is, surprisingly, at a very early stage (Greenberg, 1999). There is *some* evidence that attachment insecurity and/or disorganisation might act as risk factors for anxiety disorders, particularly where children are also high BI (Shamir-Essakow et al., 2005). Furthermore, as we have seen, maltreatment and domestic violence may raise a child's risk of experiencing an anxiety disorder *via* processes of attachment disorganisation.

Parents, carers, and families: protecting children, and providing encouragement to explore and problem-solve

Throughout the sections on anxiety and attachment relationships I have touched on the roles of parents and the family.

Caregiving and protection

One primary role of parents, and carers such as foster parents, is to act as caregivers, providing protection for their child or adolescent. Protection, as we have seen, is usefully thought of as providing a 'secure base' (Ainsworth et al., 1971; George and Solomon, 1999). In the words of attachment theorists Everett Waters and Mark Cummings:

> For Bowlby, the function of secure base relationships is always to support competence development and promote safety. This function is enhanced by access to (and confidence in) a sensitive and responsive secure base figure.
>
> (Waters and Cummings, 2000, p. 9)

Or in Bowlby's own words:

> a central feature of my concept of parenting – the provision by both parents of a secure base from which a child or an adolescent can make sorties into the outside world and to which he can return knowing for sure that he will be welcomed when he gets there, nourished physically and emotionally, comforted if distressed, reassured if frightened. In essence this role is one of being available, ready to respond when called upon to encourage and perhaps assist, but to intervene actively only when clearly necessary.
>
> (Bowlby, 1988, p. 11)

Protection of the child, as we have seen in the two quotations above, involves two distinct and interrelated elements of provision of emotional security. First, to support the child being able to explore, problem-solve, approach novel and interesting things and people, and to be autonomous in an age or stage-appropriate manner. Second, to be genuinely emotionally available when a child is distressed or frightened. In older children, *perceived* availability becomes crucial, as it does in adolescents and adults. Ainsworth (citing personal communication with Bowlby) has argued that cognitions (or beliefs) about emotional availability of the attachment figure include (a) belief that lines of communication with the attachment figure are open, (b) that physical accessibility exists, and (c) that the attachment figure will respond if called upon for help (Ainsworth, 1990, p. 474).

Providing emotional security in the family

Provision of support for exploration, and genuine emotional availability, do of course go beyond individual relationships between one parent (or carer) and a child – the child may have access to two parents, and sometimes additional parent figures, such as grandparents, step-parents, older siblings, and so on. Family systems theorists and family therapists have for many years drawn attention to the *interplay* between all relationships and people in the family, focusing on relationship structures (e.g. the marital or partner relationship), interpersonal boundaries, the distribution of power, and patterns of communication (Davies and Cicchetti, 2004). It is thought that the *child's* sense of emotional security derives from family-wide processes – the sense that family bonds are positive and stable, and that family members are likely to remain responsive, even in times of difficulty (Cummings et al., 2006).

Part of the child's sense of emotional security is likely to be determined by clarity of communication, and a shared understanding of the meaning of emotions expressed by individuals in the family. For instance, if a child's normal anxiety about early days in school is understood for what it is, particularly taking into account the individual child's personality, the child is likely to feel supported within the family, and to understand and interpret their own internal experience. If, on the other hand, parents disagree, in an unresolved and conflictful manner, about the child's expressed experience, the child may feel unsure how to interpret their own experience. Jonathan Hill and colleagues talk about shared understanding as follows:

> When communications lack clarity and family members are unsure of the demarcations among domains, individuals' experiences of their own emotional reactions are likely to become a source of confusion to themselves, and in turn this may make their membership in the family fragile, further undermining their sense of knowing who they are. Self-expression is likely to be misunderstood or responded to in ways that are incoherent and confusing. In these instances, the individuals lose confidence in the communicative capacity of their own voice to effectively express their feelings, beliefs, and desires.
>
> (Hill et al., 2003, p. 216)

If a child's concerns or fears are routinely misunderstood, then they will not be spoken about confidently (I shall have more to say about this in Chapter 3). Research has shown (Forman and Davies, 2005; Hill et al., 2003) that defences against emotional insecurity include *preoccupation* – worries about the future well-being of themselves and their families (e.g. 'I feel like something could go very wrong in my family at any time'), or *disengagement* – apparently minimizing the importance of the family, or wishing to escape to another family (e.g. 'I don't care what goes on in my family').

Clarity of communication, and a 'shared interpretive frame', is also crucial for family understanding of the child's or young person's exploratory and experimental 'sorties' into worlds outside the family – forays that may, by definition, surprise parents. For instance, if a young teenager starts to mix with peers one parent disapproves of. What circumstances might lead a parent to find it difficult to understand this (or indeed any developmentally typical exploratory behaviour)? One suggestion, from Mary Main and colleagues (Main et al., 2005), is that exploratory behaviours by a child or teenager may lead an insecure-preoccupied parent away from the state of mind that had seemed optimal for maintenance of the relationship to *their own* parents during childhood, and may still therefore create feelings of anxiety. The parent may discourage the child from exploration. Current family relationship patterns might either maintain this negative process (if for instance the other parent is distanced) or challenge it in a helpful way (if for instance the other parent is able to enter a family conversation, or create 'open communication', about the meaning of the young person's behaviour).

Some studies of parenting and child anxiety suggest that if parents are unable to understand and 'scaffold' a young child's independence and learning of self-motivated and age-appropriate behaviour, then it is possible that the child, as they grow older, may find new and challenging situations anxiety-provoking. The available research on parent–child interactions and child anxiety is summarised by Mark Dadds as follows: 'high levels of control, restriction, attention to social threat, and endorsement of avoidant coping strategies are characteristic of families of anxious children' (Dadds, 2002, p. 87).

We now examine two contexts of parenting and family life which can act as risk factors for anxiety.

Family transitions

Parental separation and divorce are one of the commonest major life stressors experienced by children and teenagers. Many children come through this major life event strengthened, and with a wider range of coping skills. However, some children experience increased levels of aggressive behaviour, school and academic difficulties, peer relationship problems, and anxiety and depression. These effects can be persistent, and are made worse by ongoing parental conflict, shifting roles and responsibilities for family members, decreased emotional availability with either or both parents, reduced or changed discipline, problematic stepfamily formation, or repeated change of partner (Hetherington and Elmore, 2003).

Although the divorce literature is extremely complex, and any one factor (e.g. child's age at divorce) has a variable outcome, depending on other contextual factors (e.g. gender of child, and level of pre-divorce family conflict), a key finding is that there are certain family processes which protect the young person, and others which raise the risk of psychological difficulties. Processes which have been researched include financial status,

ongoing interparental conflict, the quality of the relationships between child
and both parents, stepfamily formation issues, the role of siblings and the
role of grandparents (Hetherington and Elmore, 2003). It is well established
that, as in stable families, a close relationship with an important adult,
usually one parent, plays a critical role in promoting the well-being of the
child (Hetherington and Elmore, 2003).

Children may express their hurt via difficult, angry, and aggressive
behaviour, which runs alongside anxiety, including sleeping problems, and
reluctance to go to school. Either or both parents may be struggling with
less money and poorer housing. Young people may have less pocket money,
and therefore have less credibility with peers. Thoughtful teenagers may
also be extremely worried, on their parents' behalf, about financial issues.
Excessive responsibilities, or over-reliance by a parent on a young person's
empathy, can contribute to anxiety and depression, and lowered self-esteem
in teenagers. Moderate degrees of responsibility, on the other hand, can
lead to greater resilience, especially among girls (Hetherington and Elmore,
2003).

Adults, including professionals, may underestimate the younger child's
ongoing anxiety about abandonment, following parental divorce. In a
recent follow-up study of 216 post-divorce children in Arizona (Wolchik et
al., 2002), aged 8 to 12 years, internalising symptoms were associated with
the following specific worries:

'I worry that my parents will want to live without me'
'It's possible that my parents will never want to see me again'
'I worry that I will be left all alone', and
'I think that one day I may have to live with a friend or relative'

Fears of abandonment 'explained' the statistical link between family
divorce stressors, and the child's psychological difficulties.

Domestic violence and child abuse

Domestic violence and abuse within the family are profoundly disturbing
for a child. One study showed that a frequent consequence of witnessing
life-threatening violence to mother is post-traumatic stress disorder (PTSD),
involving sleep disorders, severe anxiety, phobic responses, and compulsive
re-enactment of the event in play (McCloskey et al., 1995). In a study of
children of battered mothers in Arizona, children had witnessed repeated
verbal arguments, physical attacks, escalated physical attacks (e.g. kicking,
beating, choking), and sexual attacks. Not surprisingly, significantly more
of the children of battered women (compared with a community control
sample) showed clinical levels of separation anxiety or obsessive-compulsive
symptoms. These children also showed high levels of distractibility and

behaviour problems. Many of the children had themselves also been attacked, adding to their extreme trauma (McCloskey et al., 1995).

Child abuse is a known contributor to anxiety and depression (and behaviour problems) in children. In a longitudinal study (Bolger and Patterson, 2001; Bolger and Patterson, 2003) looking specifically at anxiety and depression as outcomes of abuse, it was found that sexual abuse and neglect were each linked to later 'internalising difficulties' (a composite measure of anxiety and depression). Children who were both neglected and sexually abused showed particularly high levels of anxiety and/or depression. Low family income also predicted internalising symptoms, independently of the abuse experience. In this study, one protective factor which, it was thought, might contribute to resilience, was carefully measured: the child's belief about whether successes and failures are caused by their own attributes ('internal control'), or other people's attributes ('powerful others control'), or unknown factors. Greater internal control was linked to fewer internalising symptoms among the abused children, but not among the non-abused children, suggesting that this might be a protective factor. The authors speculate that successes in areas of life important to the child may have contributed to the sense of internal control.

The key role of peers and friends in understanding children's anxiety and confidence

In the developmental framework I have focused on the contexts of the child's attachment relationships, and on family communication. But peer relationships, including friendships, become ever more important as a child begins school, moving into middle childhood and adolescence. His or her developing agency, and sense of worth as a person, is governed increasingly by the quality of relationships with peers, in tandem with important and continuing attachment relationships with parents and parent figures.

Peer relationships include not only friendships, but also a sense of participation in, and acceptance by, a peer group. This begins very early, but starts consciously to matter during middle childhood, and becomes deeply important during adolescence (Harter, 1999).

By middle childhood (age 6 to 12) children may be spending around 40 per cent of their waking hours with age-mates. They may be just hanging-out, or playing computer games, or doing sport, but this is real time during which important social experience is being gained. Children have to find their own ways of establishing and maintaining social order, and at least some of this is discovered through game-playing, where explicit rules have to be followed, and clear roles have to be maintained. Concepts of justice are developed (Cole and Cole, 1996).

Another key aspect of middle childhood is the fascinating phenomenon of strict gender segregation. Boys and girls develop their own cultures and interests, with boys tending to have larger groups, with strong dominance hierarchies, and girls more concerned with friendships and the maintenance of group cohesion. At least in many Western cultures, it is perceived negatively by peers to be seen mixing across gender, and clear boundary rules seem to be maintained (Maccoby, 1995).

Social comparison, the process by which an individual child routinely compares him or her self with peers, becomes important during middle childhood. The majority of children are cognitively competent to compare themselves in a range of specific areas, including physical appearance, ability in learning at home and school, athletic competence, peer acceptance, perceived 'good behaviour', and overall self-worth. Each of these areas may be more or less important to the individual child, and may therefore be either a source of positive self-esteem (if relatively 'successful' in those areas), or a source of negative self-views (if the individual child feels they do not 'measure up' in comparison with peers). It is helpful to check out with children which specific areas of their lives they feel happy about (in comparison with other children), and which areas they feel they are doing less 'well' – this conversation shows one's interest in the child's individuality, and also moves beyond the unhelpful label of 'has low self-esteem' (Harter, 1999).

Adolescence brings new and qualitatively different peer social experiences. There is a progressive involvement, for many young people, with mixed sex groups. The transition to romantic and sexual relationships brings with it an extraordinary spectrum of emotions, blending the young person's previous experience of both peers, and attachment figures (Furman et al., 1999).

Social comparison becomes more complex, now including a more differentiated sense of peer involvement: not only broad peer acceptance, but also perceived success in close friendships, and perceived success in romantic relationships. Gender differences in each of these areas may be important in understanding risk for anxiety and depression.

With the gradual transition to work environments, social comparison begins to include perceived competence at work.

Peer relationships are so important to children and adolescents, and they are so dependent, especially in Western materialistic cultures, on fine discrimination of perceived social success, that children who are 'different', and children who feel different, or excluded, may experience problematic anxiety.

There are many reasons why a child may have difficulty in maintaining good peer relationships, and there will be a number of examples of this in our clinical case chapters.

Peer victimisation

The extreme example of peer isolation and rejection that occurs when a child is systematically victimised over a significant period of time, is one of continuing major public concern, as a contributory cause of anxiety and other psychological problems (Bond et al., 2001). Being frequently teased, having rumours spread about you, being deliberately excluded from your peer group on a regular basis, or experiencing physical threats or violence from peers, are now generally regarded as events which should be prevented, however difficult a task that might be (Berger, 2007). Studies into the specific impact of bullying are difficult to do, as many factors other than the bullying will also contribute to a victim's distress. However, in a longitudinal study in Australia, experience of victimisation predicted self-reported anxiety or depression, independently of co-existing levels of social adversity (Bond et al., 2001).

A distinction is usually made between physical and relational victimisation. Relational violence is aimed at damaging another's self-esteem or social status, and may take direct forms such as verbal rejection, negative facial expressions or body movements, or more indirect forms such as slanderous rumours or social exclusion (Underwood et al., 2001). Although relational aggression is frequently assumed to be used more by girls, studies have not consistently shown this to be the case. It is likely that both sexes use both types of aggression, varying by context and by age. In addition it is clear that physical aggression can hurt another child's relational position in a group, raising questions about the specificity of definitions (Underwood et al., 2001).

Victimisation and rejection, by definition, hurt. Recent studies of the brain suggest that the word 'hurt', when applied to social rejection, may be rather accurate. There is now evidence that one of the specific parts of the brain involved in perceptions of physical pain (the anterior cingulate cortex) is also implicated in processing 'social pain' (Eisenberger and Lieberman, 2004). The overlap in neural circuitry suggests a common neural alarm system which has evolved to deal with both physical and social attack.

The linkages between social and physical pain perception may also apply to numbing. Physical pain can of course lead to numbing, but there is now evidence that social rejection not only leads to psychological shock, but also to reduced physical pain sensitivity (Baumeister, 2005), providing further evidence for the overlap between social and physical pain.

Interviews with young people who have experienced bullying and social exclusion within school systems suggest that moving on to Further Education can bring new opportunities of peer acceptance and friendship (Osler, 2006). An individual clinical example is provided in Chapter 12.

The developing self and anxiety

> But talk does not construct the self. Only the individual can undertake that project, through re-experiencing on a new reflective level the narratives about the self that have been the topic of talk. Out of these narratives continuity of self-conceptions (a 'theory' of self) must be wrung.
>
> (Nelson, 2001, p. 30)

Throughout the sections on anxiety, attachment relationships, family functioning, and peer relationships, we have touched on the role of the self – the child's sense of his or her agency, coherence, continuity in time – and the sense that feelings, thoughts and emotions are one's own. We have also touched on the self-concept – the detailed set of ideas children have about different areas of their lives, e.g. in middle childhood concepts of academic functioning, athletic competence, physical appearance, peer acceptance and behavioural conduct. And we have mentioned the child's overall *evaluative* sense of self-worth, or global self-esteem (Harter, 1999).

The child's self is important in our developmental framework for several reasons. First, anxiety is experienced in some sense as part of the self, or part of the self's response to certain events. Second, recent studies of the development of language, memory, and the self, throw much light on the ways in which children learn to communicate emotions and thoughts – and thereby, through social interactions with important others, learn to create meaning (Bruner, 1990; Fivush, 2001; Nelson, 2001, 2007). The capacity to organise and construct meaning, and make sense of emotionally significant events, has profound relevance for the growth of the child's self, and for children's well-being (Oppenheim, 2006). Third, attachment theory, which has formed an important part of some developmental models of anxiety (Warren and Sroufe, 2004), suggests that the growth of the self is profoundly affected by the child's experience of *close* relationships (Cassidy, 1990; Stern, 1985). Finally, the individual child will have goals and aspirations, and areas of their lives they feel positive about, which will be critical to identify in any professional work with a child experiencing problematic anxiety.

To illustrate the link between young children's experience, their descriptions of specific experiences, and the role of important others in interpreting the child's expressed experience, we can take an example from the work of developmental psychologist Robyn Fivush. Late in the second year, or early in the third, children start to use words to describe their own feelings. Later in the third year, toddlers can also describe 'what happened' in the recent past, and what feelings were experienced. Parents help interpret these thoughts and feelings. Robyn Fivush recorded a 35-month old and her mother talking about bears at a carnival:

Mother: They were big bears. Did they scare you?
Child: Um-mmm (no)
Mother: A little bit? Just a little bit?
Child: Oh, I'm not scared of bears.
Mother: You're not scared of bears. Well that's good.

Fivush remarks that the mother appears to accept the child's perception, and goes on to chat about other aspects of the carnival. But then the child returns to the bears:

Child: Bears scare me.
Mother: They scare you. I thought they didn't scare you.
Child;   I'm scary (i.e. I'm scared)

(Fivush, 2001, p. 46)

During this conversation the little girl does seem to develop an idea that she is someone who is scared of bears – we don't know what the original internal experience was, but the conversation illustrates clearly the social construction of the self's memory for events – including how anxious she thinks she was at a specific event (see also Field, 2006).

But attachment theory (and family process theory) has helped us understand something more fundamental about the origins of anxiety and the self, i.e. that the emotional availability of a parent or carer, and the capacity of a parent of carer to encourage exploration and autonomy, and indeed their capacity to engage in clear and open communication about emotions, forms the basis for a child's 'secure attachment and the growth of self-reliance' (Bowlby, 1973, pp. 322–362).

One approach to thinking about the child's growing self is the notion of an 'internal working model' (Bowlby, 1969).

A working model of self as valued and competent . . . is constructed in the context of a working model of parents as emotionally available, but also as supportive of exploratory activities. Conversely, a working model of self as devalued and incompetent is the counterpart of a working model of parents as rejecting or ignoring of attachment behaviour and/or interfering with exploration.

(Bretherton and Munholland, 1999, p. 91)

Attachment researchers have studied the development of children's internal working models through from the preschool years (using structured play-based tasks), middle childhood, and into adolescence (Bretherton and Munholland, 1999). Clinicians have been particularly interested in Bowlby's notion of 'segregated systems' – two (or more) inconsistent working models of the self in relation to a significant other (Bowlby, 1980; Bretherton, 2005). On the basis of clinical case studies Bowlby suggested that when parents reject or ridicule attachment behaviours during stressful or challenging situations, the child may respond by 'repressing' those experiences (or, not integrating those experiences into an evolving and potentially coherent self). The child may be particularly at risk of this defence if the parent or carer is *routinely* critical of the child in this type of situation. Contradictory working models of the self may develop, one based on the child's own memories of individual experience, and the other based on parental attributions or misinterpretations (Bowlby, 1980; Bretherton, 2005). As Mary Main has pointed out, children undergoing these interactional experiences will have less 'epistemic space', or less working memory capacity, to review, consider, and integrate thoughts about the self (Main, 1991).

Children experiencing hidden family violence are 'caught between their need to protect parenting relationships and their experience of physical injury, threat and anger' (Ayoub et al., 2003). Catherine Ayoub and colleagues provide the following example of play from a preschooler experiencing family violence:

> At 3.5 years, when alone in his playroom, Roger enacted a story about his father being mean to him. First, Mr K. said 'Roger, shut-up! You are the stupidest boy. You will never learn. You embarrass me; you must not be my son. Your mother must be a slut! Slut, slut, slut!' In response, Roger banged the trucks together until one of the toys broke. Suddenly he panics and hides the broken toy, knowing that his father will rage at him for this transgression. 'You dumb boy! How many times have I told you not to break your toys! You are stupid, stupid, stupid, just like your mother!'
> Later, when Roger was playing with his baby sister he called her a slut and pushed her forcefully into the chair. He ran from the room as she cried. When asked by his mother what happened to his sister, he said, 'I don't know, mommy. Poor baby, poor baby.'
>
> (Ayoub et al., 2003, p. 108)

Developmental pathways for working models of the self are still poorly understood, but it is likely that research in this area will provide important insights into the nature of children's anxiety and other aspects of psychological distress (Ayoub et al., 2003; Harter, 1999; Toth et al., 2002; Warren et al., 2000). Chapter 5 provides a clinical case example of the use of play therapy with a maltreated child who uses both narrative and symbolic play to make possible a revision of his models of self, in preparation for a potential turning point in his life.

The concept of pathways – the individual child's 'trajectory' through his or her development

> Instead of jumping from *early* to *late*, from experiences at the beginning of life to the point at which outcome is to be assessed, it has become clear that the early experience needs to be seen in the context of individual children's life paths, and that instead of expecting some particular trauma uniformly to lead to pathological outcomes it is necessary to recognise the modifying role of intervening events. Recognition has to be given, that is, to the fact that the developmental trajectories leading from early adversity to later personality functioning can take diverse forms in different individuals.
>
> (Schaffer, 2004, p. 338)

The idea of a journey or safari (Ainsworth, 1967) through life is a well-established metaphor, with many examples in literature such as John Bunyan's *Pilgrim's Progress*. But in child psychology it is only in the last 50 years that life-course metaphors have come into focus. A *pathways* model of thinking about children's development can be represented as the branching of railway tracks (Bowlby, 1973), or pictorially as a tree (Sroufe, 1997). The model is set in real-time, as a child develops from the fertilized egg, via life in the womb, infancy, childhood, adolescence, and beyond. Each developmental 'step' is influenced by both environmental and genetically-driven processes, and the child's sense of his or her own agency contributes to his or her ability to influence this process. Starting school, moving house, and other life events, may act as turning points in this process. Hormonal changes, increases in body-size, and other physical changes are equally important.

Alan Sroufe sets out five implications that follow from a developmental life-course, or *pathway*, a framework of thinking about psychological problems, such as problematic levels of anxiety (Sroufe, 1997). First, over time a child may accumulate experiences which have been stressful and restrictive, pushing the child off a potentially positive individual pathway, and on to a pathway towards further stresses, or fewer openings and choices. For instance, a bullying episode at school can lead to a positive response by school and home, giving a child confidence that he will be protected, and that he is more able to deal successfully with peer attacks. Alternatively, with less support from a school, or a fearful parental response, or a response by the child reflecting previous experience of assaults, withdrawal from usual peer relationships can be provoked, perhaps leading to restrictions of experience in dealing with stresses. The resulting pathway might take the child further away from a positive pathway of development for him as an individual, but it may also be 'corrected' by thoughtful and committed adults, or peers, or the young person himself.

The second implication of the metaphor follows from the idea of a developmental history of a 'succession of branchings', or turning points. The same end-point, i.e. problematic anxiety of a particular type, will result from a variety of different life-course pathways. It has been suggested that even with one specific type of phobia, wide variation in history and cause is likely to be found. So, despite having the same label, and similar behaviour, two different children are likely to have reached the same 'diagnostic point' via different routes (Vasey and Dadds, 2001). Clearly, the form of help required in the two cases will probably be different.

The third implication of a pathways model is that routes may begin at a similar place (e.g. with high behavioural inhibition), but will end in widely different places, some appropriate for the individual's interests and abilities, but others placing a child on 'high alert', or showing some other problematic experience or behaviour.

Fourth, change is possible at many points (Sroufe, 1997). After a worrying parental divorce, a young person may initially experience traumatic changes of residence, and uncertainty of who will be in the household: a series of turning points, each of which include finely balanced costs and benefits.

Finally, change is limited by prior experience. The longer a problematic pathway has been followed, the more difficult it is for the young person to return to a more positive route.

But is this always true? John Laub and Robert Sampson, two American social scientists, followed up to age 70 a cohort of 500 men who had been in reform school for delinquency in the 1940s. Although the study was *not* about anxiety, it perhaps has something important to tell us about a strategic, or long-term view about life-course development.

They found that many so-called 'life-course persistent offenders', irrespective of the number of early risk factors, began to desist from crime in adulthood (Laub and Sampson, 2003). Key turning points were marriage, military service, and employment stability, helped by active 'subjective reconstruction of the self' (p. 141). Other participants persisted in crime, and yet others followed 'zigzag criminal careers'. Art, a zigzag participant who desisted in later adulthood, grew up in an abusive, violent, criminal, and drug-misusing home. He was in several foster care placements. When asked, at the age of 71, if he had had any troubles as a child, Art said he had had some 'minor problems' (p. 222). Asked whether he thought that there are turning points in people's lives, he replied:

'Yes, but see, it's conditional on happenstance. It's conditional on your feeling, the event, the time the event occurs, or who you were with. It's something that's, I'd say, strictly emotional. I mean there's nothing you can put down on a piece of paper, after X amount of years, you gotta do this. You can't, because I know people, for crying out loud.'

(Laub and Sampson, 2003, p. 225)

Pathways to change, and turning points

As we have said, problematic anxiety may be thought of as a 'high alert' warning signal to the child, and his or her family, that threats to self-development have reached a level beyond the coping capacity of the young person (see Box 1.2). It is therefore a chance to review the young person's life situation, and to recognise that choices, opportunities, and changes are possible. Parents (or carers) and children are right in the middle of the process of the young person's development.

Psychological therapy assists some children, teenagers, and their families in constructing change, or creating a turning point. Many of the clinical case chapters provide examples of therapy occurring in a wider context of individual and family change.

References

Ainsworth, M. D. S. (1967) *Infancy in Uganda: Infant Care and the Growth of Love.* Baltimore, The Johns Hopkins Press.

Ainsworth, M. D. S. (1990) Epilogue: Some considerations regarding theory and assessment relevant to attachment beyond infancy. In Greenberg, M. T., Cicchetti, D. and Cummings, E. M. (eds) *Attachment in the Preschool Years: Theory, Research, and Intervention.* London, University of Chicago Press.

Ainsworth, M. D. S., Bell, S. M. V. and Stayton, D. J. (1971) Individual differences in strange-situation behaviour of one-year-olds. In Schaffer, H. R. (ed.) *The Origins of Human Social Relations.* London, Academic Press.

Albano, A. M. and Hayward, C. (2004) Social anxiety disorder. In Ollendick, T. H. and March, J. S. (eds) *Phobic and Anxiety Disorders in Children and Adolescents: A Clinician's Guide to Effective Psychosocial and Pharmacological Interventions.* Oxford, Oxford University Press.

Ayoub, C. C., Fischer, K. W. and O'Connor, E. E. (2003) Analysing development of working models for disrupted attachments: the case of hidden family violence. *Attachment and Human Development*, 5, 97–119.

Barlow, D. H. (2002) *Anxiety and Its Disorders: The Nature and Treatment of Anxiety and Panic.* New York, Guilford Press.

Bateson, P. and Martin, P. (1999) *Design for a Life: How Behaviour Develops.* London, Jonathan Cape.

Baumeister, R. (2005) Rejected and alone. *The Psychologist*, 18, 732–735.

Berger, K. S. (2007) Update on bullying at school: science forgotten? *Developmental Review*, 27, 90–126.

Bolger, K. E. and Patterson, C. J. (2001) Pathways from child maltreatment to internalizing problems: perceptions of control as mediators and moderators. *Development and Psychopathology*, 13, 913–940.

Bolger, K. E. and Patterson, C. J. (2003) Sequelae of child maltreatment: vulnerability and resilience. In Luthar, S. S. (ed.) *Resilience and Vulnerability: Adaptation in the Context of Childhood Adversities.* Cambridge, Cambridge University Press.

Bond, L., Carlin, J. B., Thomas, L., Rubin, K. and Patton, G. (2001) Does bullying cause emotional problems? A prospective study of young teenagers. *British Medical Journal*, 323, 480–484.

Bowlby, J. (1969) *Attachment and Loss. Volume 1. Attachment.* London, The Hogarth Press and the Institute of Psycho-analysis.

Bowlby, J. (1973) *Attachment and Loss. Volume 2. Separation: Anxiety and Anger.* London, The Hogarth Press and the Institute of Psycho-analysis.

Bowlby, J. (1980) *Attachment and Loss. Volume 3. Loss: Sadness and Depression.* London, The Hogarth Press and the Institute of Psycho-analysis.

Bowlby, J. (1988) *A Secure Base: Clinical Applications of Attachment Theory.* London, Routledge.

Bretherton, I. (2005) In pursuit of the internal working model construct and its relevance to attachment relationships. In Grossman, K. E., Grossman, K. and Waters, E. (eds) *Attachment from Infancy to Adulthood: The Major Longitudinal Studies*. London, The Guilford Press.

Bretherton, I. and Munholland, K. A. (1999) Internal working models in attachment relationships: a construct revisited. In Cassidy, J. and Shaver, P. R. (eds) *Handbook of Attachment: Theory, Research, and Clinical Applications*. London, The Guilford Press.

Broberg, A. G., Dyregrov, A. and Lilled, L. (2005) The Göteborg discotheque fire: posttraumatic stress, and school adjustment as reported by the primary victims 18 months later. *Journal of Child Psychology and Psychiatry*, 46, 1279–1286.

Bronfenbrenner, U. (1979) *The Ecology of Human Development: Experiments by Nature and Design*. London, Harvard University Press.

Bronfenbrenner, U. (1992) Ecological systems theory. In Vasta, R. (ed.) *Six Theories of Child Development*. London, Jessica Kingsley Publishers.

Bruner, J. S. (1990) *Acts of Meaning*. London, Harvard University Press.

Cassidy, J. (1990) Theoretical and methodological considerations in the study of attachment and the self in young children. In Greenberg, M. T., Cicchetti, D. and Cummings, E. M. (eds) *Attachment in the Preschool Years: Theory, Research, and Intervention*. London, The University of Chicago Press.

Cassidy, J. and Berlin, L. J. (1994) The insecure/ambivalent pattern of attachment: theory and research. *Child Development*, 65, 971–991.

Chen, X., Hastings, P. D., Rubin, K. H., Chen, H., Cen, G. and Stewart, S. L. (1998) Child-rearing attitudes and behavioral inhibition in Chinese and Canadian toddlers: a cross-cultural study. *Developmental Psychology*, 34, 677–686.

Cicchetti, D. (2004) An odyssey of discovery: lessons learned through three decades of research on child maltreatment. *American Psychologist*, 59, 731–741.

Cole, M. and Cole, S. R. (1996) *The Development of Children*. New York, W. H. Freeman and Company.

Cummings, E. M., Schermerhorn, A. C., Davies, P. T., Goeke-Morey, M. C. and Cummings, J. S. (2006) Interparental discord and child adjustment: prospective investigations of emotional security as an explanatory mechanism. *Child Development*, 77, 132–152.

Dadds, M. R. (2002) Learning and intimacy in the families of anxious children. In McMahon, R. J. and Peters, R. D. (eds) *The Effects of Parental Dysfunction on Children*. New York, Kluwer Academic.

Davies, P. T. and Cicchetti, D. (2004) Toward an integration of family systems and developmental psychopathology approaches. *Development and Psychopathology*, 16, 477–481.

Eisenberger, N. I. and Lieberman, M. D. (2004) Why rejection hurts: a common neural alarm system for physical and social pain. *Trends in Cognitive Sciences*, 8, 294–300.

Espejo, E. P., Hammen, C. L., Connolly, N. P., Brennan, P. A., Najman, J. M. and Bor, W. (2007) Stress sensitization and adolescent depressive severity as a function of childhood adversity: a link to anxiety disorders. *Journal of Abnormal Child Psychology*, 35, 287–299.

Fergusson, D. M. and Horwood, L. J. (2003) Resilience to childhood adversity. In Luthar, S. S. (ed.) *Resilience and Vulnerability: Adaptation in the Context of Childhood Adversities*. Cambridge, Cambridge University Press.

Field, A. P. (2006) The behavioral inhibition system and the verbal information pathway to children's fears. *Journal of Abnormal Psychology*, 115, 742–752.

Fivush, R. (2001) Owning experience: developing subjective perspective in autobiographical narratives. In Moore, C. and Lemmon, K. (eds) *The Self in Time: Developmental Perspectives*. London, Lawrence Erlbaum Associates.

Fonagy, P. and Target, M. (2005) Bridging the transmission gap: an end to an important mystery of attachment research? *Attachment and Human Development*, 7, 333–343.

Forman, E. M. and Davies, P. T. (2005) Assessing children's appraisals of security in the family system: the development of the Security in the Family System (SIFS) scales. *Journal of Child Psychology and Psychiatry*, 46, 900–916.

Fox, N. A. and Card, J. A. (1999) Psychophysiological measures in the study of attachment. In Cassidy, J. and Shaver, P. R. (eds) *Handbook of Attachment: Theory, Research, and Clinical Applications*. London, The Guilford Press.

Furman, W., Brown, B. B. and Feiring, C. (eds) (1999) *The Development of Romantic Relationships in Adolescence*. Cambridge, Cambridge University Press.

George, C. and Solomon, J. (1999) Attachment and caregiving: the caregiving behavioral system. In Cassidy, J. and Shaver, P. R. (eds) *Handbook of Attachment: Theory, Research, and Clinical Applications*. London, The Guilford Press.

Gray, J. A. and McNaughton, N. (2000) *The Neuropsychology of Anxiety: An Enquiry into the Functions of the Septo-Hippocampal System*. Oxford, Oxford University Press.

Greenberg, M. T. (1999) Attachment and psychopathology in childhood. In Cassidy, J. and Shaver, P. R. (eds) *Handbook of Attachment: Theory, Research, and Clinical Applications*. New York, The Guilford Press.

Grossman, K. E., Grossman, K. and Zimmerman, P. (1999) A wider view of attachment and exploration: stability and change during the years of immaturity. In Cassidy, J. and Shaver, P. R. (eds) *Handbook of Attachment: Theory, Research, and Clinical Applications*. London, The Guilford Press.

Harter, S. (1999) *The Construction of the Self: A Developmental Perspective*. London, The Guilford Press.

Harvey, A. G., Watkins, E., Mansell, W. and Shafran, R. (2004) *Cognitive-behavioural Processes across the Psychological Disorders: A Transdiagnostic Approach to Research and Treatment*. Oxford, Oxford University Press.

Hatton, C. and Emerson, E. (2004) The relationship between life events and psychopathology amongst children with intellectual disabilities. *Journal of Applied Research in Intellectual Disabilities*, 17, 109–117.

Hesse, E. (1999) The adult attachment interview: historical and current perspectives. In Cassidy, J. and Shaver, P. R. (eds) *Handbook of Attachment: Theory, Research, and Clinical Applications*. London, The Guilford Press.

Hetherington, M. E. and Elmore, A. M. (2003) Risk and resilience in children coping with their parents' divorce and remarriage. In Luthar, S. S. (ed.) *Resilience and Vulnerability: Adaptation in the Context of Childhood Adversities*. Cambridge, Cambridge University Press.

Hill, J., Fonagy, P., Safier, E. and Sargent, J. (2003) The ecology of attachment in the family. *Family Process*, 42, 205–221.

Hirshfeld-Becker, D. R., Biederman, J. and Rosenbaum, J. F. (2004) Behavioral inhibition. In Morris, T. L. and March, J. S. (eds) *Anxiety Disorders in Children and Adolescents*, 2nd edn. London, The Guilford Press.

Kagan, J. and Snidman, N. (2004) *The Long Shadow of Temperament*. London, Harvard University Press.

Klein, R. G. and Pine, D. S. (2002) Anxiety disorders. In Rutter, M. and Taylor, E. (eds) *Child and Adolescent Psychiatry*, 4th edn. Oxford, Blackwell Science.

Kochanska, G., Aksan, N. and Joy, M. E. (2007) Children's fearfulness as a moderator of parenting in early socialization: two longitudinal studies. *Developmental Psychology*, 43, 222–237.

Laub, J. H. and Sampson, R. J. (2003) *Shared Beginnings, Divergent Lives: Delinquent Boys to Age 70*. London, Harvard University Press.

Luthar, S. S. (ed.) (2003) *Resilience and Vulnerability: Adaptation in the Context of Childhood Adversities*. Cambridge, Cambridge University Press.

Lyons-Ruth, K., Yellin, C., Melnick, S. and Atwood, G. (2005) Expanding the concept of unresolved mental states: hostile/helpless states of mind on the Adult Attachment Interview are associated with disrupted mother–infant communication and infant disorganization. *Development and Psychopathology*, 17, 1–23.

Maccoby, E. E. (1995) The two sexes and their social systems. In Moen, P., Elder, G. H. J. and Luscher, K. (eds) *Examining Lives in Context: Perspectives on the Ecology of Human Development*. Washington DC, American Psychological Association.

Main, M. (1991) Metacognitive knowledge, metacognitive monitoring, and singular (coherent) vs. multiple (incoherent) model of attachment: findings and directions for future research. In Parkes, C. M., Stevenson-Hinde, J. and Marris, P. (eds) *Attachment Across the Life Cycle*. London, Routledge.

Main, M. (1996) Introduction to the special section on attachment and psychopathology: 2. Overview of the field of attachment. *Journal of Consulting and Clinical Psychology*, 64, 237–243.

Main, M. (1999a) Epilogue. Attachment theory: eighteen points with suggestions for future studies. In Cassidy, J. and Shaver, P. R. (eds) *Handbook of Attachment: Theory, Research, and Clinical Applications*. London, The Guilford Press.

Main, M. (1999b) Mary D. Salter Ainsworth: Tribute and Portrait. *Psychoanalytic Inquiry*, 19, 682–776.

Main, M. and Solomon, J. (1990) Procedures for identifying infants as disorganised/disoriented during the Ainsworth Strange Situation. In Greenberg, M. T., Cicchetti, D. and Cummings, E. M. (eds) *Attachment in the Preschool Years*. Chicago, University of Chicago Press.

Main, M., Hesse, E. and Kaplan, N. (2005) Predictability of attachment behavior and representational processes at 1, 6, and 19 years of age: the Berkeley Longitudinal Study. In Grossman, K. E., Grossman, K. and Zimmerman, P. (eds) *Attachment from Infancy to Adulthood: The Major Longitudinal Studies*. London, The Guilford Press.

Maughan, A. and Cicchetti, D. (2002) Impact of child maltreatment and interadult violence on children's emotion regulation abilities and socioemotional adjustment. *Child Development*, 73, 1525–1542.

McCloskey, L. A., Figueredo, A. J. and Koss, M. P. (1995) The effects of systemic family violence on children's mental health. *Child Development*, 66, 1239–1261.

Mogg, K. and Bradley, B. P. (2004) A cognitive-motivational perspective on the processing of threat information and anxiety. In Yiend, J. (ed.) *Cognition, Emotion and Psychopathology*. Cambridge, Cambridge University Press.

Nelson, K. (2001) Language and the self: From the 'Experiencing I' to the 'Continuing Me'. In Moore, C. and Lemmon, K. (eds) *The Self in Time: Developmental Perspectives*. London, Lawrence Erlbaum Associates.

Nelson, K. (2007) *Young Minds in Social Worlds: Experience, Meaning, and Memory*. London, Harvard University Press.

Oppenheim, D. (2006) Child, parent, and parent–child emotion narratives: implications for developmental psychopathology. *Development and Psychopathology*, 18, 771–790.

Oppenheim, D., Koren-Karie, N. and Sagi-Schwartz, A. (2007) Emotion dialogues between mothers and children at 4.5 and 7.5 years: relations with children's attachment at 1 year. *Child Development*, 78, 38–52.

Osler, A. (2006) Excluded girls: interpersonal, institutional and structural violence in schooling. *Gender and Education*, 18, 571–589.

Phillips, N. K., Hammen, C. L., Brennan, P. A., Najman, J. M. and Bor, W. (2005) Early adversity and the prospective prediction of depressive and anxiety disorders in adolescents. *Journal of Abnormal Child Psychology*, 33, 13–24.

Rachman, S. (2004) *Anxiety*. Hove, Psychology Press.

Rothbart, M. K. and Putnam, S. P. (2002) Temperament and socialization. In Pulkkinen, L. and Caspi, A. (eds) *Paths to Successful Development*. Cambridge, Cambridge University Press.

Rutter, M. (1982) Prevention of children's psychosocial disorders: myths and substance. *Pediatrics*, 70, 883–894.

Rutter, M. (1987) Psychosocial resilience and protective mechanisms. *American Journal of Orthopsychiatry*, 57, 316–331.

Sameroff, A. (2006) Identifying risk and protective factors for healthy child development. In Clarke-Stewart, A. and Dunn, J. (eds) *Families Count: Effects on Child and Adolescent Development*. Cambridge, Cambridge University Press.

Sameroff, A., Gutman, L. M. and Peck, S. C. (2003) Adaptation among youth facing multiple risk. In Luthar, S. S. (ed.) *Resilience and Vulnerability: Adaptation in the Context of Childhood Adversities*. Cambridge, Cambridge University Press.

Schaffer, H. R. (2004) *Introducing Child Psychology*. Oxford, Blackwell Publishing.

Scheeringa, M. S., Zeanah, C. H., Drell, M. J. and Larrieu, J. A. (1995) Two approaches to the diagnosis of posttraumatic stress disorder in infancy and early childhood. *Journal of the American Academy of Child and Adolescent Psychiatry*, 34, 191–200.

Scheeringa, M. S., Zeanah, C. H., Myers, L. and Putnam, F. W. (2005) Predictive validity in a prospective follow-up of PTSD in preschool children. *Journal of the American Academy of Child and Adolescent Psychiatry*, 44, 899–906.

Schoon, I. (2006) *Risk and Resilience: Adaptations in Changing Times*. Cambridge, Cambridge University Press.

Shamir-Essakow, G., Ungerer, J. A. and Rapee, R. M. (2005) Attachment, behavioral inhibition, and anxiety in preschool children. *Journal of Abnormal Child Psychology*, 33, 131–143.

Slade, A. (2005) Parental reflective functioning: an introduction. *Attachment and Human Development*, 7, 269–281.

Solomon, J. and George, C. (1999) The place of disorganization in attachment theory: linking classic observations with contemporary findings. In Solomon, J. and George, C. (eds) *Attachment Disorganization*. London, The Guilford Press.

Sroufe, L. A. (1997) Psychopathology as an outcome of development. *Development and Psychopathology*, 9, 251–268.

Sroufe, L. A., Egeland, B., Carlson, E. and Collins, W. A. (2005) Placing early attachment experiences in developmental context: the Minnesota Longitudinal Study. In Grossman, K. E., Grossman, K. and Zimmerman, P. (eds) *Attachment from Infancy to Adulthood: The Major Longitudinal Studies*. London, The Guilford Press.

Stallard, P. and Smith, E. (2007) Appraisals and cognitive coping styles associated with chronic post-traumatic symptoms in child road traffic accident survivors. *Journal of Child Psychology and Psychiatry*, 48, 194–201.

Stern, D. (1985) *The Interpersonal World of the Infant: A View from Psychoanalysis and Developmental Psychology*. New York, Basic Books.

Stevenson-Hinde, J. (2005) The interplay between attachment, temperament, and maternal style: a Madingley perspective. In Grossman, K. E., Grossman, K. and Waters, E. (eds) *Attachment from Infancy to Adulthood: The Major Longitudinal Studies*. London, The Guilford Press.

Teti, D. (1999) Conceptualizations of disorganization in the preschool years: an integration. In Solomon, J. and George, C. (eds) *Attachment Disorganization*. London, The Guilford Press.

Toth, S. L., Maughan, A., Manly, J. T., Spagnola, M. and Cicchetti, D. (2002) The relative efficacy of two interventions in altering maltreated preschool children's representational models: implications for attachment theory. *Development and Psychopathology*, 14, 877–908.

Underwood, M. K., Galen, B. R. and Paquette, J. A. (2001) Top ten challenges for understanding gender and aggression in children: Why can't we all just get along? *Social Development*, 10, 248–266.

Vasey, M. W. and Dadds, M. R. (eds) (2001) *The Development and Psychopathology of Anxiety*. Oxford, Oxford University Press.

Warren, S. L. and Sroufe, L. A. (2004) Developmental issues. In Ollendick, T. H. and March, J. S. (eds) *Phobic and Anxiety Disorders in Children and Adolescents: A Clinician's Guide to Effective Psychosocial and Pharmacological Interventions*. Oxford, Oxford University Press.

Warren, S. L., Emde, R. N. and Sroufe, L. A. (2000) Internal representations: predicting anxiety from children's play narratives. *Journal of the American Academy of Child and Adolescent Psychiatry*, 39, 100–107.

Warren, S. L., Huston, L., Egeland, B. and Sroufe, L. A. (1997) Child and adolescent anxiety disorders and early attachment. *Journal of the American Academy of Child and Adolescent Psychiatry*, 36, 637–644.

Waters, E. and Cummings, E. M. (2000) A secure base from which to explore close relationships. *Child Development*, 71, 164–172.

Weinfield, N. S., Sroufe, L. A., Egeland, B. and Carlson, E. (1999) The nature of individual differences in infant–caregiver attachment. In Cassidy, J. and Shaver, P. R. (eds) *Handbook of Attachment: Theory, Research, and Clinical Applications*. London, The Guilford Press.

Wolchik, S. A., Tein, J. Y., Sandler, I. N. and Doyle, K. W. (2002) Fear of abandonment as a mediator of the relations between divorce stressors and mother–child relationship quality and children's adjustment problems. *Journal of Abnormal Child Psychology*, 30, 401–418.

Chapter 2

Anxiety disorders in children and adolescents: a brief outline

Peter Appleton

> Diagnosis is a moment in a biography. But biography is a story, told according to some narrative convention, and the meaning and hence the effect of a diagnosis will depend upon the kind of story in which it appears.
>
> (Taylor and Harrison, 1976, p. 21)

> Clearly, no behaviour or pattern of adaptation can be viewed as psychopathological except in particular contexts.
>
> (Cicchetti and Aber, 1998, p. 137)

Anxiety disorders are one of the commonest forms of psychological disorder in children and adolescents, with a prevalence of between 5 and 10 per cent (Klein and Pine, 2002). Prevalence rates of *specific* anxiety disorders are poorly understood at the present time, as are the range of trajectories, or pathways of development, of particular disorders (Vasey and Dadds, 2001). However, it is clear that many adults with anxiety disorders experienced mental health problems as children or teenagers (see e.g. Gregory et al., 2007). Fortunately, it is also true that *not all* children and adolescents with anxiety disorders will inevitably continue to experience problematic levels of anxiety into adulthood – some children will overcome their difficulties through resilience processes played out between themselves, their families, friends, school, and other supportive systems (including, for a few children, therapy).

A useful preamble is provided by the American Academy of Child and Adolescent Psychiatry Practice Parameter (Connolly and Bernstein, 2007) for child and adolescent anxiety disorders:

> Children with anxiety disorders may present with fear or worry and may not recognise their fear as unreasonable. Commonly they have somatic complaints of headache and stomach-ache. The crying, irritability, and angry outbursts that often accompany anxiety disorders in

youths may be misunderstood as oppositionality or disobedience, when in fact they represent the child's expression of fear or effort to avoid the anxiety-provoking stimulus at any cost. A specific diagnosis is determined by the context of these symptoms.

(Connolly and Bernstein, 2007, p. 268)

This chapter will briefly describe each of the major anxiety disorders, and then discuss the important issue of co-occurrence of disorders. It is not the purpose of this chapter to provide precise guidance on diagnosis – detailed and excellent texts are available (see e.g. Ollendick and March, 2004).

Panic disorder

The experience of panic entails extreme fear and terror, thoughts of dying, and an overwhelming wish to escape the situation (Barlow, 2002). Some of the following cognitions and physical symptoms occur during *panic attacks*: palpitations, sweating, trembling, shortness of breath, feeling of choking, fear of dying, chest pain, nausea, dizziness, feelings of unreality or depersonalisation, fear of going crazy, numbing or tingling sensations, and chills or hot flushes. Panic attacks can occur during sleep.

Episodes of fear and panic have an abrupt onset, either in a situation causing fear (e.g. a car speeding out of control towards you), or in an 'uncued' (out of the blue) circumstance. True panic attacks last for between 5 and 20 minutes, but seem endless to the person experiencing them (Rachman, 2004).

Panic disorder (PD) is characterised by recurrent uncued panic attacks. Young people who have experienced a panic attack understandably tend to become anxious about future panic episodes, and may avoid going out (see agoraphobia below), or refuse to go to school, or not want to be far from a parent. PD is uncommon before adolescence.

According to the cognitive theory of PD, panic attacks are viewed as resulting from catastrophic misinterpretation of certain bodily sensations such as palpitations, breathlessness, dizziness, and other sensations (Clark, 1996). The person's misinterpretation suggests immediate and impending death, or heart attack, or insanity, or some other extremely serious outcome. Cognitive therapy, focusing on reducing clients' tendency to interpret sensations in a catastrophic fashion, has been found to be very effective for adults (Barlow, 2002; Hofmann, 2004).

Specific phobias

A specific phobia is a persistent and excessive fear of a particular object or event – usually specific animals, natural events (e.g. storms), blood, situational events (e.g. the dark, going in lifts/elevators), and other particular objects (e.g. dogs, costumed characters).

It is distinguished from Separation Anxiety Disorder, social and performance anxieties, anxiety about dirt, fear of having a panic attack, or Post-traumatic Stress Disorder (PTSD), which are described below.

Average age of onset for specific phobias is 6, with a range from infancy through to adolescence (Costello et al., 2004).

PTSD

Diagnosis of PTSD requires exposure to a traumatic event – the child will have witnessed actual or threatened death or serious injury, and will have responded with fear, horror or helplessness, which can be inferred from disorganised and agitated behaviour. Exposure to the event may be followed by re-experiencing, repetition or re-enactments (sometimes through play and art). Frightening dreams may also occur. Places and people that arouse memories may be avoided. There is usually strong effort to avoid thoughts, feelings or conversations associated with the trauma. Hyperarousal is signalled by exaggerated startle, difficulties in concentration, hypervigilance for all threat, sleeping difficulties, and physical symptoms such as headaches (Dyregrov and Yule, 2006; Stallard, 2006).

PTSD can occur in preschool children (Scheeringa et al., 2005), and throughout childhood and adolescence.

For some children, PTSD can follow sexual abuse (Kaplow et al., 2005) or the witnessing of violence against a parent (Scheeringa et al., 2005).

Agoraphobia

Agoraphobia used to be thought of as a fear of public places. It is now regarded, not as a phobia, but as a form of anxiety (Gray and McNaughton, 2000), frequently associated with panic disorder. It is diagnosed when the core anxiety is about a situation from which it might be difficult to escape, or in which the consequences of having a panic attack might be regarded as extremely upsetting (e.g. in a public place, or in school assembly).

Generalised Anxiety Disorder (GAD)

GAD refers to excessive worry in several areas of life – concerns such as academic or social events, or health of family members, and sometimes world events. For diagnosis, the worry must be present for at least six months, must involve several domains of the child's life, and must be difficult to control. There must also be physical symptoms associated with the worry (e.g. headaches).

It more frequently affects children from age 10 upwards (Beidel and Turner, 2005).

As with other disorders, avoidance is a common problem (Kendall et al., 2004) – school work (worrying about mistakes), school (worrying about academic evaluation), sports (worrying about social or performance factors). Repeated requests for reassurance (by the young person) are problematic for family members.

Social Anxiety Disorder

Social Anxiety Disorder is defined as anxiety about social situations in which the young person expects negative evaluation by others. These situations, which obviously may include school, are avoided, or endured with significant stress. For young people experiencing severe symptoms, there may be active avoidance of all social and evaluative situations, yet with no acknowledgement of the specific concerns by the young person him or herself. They may have few or no friendships (Albano and Hayward, 2004), and may be negatively treated by peers (Blöte and Westenberg, 2007).

Highest risk for onset is during adolescence, but it can occur in younger children (Beidel and Turner, 2005).

Separation Anxiety Disorder

Separation Anxiety Disorder includes distress prior to and during times of separation, anxiety about being separated from an attachment figure, worries about harm to an attachment figure, difficulty sleeping alone, nightmares and somatic complaints. These problems are beyond what would be expected given the child's developmental stage. It is the commonest anxiety disorder of childhood. The majority of cases develop before puberty (Costello et al., 2004).

Children who refuse to go to school may be diagnosed with Separation Anxiety Disorder, but may also experience other anxiety disorders (e.g. Social Anxiety Disorder) and depression (Heyne et al., 2004).

Selective mutism

Selective mutism is characterised by a consistent failure to speak in certain important social situations (e.g. school). It must be carefully distinguished from other types of non-communication (e.g. pervasive developmental disorders such as autism), and from normal shyness. Selective mutism is regarded as rare (Standart and Le Couteur, 2003).

Although it tends mainly to occur in young children at school entry, it can present at any age, usually as part of a broader set of anxiety disorders, especially social anxiety (Cohan et al., 2006; Sharp et al., 2006).

Obsessive-Compulsive Disorder (OCD)

OCD is characterised by anxiety-evoking intrusive thoughts and mental pictures (obsessions), which lead to behaviours and thoughts (compulsions) aimed at *neutralising* the intrusive thoughts, avoiding further distress, and avoiding feared consequences (Franklin et al., 2003).

Ritualistic hand-washing is a common compulsion (in childhood OCD), as is repetitive checking. Both behaviours are aimed at prevention of a catastrophic event (illness in the case of hand-washing, or, for instance repeatedly checking window security to avoid burglary). Child and adolescent primary obsessive-compulsive symptoms may also include aggressive or sexual obsessions, magical thoughts and superstitions, or hoarding and ordering (McKay et al., 2006).

Average age of onset is 10, with a wide range, including preschool children (Beidel and Turner, 2005).

Health Anxiety

Health anxiety refers to health-related anxieties and beliefs, based on interpretations, or misinterpretations, of bodily signs and symptoms as being indicative of serious illness (Asmundson et al., 2001). Safety behaviours include avoidance of perceived sources of threat, reassurance-seeking, body checking, and frequent use of medical facilities. Related concepts include hypochondriasis, somatisation, and abnormal illness behaviour.

Functional somatic disorders, such as 'unexplained' aches and pains, are well documented in children (Gledhill and Garralda, 2006). About 10 per cent of children attending paediatric or general practice clinics have medically unexplained symptoms. Although these disorders are *not* usually regarded as primary anxiety disorders, they are part of a spectrum of psychological phenomena which involve expression of worry and fear about the body. Cultural aspects of somatisation are critical.

Co-occurrence between anxiety disorders

Anxiety disorders rarely occur in isolation. For instance, 90 per cent of children receiving help for GAD may also be experiencing a second anxiety disorder (Klein and Pine, 2002). Between 35 and 50 per cent of children with a diagnosis of Separation Anxiety Disorder may have another anxiety disorder. Social Anxiety Disorder is strongly associated with GAD and somatising disorders. Panic disorder tends to be accompanied by Separation Anxiety Disorder or GAD (Beidel and Turner, 2005). Many other linkages can occur.

Of course the boundaries between anxiety disorders may be artificial. In a study of over 2000 Dutch children aged 10 to 12 years, the distinctions between separation anxiety, social anxiety, panic disorder, and GAD appeared not to be valid (Ferdinand et al., 2006). Similar anxiety and fear processes occur across disorders: hypervigilance and focusing of attention, hyperarousal, overestimation of risk, and avoidance of threat (Craske, 2003). Some interventions, as we will see, work with across-disorder aspects of anxiety.

Key messages at this early stage of understanding about the nature of co-occurrence of specific anxiety disorders in childhood are as follows (Curry et al., 2004):

- Ensure a child with problematic anxiety has access to specialist assessment and help;
- The young person's *own* account of their worries, fears and concerns is crucial, as well as observations and accounts from parents and concerned others;
- Specialist assessments should be for a *range* of possible anxiety disorders (and other disorders – see below).

Co-occurrence between anxiety and depressive symptoms

Anxiety disorders are also strongly associated with depression in young people. Sadness, unhappiness, irritable mood, and very low mood, frequently accompany anxiety disorders (Curry et al., 2004). Among young people seeking help for anxiety problems, between 30 and 50 per cent may also be experiencing depression.

Again there is evidence that the boundaries between anxiety disorders and depression may not be entirely distinct or clear. The following anxiety and depressive symptoms tend to co-occur: fears he/she might think or do something bad; feels he/she has to be perfect; feels others are out to get him/her; nervous, highly strung or tense; too fearful or anxious; self-conscious or easily embarrassed; suspicious; worries; complains of loneliness; cries a lot; feels or complains that no one loves him or her; feels worthless or inferior; feels too guilty; unhappy, sad or depressed (Wadsworth et al., 2001). This cluster of 'symptoms', which represent a mixture of anxious and depressive problems, is usually referred to as 'internalising difficulties'.

In children's trajectories of development, anxiety usually *precedes* depression (Crick and Zahn-Waxler, 2003). This important finding, confirmed in recent research (Espejo et al., 2007), helps us begin to understand possible pathways of development of children's psychological difficulties. This discovery is compatible with attachment theory – agitation, anxiety (and anger) are first responses to perceived threats and loss. Sadness, depression and despair may then gradually develop if there is chronic stress, lack of opportunity to 'process' loss and change, or incomplete resolution of difficulties. Learned helplessness theory would also predict this order of development of difficulties, as anxious arousal depletes psychological resources, leading to further loss of self-worth and lowered expectations for the future (Crick and Zahn-Waxler, 2003).

Co-occurrence between anxiety and aggression/ rule-breaking behaviours

Research with children with anxiety disorders, and with the more broadly defined 'internalising difficulties', shows a raised probability of the co-occurrence of antisocial, aggressive, and oppositional behaviour (Marmorstein, 2007). Equally, studies of aggressive children show raised prevalence, compared with non-aggressive children, of both anxiety disorders and depression (Maughan et al., 2004).

A recent large twin study of preschool children (Gregory et al., 2004) suggested that the *overlap* between aggressive behaviour and anxiety difficulties might be explained at least partly by risk factors within the family environment (i.e. operating for all children within any one family). The authors of the study suggest that parent–child relationships, including attachment insecurity or disorganisation, could act as risk factors for 'joined-up' anxiety and aggressive behaviour in young children.

Selective attention to threat cues is of course a key characteristic of anxiety disorders, both in adults (Bar-Haim et al., 2007; Harvey et al., 2004) and children (Vasey and MacLeod, 2001). In a longitudinal-epidemiological study of 684 first-grade children in the United States it was found that stability of aggressive behaviour was strengthened in the presence of co-occurring anxiety, when compared with aggression alone (Ialongo et al., 1996). The authors suggest that one possible explanation for increased stability of aggression in anxious/aggressive children may be an 'enduring perception of their environments as hostile and potentially harmful' (Ialongo et al., 1996, p. 453). They suggest that Jeffrey Gray's theory of anxiety and defensive aggression might help explain these findings, specifically that co-occurring anxiety may precipitate defensive aggression as the individual perceives threat by another, and 'strikes' pre-emptively (Gray and McNaughton, 2000).

Specific clinical examples of mixed anxiety and aggression in boys are provided in Chapters 5, 7 and 8.

Additional co-occurrences of anxiety and psychological disorders

Anxiety disorders are frequently associated with ADHD (CME, 2007), and with substance misuse (Connolly and Bernstein, 2007).

Learning disabilities double the risk of an anxiety disorder, compared with children without a learning disability (Emerson, 2003, and see Chapter 9, this book).

Severe anxiety is usually part of the experience of children with a diagnosis of Asperger's Disorder (Attwood, 1998, and see Chapter 8, this book).

Disorders, co-occurrence and context

A developmental approach (see Box 1.1) to children's problematic anxiety, and studies of co-occurrence of disorders, suggests a circumspect approach to diagnostic categories (Jensen and Hoagwood, 1997; Wakefield, 1997). Diagnostic categories can of course aid careful description (and therefore formulation and treatment) of a child's difficulties – this benefit should not be underestimated (see Chapter 8 for a useful example of the benefits of careful diagnosis). However, diagnostic categories can also draw attention away from the real-life context of the child's family and social circumstances. Jerome Wakefield provides an example of a study of children of US military personnel which took place at the time of 'Desert Storm', when many parents were leaving for the Middle East. The level of separation anxiety was high enough among many of the children that they would qualify for diagnosis of Separation Anxiety Disorder. In fact the children were responding normally to a situation in which they knew the risks of loss of a parent (Wakefield, 1997).

The two epigraphs for this chapter provide useful starting points for thinking about children's presenting difficulties.

References

Albano, A. M. and Hayward, C. (2004) Social anxiety disorder. In Ollendick, T. H. and March, J. S. (eds) *Phobic and Anxiety Disorders in Children and Adolescents: A Clinician's Guide to Effective Psychosocial and Pharmacological Interventions.* Oxford, Oxford University Press.

Asmundson, G. J. G., Taylor, S., Sevgur, S. and Cox, B. J. (2001) Health anxiety: classification and clinical features. In Asmundson, G. J. G., Taylor, S. and Cox, B. J. (eds) *Health Anxiety: Clinical and Research Perspectives on Hypochondriasis and Related Conditions.* Chichester, John Wiley and Sons, Ltd.

Attwood, T. (1998) *Asperger's Syndrome: A Guide for Parents and Professionals.* London, Jessica Kingsley Publishers.

Bar-Haim, Y., Lamy, D., Pergamin, L., Bakermans-Kranenburg, M. J. and Van, I. M. H. (2007) Threat-related attentional bias in anxious and nonanxious individuals: a meta-analytic study. *Psychological Bulletin*, 133, 1–24.

Barlow, D. H. (2002) *Anxiety and Its Disorders: The Nature and Treatment of Anxiety and Panic.* New York, Guilford Press.

Beidel, D. C. and Turner, S. M. (2005) *Childhood Anxiety Disorders: A Guide to Research and Treatment.* Hove, Routledge.

Blöte, A. and Westenberg, P. M. (2007) Socially anxious adolescents' perception of treatment by classmates. *Behaviour Research and Therapy*, 45, 189–198.

Cicchetti, D. and Aber, J. L. (1998) Contextualism and developmental psychopathology. *Development and Psychopathology*, 10, 137–141.

Clark, D. M. (1996) Panic disorder: from theory to therapy. In Salkovskis, P. M. (ed.) *Frontiers of Cognitive Therapy.* New York, The Guilford Press.

CME Institute of Physicians Postgraduate Press, Inc. (2007) Managing ADHD in children, adolescents, and adults with comorbid anxiety. *Journal of Clinical Psychiatry*, 68, 451–462.

Cohan, S. L., Chavira, D. A. and Stein, M. B. (2006) Practitioner review: psychosocial interventions for children with selective mutism: a critical evaluation of the literature from 1990–2005. *Journal of Child Psychology and Psychiatry*, 47, 1085–1097.

Connolly, S. D. and Bernstein, G. A. (2007) Practice parameter for the assessment and treatment of children and adolescents with anxiety disorders. *Journal of the American Academy of Child and Adolescent Psychiatry*, 46, 267–283.

Costello, E. J., Egger, H. L. and Angold, A. (2004) Developmental epidemiology of anxiety disorders. In Ollendick, T. H. and March, J. S. (eds) *Phobic and Anxiety Disorders in Children and Adolescents: A Clinician's Guide to Effective Psychosocial and Pharmacological Interventions.* Oxford, Oxford University Press.

Craske, M. G. (2003) *Origins of Phobias and Anxiety Disorders: Why More Women than Men?* London, Elsevier.

Crick, N. R. and Zahn-Waxler, C. (2003) The development of psychopathology in females and males: current progress and future challenges. *Development and Psychopathology*, 15, 719–742.

Curry, J. F., March, J. S. and Hervey, A. S. (2004) Comorbidity of childhood and adolescent anxiety disorders. In Ollendick, T. H. and March, J. S. (eds) *Phobic and Anxiety Disorders in Children and Adolescents: A Clinician's Guide to Effective Psychosocial and Pharmacological Interventions.* Oxford, Oxford University Press.

Dyregrov, A. and Yule, W. (2006) A review of PTSD in children. *Child and Adolescent Mental Health*, 11, 176–184.

Emerson, E. (2003) Prevalence of psychiatric disorders in children and adolescents with and without intellectual disability. *Journal of Intellectual Disability Research*, 47, 51–58.

Espejo, E. P., Hammen, C. L., Connolly, N. P., Brennan, P. A., Najman, J. M. and Bor, W. (2007) Stress sensitization and adolescent depressive severity as a function of childhood adversity: a link to anxiety disorders. *Journal of Abnormal Child Psychology*, 35, 287–299.

Ferdinand, R. F., Van Lang, N. D., Ormel, J. and Verhulst, F. C. (2006) No distinctions between different types of anxiety symptoms in pre-adolescents from the general population. *Journal of Anxiety Disorders*, 20, 207–221.

Franklin, M. E., Rynn, M., Foa, E. B. and March, J. S. (2003) Treatment of obsessive-compulsive disorder. In Reinicke, M. A., Dattilio, F. M. and Freeman, A. (eds) *Cognitive Therapy with Children and Adolescents: A Casebook for Clinical Practice*, 2nd edn. London, The Guilford Press.

Gledhill, J. and Garralda, E. (2006) Functional symptoms and somatoform disorders in children and adolescents: the role of standardised measures in assessment. *Child and Adolescent Mental Health*, 11, 208–214.

Gray, J. A. and McNaughton, N. (2000) *The Neuropsychology of Anxiety: An Enquiry into the Functions of the Septo-Hippocampal System*. Oxford, Oxford University Press.

Gregory, A. M., Caspi, A., Moffitt, T. E., Koenen, K., Eley, T. C. and Poulton, R. (2007) Juvenile mental health histories of adults with anxiety disorders. *American Journal of Psychiatry*, 164, 301–308.

Gregory, A. M., Eley, T. C. and Plomin, R. (2004) Exploring the association between anxiety and conduct problems in a large sample of twins aged 2–4. *Journal of Abnormal Child Psychology*, 32, 111–122.

Harvey, A. G., Watkins, E., Mansell, W. and Shafran, R. (2004) *Cognitive-behavioural Processes across the Psychological Disorders: A Transdiagnostic Approach to Research and Treatment*. Oxford, Oxford University Press.

Heyne, D., King, N. J. and Tonge, B. (2004) School refusal. In Ollendick, T. H. and March, J. S. (eds) *Phobic and Anxiety Disorders in Children and Adolescents: A Clinician's Guide to Effective Psychosocial and Pharmacological Interventions*. Oxford, Oxford University Press.

Hofmann, S. G. (2004) The cognitive model of panic. In Reinicke, M. A. and Clark, D. A. (eds) *Cognitive Therapy across the Lifespan*. Cambridge, Cambridge University Press.

Ialongo, N., Edelsohn, G., Werthamer-Larsson, L., Crockett, L. and Kellam, S. (1996) The course of aggression in first-grade children with and without comorbid anxious symptoms. *Journal of Abnormal Child Psychology*, 24, 445–456.

Jensen, P. S. and Hoagwood, K. (1997) The book of names: DSM-IV in context. *Development and Psychopathology*, 9, 231–249.

Kaplow, J. B., Dodge, K. A., Amaya-Jackson, L. and Saxe, G. N. (2005) Pathways to PTSD, part II: sexually abused children. *American Journal of Psychiatry*, 162, 1305–1310.

Kendall, P. C., Pimentel, S., Rynn, M. A., Angelosante, A. and Webb, A. (2004) Generalized anxiety disorder. In Ollendick, T. H. and March, J. S. (eds) *Phobic and Anxiety Disorders in Children and Adolescents: A Clinician's Guide to Effective Psychosocial and Pharmacological Interventions*. Oxford, Oxford University Press.

Klein, R. G. and Pine, D. S. (2002) Anxiety disorders. In Rutter, M. and Taylor, E. (eds) *Child and Adolescent Psychiatry*, 4th edn. Oxford, Blackwell Science.

Marmorstein, N. R. (2007) Relationships between anxiety and externalizing disorders in youth: the influences of age and gender. *Journal of Anxiety Disorders*, 21, 420–432.

Maughan, B., Rowe, R., Messer, J., Goodman, R. and Meltzer, H. (2004) Conduct disorder and oppositional defiant disorder in a national sample: developmental epidemiology. *Journal of Child Psychology and Psychiatry*, 45, 609–621.

McKay, D., Piacentini, J., Greisberg, S., Graae, F., Jaffer, M. and Miller, J. (2006) The structure of childhood obsessions and compulsions: dimensions in an outpatient sample. *Behaviour Research and Therapy*, 44, 137–146.

Ollendick, T. H. and March, J. S. (2004) *Phobic and Anxiety Disorders in Children and Adolescents: A Clinician's Guide to Effective Psychosocial and Pharmacological Interventions*. Oxford, Oxford University Press.

Rachman, S. (2004) *Anxiety*. Hove, Psychology Press.

Scheeringa, M. S., Zeanah, C. H., Myers, L. and Putnam, F. W. (2005) Predictive validity in a prospective follow-up of PTSD in preschool children. *Journal of the American Academy of Child and Adolescent Psychiatry*, 44, 899–906.

Sharp, W. G., Sherman, C. and Gross, A. M. (2006) Selective mutism and anxiety: a review of the current conceptualization of the disorder. *Journal of Anxiety Disorders*, 21, 568–578.

Stallard, P. (2006) Post-traumatic stress disorder. In Gillberg, C., Harrington, R. and Steinhausen, H.-C. (eds) *A Clinician's Handbook of Child and Adolescent Psychiatry*. Cambridge, Cambridge University Press.

Standart, S. and Le Couteur, A. (2003) The quiet child: a literature review of selective mutism. *Child and Adolescent Mental Health*, 8, 154–160.

Taylor, D. C. and Harrison, R. M. (1976) On being categorized in the speech of others: medical and psychiatric diagnosis. In Harré, R. (ed.) *Life Sentences: Aspects of the Social Role of Language*. London, John Wiley and Sons.

Vasey, M. W. and Dadds, M. R. (eds) (2001) *The Developmental Psychopathology of Anxiety*. Oxford, Oxford University Press.

Vasey, M. W. and MacLeod, C. (2001) Information-processing factors in childhood anxiety: a review and developmental perspective. In Vasey, M. W. and Dadds, M. R. (eds) *The Developmental Psychopathology of Anxiety*. Oxford, Oxford University Press.

Wadsworth, M. E., Hudziak, J. J., Heath, A. C. and Achenbach, T. M. (2001) Latent class analysis of child behavior checklist anxiety/depression in children and adolescents. *Journal of the American Academy of Child and Adolescent Psychiatry*, 40, 106–114.

Wakefield, J. C. (1997) When is development disordered? Developmental psychopathology and the harmful dysfunction analysis of mental disorder. *Development and Psychopathology*, 9, 269–290.

Chapter 3

Help for children experiencing severe and complex anxiety: a brief outline

Peter Appleton

This chapter will first discuss the differences between providing help for adult and child anxiety difficulties, and then focus on planning a first family meeting, obtaining a history and assessment, formulation, and referral for specialist help. Finally psychological treatments are outlined. It is not the purpose of this chapter to provide a detailed guide to specialist treatment: several excellent books on specialist aspects of assessment and treatment of child and adolescent anxiety disorders have been published in the last few years (Beidel and Turner, 2005; Morris and March, 2004; Ollendick and March, 2004; Weisz, 2004). This chapter examines some of the issues that may arise (for children with complex anxiety difficulties, living in adverse family and social circumstances) in the very first stages of help-seeking in community settings (Sayal, 2006).

Helping children and families is different from helping adults

For adults experiencing severe and complex anxiety, therapies are available for which there is a clear evidence base. The adult can seek professional help, and as long as help is available, he or she can start to deal specifically with their anxiety disorder. For children it is not quite so straightforward.

There are many detailed differences, many of which have been discussed throughout the previous chapters, as part of the developmental framework (see Boxes 1.1 and 1.2). Probably the primary difference is that the young person is not independent. He or she is embedded within a complex developmental and social context of family, peers, and school (usually), and is not free to make changes in the same way as an adult.

Unfortunately, many of the well-researched interventions for childhood anxiety have been developed from *adult* psychological models of anxiety, with implicit assumptions that:

(a) children are little adults; (b) children at all stages of development will have their needs met with a single treatment approach; and (c) all children respond equally to treatment, independently of cultural background.

. . .

A further concern is the implicit dependence upon intrapsychic or individualistic models of treatment that may be applicable to adult patients seen in clinical settings. As children are heavily dependent on their immediate family and peer environment, a better mode of treatment may be one founded on interpersonal and systemic factors . . .

(Barrett, 2001, pp. 311–312)

Paula Barrett, together with a number of other researchers in Australia and elsewhere, has led the field in designing family-based interventions for children (Barrett et al., 1996).

Later in this section we will look at some of the interventions that have been developed for anxiety-related problems in children, but before doing that we need to consider the first contact professionals have with children whose families are concerned about a child who is anxious.

Planning a first meeting

If a child is anxious, then perhaps the last thing they want to do is talk to a GP or a teacher or a paediatrician, or a child psychologist. First, it is not easy meeting someone grown up, powerful, and perhaps new, especially if they are going to ask personal questions. Second, the child may have reason to think that they will be sent away, or may fear some other catastrophic outcome. Third, they may have learned to be suspicious of adults, and to be very careful about what they say. Fourth, it is painful to talk about painful thoughts. Fifth, parents or teachers may have underestimated the severity of the child's anxiety (Connolly and Bernstein, 2007), leading the child to expect other adults not to understand. So, whatever the age of the child or young person, talking may not be high on their agenda! It is always worth remembering that for a child who, by definition, may expect negative outcomes, and may overestimate risk, meeting someone who asks searching questions is likely to provoke further anxiety. Some young people will also have the additional burden of hearing critical things said about them in front of the professional, at a first meeting.

For the child who is experiencing problematic anxiety, it is usually a parent who actively seeks help on the child's behalf (Sayal, 2006). It is therefore crucial that the professional is able to listen to what the parent(s) have to say, while also showing that one is keen to understand the young person's point of view. Parents and teachers may appreciate the impact of anxiety on the child's functioning at home and school (although they are unlikely fully to understand the nature of the child's internal distress). With teenagers it is important to see the young person on their own, and with younger children it is vital to ensure that he or she can communicate with one as freely as possible. Children, especially anxious children, are acutely tuned in to adult criticism, so a 'listening stance', with zero advice, is a good starting point. Both the parents and the child are likely to have received a great deal of well-meaning advice from many different sources. So the first meeting is an opportunity to break the mould, by simply *listening*, and showing one has heard what the different family members have said. Parents may be desperate for someone to *do* something, but it is usually useful to set up a further meeting to do some more listening, and ask some more focused questions – normally the family will go away from the first meeting relieved that someone is listening, will reflect on what has been discussed, and will come back next time with more to say. For pre-adolescents, a room should have age-appropriate play and drawing materials available, so that the child can absorb herself, watch and listen to what is going on, and communicate via play and drawing, before participating verbally as well.

Modern preoccupation with forms, comprehensive notes, and accountability, mean that many professionals now seem to spend first meetings (with families) frantically scribbling notes, and filling in forms, rather than listening, watching, and communicating that they have genuinely heard what a family has said. Some *balance* has to be achieved between making human contact, and demonstrating recordable professional accountability (Manson and O'Neill, 2007).

In summary, planning a first meeting requires the adoption of a calm, listening, and open mind-set, and the provision of a quiet, confidential environment with age-appropriate play and/or drawing materials for the child.

Obtaining a history and assessment

There are some principles which apply to the first sessions of history-taking and assessment, whether these sessions occur within community services, or in specialist services. This chapter will not deal with the details of *specialist* assessment of specific anxiety disorders, but does take account of the particular issues that may arise for anxious children and teenagers.

For medical practitioners, it is of course crucial to consider differential diagnosis of other physical conditions and psychiatric disorders that may mimic anxiety (Connolly and Bernstein, 2007).

The listening stance described above usually helps parents and young people feel more confident in explaining what the problems are, and what circumstances may have led up to the present situation.

First, it is useful to try to meet as many members of the family as one can, although not necessarily at a first meeting. In divorced families it is important to meet both parents, as well as step-parents. The views of the child or young person, and the views of the parent seeking help, are important in determining when other family members can be met, and in what circumstances (e.g. it may be necessary to meet divorced parents separately). Of course it may not be a parent who is seeking help for a child – a teacher may have noticed that a child is newly anxious in the classroom, and may have asked to meet with a parent – the same principle applies, that is that meeting additional members of the family (e.g. separated parents) may be helpful.

Second, adopting a collaborative, or 'working-alongside', approach to parents (as well as children and young people) is regarded as a golden rule (Sutton, 1999). If family members feel talked down to, or criticised, they are unlikely to return for further help.

Third, being even-handed in listening to different family members, while also respecting the family hierarchy, is appreciated. Different family members will usually have different perspectives, sometimes forcefully stated. It is important to acknowledge these different 'positions', which do of course provide information about the context within which the child is growing up.

Fourth, respect for the family's cultural and religious beliefs, and the preferred language of each family member, is critical (see Chapter 4).

Fifth, it is important to be aware that a parent who is depressed (or simply stressed) will struggle to give precise information about episodes of family life, and specific accounts of the child's difficulties. There are many reasons for this. One is situational – the interview may be in the presence of noisy and demanding young siblings! Or the parent may have many things on his or her mind, all competing for attention; it may be too difficult to think in detail about an incident a few days ago when the child failed to get to school. Alternatively the parent may feel ashamed that they have had to come to seek help (or been asked to meet with a professional) – the experience of the emotion may block careful attention to detail, especially in a first session. If there are marital difficulties, these may be associated with complex feelings of concern for the child, and profound anxieties and anger in the partner relationship. We know that both depression and post-traumatic stress disorder are associated with a particular type of difficulty with memory – over-general autobiographical memory (Williams et al., 2007). The parent is more likely to provide a general instance, for example, 'she is always seeking reassurance', or 'he sleeps poorly every night', rather than a specific example (by specific we would mean on a particular day, time, and place). There are at least two reasons why it is important to help parents gradually to provide specific accounts. First, in order to understand the child's anxiety, extremely accurate information is necessary – not only about the anxiety, but also about family interactions (who did what, or said what, and when – from everyone's particular angle), neighbourhood and school characteristics, and so on. But second, the child or young person usually finds over-general statements by a parent unsettling (and sometimes critical), whereas accuracy may appeal to the child's sense of fairness.

Sixth, for some families, accuracy is more fundamentally problematic, and initial interviewing may not lead to a coherent or clear story about the background to the child's anxiety. In a chapter entitled 'Omission, Suppression, and Falsification of Family Context', John Bowlby comments on the

> marked tendency of the parents of patients (both young and old) to keep silent about the part they themselves are or have been playing. Information about their quarrels, or about their threats to separate, to abandon or eject their children, or to commit suicide, is very rarely volunteered to clinicians trying to help.
>
> (Bowlby, 1973, p. 314)

Later, when parents have begun to trust the clinician: 'they admit frankly that in the account of events they gave during initial interviews they either suppressed or deliberately falsified key information' (Bowlby, 1973, p. 315).

Experienced clinicians will recognise that this does occur, and there is an ethical demand on the professional continually to keep an open mind about the range of risk factors that may have contributed (or be currently contributing) to the child's anxiety problems. As Bowlby points out, this is not a question of moral condemnation of the parents, but rather a continuous process of understanding the experiences both of the child and the parents. The parents' own family-of-origin experiences may have been both traumatic and unresolved (Main et al., 2005).

Finally, in obtaining a history and assessment, one hypothesis always to keep in mind (but remembering 'no single cause') is that of Ainsworth (1990), shown in Box 3.1.

Box 3.1 Attachment, emotional security, and anxiety

Does the young person's anxiety or fear about an object or situation reflect (at least partially) a concern that a parent figure, or sibling, is being hurt, or is not well, or is *not* currently emotionally available?

Cognitions (or beliefs) about emotional availability of the attachment figure include '(a) belief that lines of communication with the attachment figure are open, (b) that physical accessibility exists, and (c) that the attachment figure will respond if called upon for help' (Ainsworth, 1990, p. 474).

Listening to the child

How can a child or teenager be engaged in a first family session? We have mentioned the important issue of developmentally appropriate 'props' – thoughtfully planned play materials, art materials, etc. Jim Wilson, in a chapter entitled 'The First Encounter' (in his book *Child-Focused Practice*, 1998) provides two aims for engaging families in child-focused work:

1   To access the child's own descriptions and accounts of his/her concerns;
2   Bring these accounts into the open, to help weave them into the fabric of the views, descriptions, and account of other family members.

Detailed descriptions are provided by Wilson for the following approaches to engaging children: play-based activities; allowing yourself time to be noticed by children; not getting stuck in the therapist's chair; restraining 'problem talk' (i.e. delay problem descriptions – build a picture of the child's wider life); not expecting children to talk about feelings (find out what is permissible to talk about in the first session); using visual aids, such as whiteboards, to create a picture of significant people in the child's life (Wilson, 1998).

When parents and children disagree, this provides useful information (Wilson, 1998). The disagreement itself can be 'normalised' by the therapist – 'it is perfectly usual for children and parents to have a different view'. If the disagreement is argumentative, repetitive or hostile, it may be useful calmly to explore whether this happens frequently, what provokes it, and how it is usually resolved (or not resolved). In the majority of cases families find it helpful that the therapist has heard a disagreement, and remained neutral (i.e. not taking sides, and not trying to persuade one family member to accept, or partially accept, the view of another member). If, rarely, hostile disagreements become abusive, and calm refocusing has not been successful, it is important to 'halt the proceedings' (Wilson, 1998), and arrange alternative means of gathering information, perhaps by seeing family members separately.

More typically, anxious children may be extremely quiet in a first session. After giving them a chance to observe and listen, questions from the therapist might begin as multiple-choice, to reduce the amount of speech the child initially needs to make (Wilson, 1998). Including a humorous item within the choice can allow the child to smile, laugh, or show in some other way that they are willing to converse.

An anxious child or teenager may sit 'close-up' to a parent, and may look at the parent when asked a direct question by the therapist. Two useful ground-rules for the therapist are: 'no pressure' and 'give it time'. Clingy and vigilant behaviours are part of the territory of anxiety, and are there-fore something to accept, at least initially. Sometimes a parent will answer for a child, but will then remark that they would like the child to say what they think. For most (but not all) children, a genuine, uncritical, sympathetic and non-intrusive interest by the therapist will be picked up by the child, and he or she will 'unfreeze'.

Some children will not speak at all in certain settings (e.g. school), and will usually not speak with professionals such as the family doctor or social worker. This may lead to a specialist diagnosis of selective mutism (see Chapter 2). Many adults find mutism provocative, and regard it as hostile. In turn they feel angry with the child – 'why can't he just speak? – we know he speaks at home'. This appraisal by the adult is of course rapidly detected by the anxious child, causing further inhibition of speech. It is more useful to be interested in the child's range and style of communications (i.e. verbal and nonverbal) in different settings (e.g. home, school, friends' houses). The initial aim is simply to *describe* the child's communication patterns accurately. Selective mutism is usually associated with other anxiety behaviours, which require a full specialist assessment (Standart and Le Couteur, 2003).

A creative approach to communication in the therapist's office is helpful. A 5-year-old who does not speak to the therapist may happily engage in silent but cooperative (and committed) symbolic play. A mute teenager may willingly complete a lengthy questionnaire about feelings and experiences.

Angela Hobday and Kate Ollier have published a practical guide to activities with children and adolescents, some of which are designed specifically for first sessions. The activities were developed 'mostly out of necessity when children have found it difficult to discuss their problems or their feelings' (Hobday and Ollier, 1998).

For non-specialist first interviews, taking place in the GP surgery, or school, or professional office, or family home, the above guidance about engagement and involvement of family and child or young person might be helpful. Without engagement and the establishment of some degree of trust it is difficult to reach a balanced view about how to help the child, and whether to refer on for specialist help. On the assumption that a family has engaged with a professional, most child psychology and psychiatry texts suggest that information is gleaned about the following areas: history of presenting problems and maintaining factors; child developmental history; family composition and history; description of parent or carer relationships with child; parent–parent relationships; living conditions and resources; involvement with other agencies; child's account of problem, life circumstances, wishes for future, and approach to professional help; and school information (Carr, 1999). In addition, Chapter 1 (see Boxes 1.1 and 1.2) emphasised the importance of understanding a spectrum of relevant factors ('no single cause'); the individual child's development in the context of family, peers, neighbourhood, school and culture; resilience processes as well as risk factors; problematic anxiety as a form of 'high alert' for the child and his carers; the role of attachment relationships; the roles of parents and carers; the roles of peers and friends; the importance of the child's own sense of agency and self-concept; and the notion of pathways or trajectories – the child on a journey through development.

Formulation

One of the important contributions of psychological therapies has been the development of the idea of formulation – a distinct stage, emerging out of assessment, in which the therapist and client begin to agree a 'way forward'. Alan Carr defines formulation as follows:

> A formulation is a mini-theory that explains why the presenting problems developed, why they persist, and what protective factors either prevent them from becoming worse or may be enlisted to solve them.
>
> (Carr, 1999, p. 117)

Formulation guards against simplistic 'single-cause' explanations, it allows the child's development-in-context to be taken into account, it incorporates both risk and resilience (protective) processes, and should allow the child's sense of his or her own agency (goals, wishes, plans) to be a guiding force. Parental involvement is crucial, and differing perspectives from the child, each family member and/or carer can be built in.

Formulation also creates a 'negotiating space' for the child, family, and therapist, to engage, agree, disagree, consult other helpful parties (e.g. school), and generally prepare the ground for therapy. All therapeutic approaches emphasise the importance of developing a therapeutic alliance, or working relationship, in which the family and the therapist have a positive feeling for each other, and for the practical process of therapy (Green, 2006).

For families experiencing multiple contextual problems the formulation may identify a pre-therapy, or early therapy, stage of ensuring that the child (and sometimes the family) is *safe*. For instance, in work with children who have witnessed domestic violence, the child's safety must be given absolute priority (Vetere and Cooper, 2005). In work with children from asylum-seeking families, safety is paramount – a detailed case study is provided by David Trickey in Chapter 4, and there is further discussion of this issue in Chapter 13 (see also Bowley, 2006).

A pre-therapy stage of ensuring safety for the child and family may also be appropriate where assessment has highlighted factors that may indicate risk to a family member. For instance, a child may, as part of problematic anxiety, be experiencing nightmares or intrusive thoughts about his or her mother being hurt. This might occur as part of a 'non-trauma' anxiety disorder such as OCD. Careful assessment will determine whether there is current domestic violence, which the child may not be free to disclose.

The child him or herself may have experienced maltreatment or be at risk of maltreatment. Again, ensuring the child is safe must be a preliminary before active therapy can begin.

Treatment

Psychological treatment of anxiety disorders has been transformed during the last few decades by the development of specialist behavioural and cognitive-behavioural therapies (CBT) (Barlow, 2002; Reinecke and Clark, 2004). These therapies help clients to (a) understand the nature of anxiety and fear (psychoeducation); (b) consider alternative ways of thinking about fear and anxiety-provoking situations and responses (cognitive restructuring); (c) conduct behavioural experiments (planned experiential activities aimed at gathering specific new information about self, others, and worrying situations, and testing new beliefs); (d) gradually and systematically expose themselves to feared situations (or feared thoughts and memories); and (e) prevent relapse. Some CBT interventions also utilise relaxation and other somatic self-management treatments. Controlled outcome studies have shown beneficial and enduring effects of CBT for adults experiencing anxiety disorders (Hollon et al., 2006).

Outcome studies of CBT for children and adolescents with anxiety disorders began to emerge in the 1990s, leading to an important and detailed literature on treatments for specific disorders (James et al., 2005). These studies have shown that CBT reduces anxiety for school-aged children with GAD, separation anxiety disorder, and social phobia (Hudson et al., 2002). These studies also showed that children who were randomly allocated to a waiting list control condition did *not* improve spontaneously. A pioneering and effective CBT intervention, called Coping Cat, for 8- to 13-year-olds, included age-appropriate psychoeducation, relaxation, cognitive restructuring, planning and doing exposure work with feared situations, and noticing and rewarding oneself for trying hard (Kendall et al., 2004; Weisz, 2004).

Studies also began to emerge in which parents were actively involved in cognitive-behavioural treatment, i.e. in addition to direct child therapy (Ginsburg and Schlossberg, 2002). In Barrett's study parents were taught skills for (a) managing child distress and avoidance, (b) managing their own anxiety, and (c) parent communication and problem-solving (Barrett et al., 2001; Ferdinand et al., 2004). The evidence suggests that involving parents in 'family treatment' is as effective, or more effective, than individual child CBT (Ginsburg and Schlossberg, 2002; Wood et al., 2006).

Research has also begun to address CBT for other child anxiety disorders, with very promising work on OCD (Franklin et al., 2003), panic disorder (Birmaher and Ollendick, 2004), and PTSD (Dyregrov and Yule, 2006). A group intervention for *parents* of young anxious children shows promising results (Cartwright-Hatton et al., 2005).

CBT is of course not effective for all children with specific anxiety disorders. About 20 per cent to 50 per cent do not overcome their disorder (Connolly and Bernstein, 2007; James et al., 2005). In addition, it is widely recognised that outcome-oriented research will need to address the circumstances of children with problematic anxiety *also* experiencing co-occurring disorders and/or multiple developmental and/or social contextual risk factors. Practising clinicians are not able, at present, to use precise evidence-based approaches to work with these children. In practice, it is recommended that the choice of treatment method for a child and family involves careful consideration of a wide range of contextual issues such as psychosocial stressors, other risk factors, nature of the child's individual anxiety disorder and co-occurring disorders, age and developmental functioning of the child, and family context (Connolly and Bernstein, 2007).

Research has begun to address interventions designed to work with contextual risk processes. Here we provide two examples.

Attachment and family process-oriented therapy for anxiety disorders

In a recent study, informed by CBT models, attachment theory, and family therapy, several adjustments to CBT were made (Siqueland et al., 2005). First, the treatment model was designed specifically for adolescents, addressing their autonomy needs. Second, the intervention for parents was aimed less at helping them manage family anxiety, but focused instead on helping parents promote psychological autonomy in the young person, re-focusing factors of intimacy and protection, and promoting the increasingly important factors of respect for autonomy, difference, and normative conflict. Treatment order and structure were modified to reflect treatment goals – evidence-based CBT was a key component for the young people themselves, but *family process* sessions were fully integrated into the treatment design. Young people referred with GAD, social phobia or separation anxiety, showed significant decreases in anxiety and depressive symptoms, following treatment.

Attachment-oriented psychotherapy for maltreated preschool children

Maltreatment is a known risk factor for attachment disorganisation, anxiety, depression, and behaviour problems (see Chapter 1). There is emerging evidence that parent–child psychotherapy can engender change in childrens' and parents' internal working models of relationships, thereby potentially reducing risk for future psychological problems.

In a controlled study of preschool children who had been maltreated, mother and child were seen together weekly for almost 12 months, focusing both on the therapist–mother relationship and on the mother–child relationship (Toth et al., 2002). The mothers' relationships with therapists were expected to reflect the mothers' 'childhood histories of disturbed parent–child relationships and frequent negative experiences with social service systems, often expect(ing) rejection, abandonment, criticism, and ridicule' (Toth et al., 2002, p. 891). Therapists provided empathy and 'unfailing positive regard', helping mothers overcome negative expectations. Therapists did *not* model 'appropriate behaviours' or try to modify specific parental behaviours – instead they used the themes arising in psychotherapy with the mother and child to help the mother to increase understanding of effects of prior relationships, and develop positive expectations of self and the child. In this randomised controlled design, one of the control conditions (i.e. for randomly allocated families with equivalent history of maltreatment) was a cognitive-behavioural home-based visitation intervention with the same frequency of intensive treatment.

Narrative story-stems (structured, play-based scenarios to which the child responds by providing play-based and/or narrative story completions – 'show me and tell me what happens next') provided one of the primary outcome measures for the children (Bretherton, 2005; Bretherton et al., 1990). For mothers and children receiving psychotherapy, a considerable reduction in negative self-representations in the children's story-stems was found (from baseline to post-intervention), when compared with data from families receiving the home-based cognitive-behavioural intervention. In two other control conditions there was also no evidence for change in negative self-representations (Toth et al., 2002). This study therefore provides preliminary evidence (Cicchetti et al., 2006) for effectiveness of a *relationship-oriented* therapy for maltreated children and their mothers.

Future treatment research

Researchers working with children showing problematic anxiety have increasingly used a developmental framework (Vasey and Dadds, 2001). The child's developmental and social contexts *have* been given greater attention by clinical researchers (Cicchetti and Aber, 1998; Cicchetti and Toth, 2006). And some of the evidence-based treatments are known to be highly effective for some children and adolescents with severe anxiety disorders (Ollendick and March, 2004). But clinicians are, in many cases, unable to match the complexity of the lives of their clients with the linear simplicity of many of the treatment programmes in the research literature. John Weisz, a leading child and adolescent mental health researcher, has identified ten issues requiring research attention:

- building evidence-based treatments for a broadened array of problems and disorders;

- learning about the impact of co-occurring problems and disorders;
- expanding the array of treatment models tested;
- identifying necessary and sufficient conditions for treatment benefit;
- enriching our understanding of the effective range of specific treatments;
- understanding change processes that mediate treatment outcome;
- increased attention to therapeutic relationship and alliance building;
- more potent comparisons within research designs;
- studying the effects of treatments in real-world practice contexts;
- revisiting the model that guides treatment development and testing (Weisz, 2004, pp. 449–457).

References

Ainsworth, M. D. S. (1990) Epilogue: Some considerations regarding theory and assessment relevant to attachment beyond infancy. In Greenberg, M. T., Cicchetti, D. and Cummings, E. M. (eds) *Attachment in the Preschool Years: Theory, Research, and Intervention*. London, University of Chicago Press.

Barlow, D. H. (2002) *Anxiety and Its Disorders: The Nature and Treatment of Anxiety and Panic*. New York, The Guilford Press.

Barrett, P. (2001) Current issues in the treatment of childhood anxiety. In Vasey, M. W. and Dadds, M. R. (eds) *The Developmental Psychopathology of Anxiety*. Oxford, Oxford University Press.

Barrett, P. M., Dadds, M. R. and Rapee, R. M. (1996) Family treatment of childhood anxiety: a controlled trial. *Journal of Consulting and Clinical Psychology*, 64, 333–342.

Barrett, P. M., Duffy, A. L., Dadds, M. R. and Rapee, R. M. (2001) Cognitive-behavioral treatment of anxiety disorders in children: long-term (6-year) follow-up. *Journal of Consulting and Clinical Psychology*, 69, 135–141.

Beidel, D. C. and Turner, S. M. (2005) *Childhood Anxiety Disorders: A Guide to Research and Treatment*. Hove, Routledge.

Birmaher, B. and Ollendick, T. H. (2004) Childhood-onset panic disorder. In Ollendick, T. H. and March, J. S. (eds) *Phobic and Anxiety Disorders in Children and Adolescents: A Clinician's Guide to Effective Psychosocial and Pharmacological Interventions*. Oxford, Oxford University Press.

Bowlby, J. (1973) *Attachment and Loss. Volume 2. Separation: Anxiety and Anger*. London, The Hogarth Press and the Institute of Psycho-analysis.

Bowley, J. (2006) Working with asylum seekers. In Tarrier, N. (ed.) *Case Formulation in Cognitive Behaviour Therapy: The Treatment of Challenging and Complex Cases*. London, Routledge.

Bretherton, I. (2005) In pursuit of the internal working model construct and its relevance to attachment relationships. In Grossman, K. E., Grossman, K. and Waters, E. (eds) *Attachment from Infancy to Adulthood: The Major Longitudinal Studies*. London, The Guilford Press.

Bretherton, I., Ridgeway, D. and Cassidy, J. (1990) Assessing internal working models of the attachment relationship: an attachment story completion task for

3-year-olds. In Greenberg, M. T., Cicchetti, D. and Cummings, E. M. (eds) *Attachment in the Preschool Years: Theory, Research, and Intervention*. London, The University of Chicago Press.

Carr, A. (1999) *The Handbook of Child and Adolescent Clinical Psychology: A Contextual Approach*. London, Routledge.

Cartwright-Hatton, S., McNally, D. and White, C. (2005) A new cognitive-behavioural parenting intervention for families of young anxious children: a pilot study. *Behavioural and Cognitive Psychotherapy*, 33, 243–247.

Cicchetti, D. and Aber, J. L. (1998) Contextualism and developmental psychopathology. *Development and Psychopathology*, 10, 137–141.

Cicchetti, D., Rogosch, F. A. and Toth, S. L. (2006) Fostering secure attachment in infants in maltreating families through preventive interventions. *Development and Psychopathology*, 18, 623–649.

Cicchetti, D. and Toth, S. L. (2006) Building bridges and crossing them: translational research in developmental psychopathology. *Development and Psychopathology*, 18, 619–622.

Connolly, S. D. and Bernstein, G. A. (2007) Practice parameter for the assessment and treatment of children and adolescents with anxiety disorders. *Journal of the American Academy of Child and Adolescent Psychiatry*, 46, 267–283.

Dyregrov, A. and Yule, W. (2006) A review of PTSD in children. *Child and Adolescent Mental Health*, 11, 176–184.

Ferdinand, R. F., Barrett, P. and Dadds, M. R. (2004) Anxiety and depression in childhood: prevention and intervention. In Ollendick, T. H. and March, J. S. (eds) *Phobic and Anxiety Disorders in Children and Adolescents: A Clinician's Guide to Effective Psychosocial and Pharmacological Interventions*. Oxford, Oxford University Press.

Franklin, M. E., Rynn, M., Foa, E. B. and March, J. S. (2003) Treatment of obsessive-compulsive disorder. In Reinicke, M. A., Dattilio, F. M. and Freeman, A. (eds) *Cognitive Therapy with Children and Adolescents: A Casebook for Clinical Practice*, 2nd edn. London, The Guilford Press.

Ginsburg, G. S. and Schlossberg, M. C. (2002) Family-based treatment of childhood anxiety disorders. *International Review of Psychiatry*, 14, 143–154.

Green, J. (2006) Annotation: the therapeutic alliance–a significant but neglected variable in child mental health treatment studies. *Journal of Child Psychology and Psychiatry*, 47, 425–435.

Hobday, A. and Ollier, K. (1998) *Creative Therapy: Activities with Children and Adolescents*. Leicester, British Psychological Society.

Hollon, S. D., Stewart, M. O. and Strunk, D. (2006) Enduring effects for cognitive behavior therapy in the treatment of depression and anxiety. *Annual Review of Psychology*, 57, 285–315.

Hudson, J. L., Kendall, P. C., Coles, M. E., Robin, J. A. and Webb, A. (2002) The other side of the coin: using intervention research in child anxiety disorders to inform developmental psychopathology. *Development and Psychopathology*, 14, 819–841.

James, A., Soler, A. and Weatherall, R. (2005) Cognitive behavioural therapy for anxiety disorders in children and adolescents. *Cochrane Database of Systematic Reviews*, CD004690.

Kendall, P. C., Safford, S., Flannery-Schroeder, E. and Webb, A. (2004) Child anxiety treatment: outcomes in adolescence and impact on substance use and depression at 7.4-year follow-up. *Journal of Consulting and Clinical Psychology*, 72, 276–287.

Main, M., Hesse, E. and Kaplan, N. (2005) Predictability of attachment behavior and representational processes at 1, 6, and 19 years of age: the Berkeley Longitudinal Study. In Grossman, K. E., Grossman, K. and Zimmerman, P. (eds) *Attachment from Infancy to Adulthood: The Major Longitudinal Studies*. London, The Guilford Press.

Manson, N. C. and O'Neill, O. (2007) *Rethinking Informed Consent in Bioethics*. Cambridge, Cambridge University Press.

Morris, T. L. and March, J. S. (2004) *Anxiety Disorders in Children and Adolescents*. London, The Guilford Press.

Ollendick, T. H. and March, J. S. (2004) *Phobic and Anxiety Disorders in Children and Adolescents: A Clinician's Guide to Effective Psychosocial and Pharmacological Interventions*. Oxford, Oxford University Press.

Reinecke, M. A. and Clark, D. A. (2004) *Cognitive Therapy across the Lifespan*. Cambridge, Cambridge University Press.

Sayal, K. (2006) Annotation: pathways to care for children with mental health problems. *Journal of Child Psychology and Psychiatry*, 47, 649–659.

Siqueland, L., Rynn, M. and Diamond, G. S. (2005) Cognitive behavioral and attachment based family therapy for anxious adolescents: Phase I and II studies. *Journal of Anxiety Disorders*, 19, 361–381.

Standart, S. and Le Couteur, A. (2003) The quiet child: a literature review of selective mutism. *Child and Adolescent Mental Health*, 8, 154–160.

Sutton, C. (1999) *Helping Families with Troubled Children: A Preventive Approach*. Chichester, John Wiley and Sons.

Toth, S. L., Maughan, A., Manly, J. T., Spagnola, M. and Cicchetti, D. (2002) The relative efficacy of two interventions in altering maltreated preschool children's representational models: implications for attachment theory. *Development and Psychopathology*, 14, 877–908.

Vasey, M. W. and Dadds, M. R. (eds) (2001) *The Developmental Psychopathology of Anxiety*. Oxford, Oxford University Press.

Vetere, A. and Cooper, J. (2005) Children who witness violence at home. In Vetere, A. and Dowling, E. (eds) *Narrative Therapies with Children and their Families: A Practitioner's Guide to Concepts and Approaches*. London, Routledge.

Weisz, J. R. (2004) *Psychotherapy for Children and Adolescents: Evidence-Based Treatments and Case Examples*. Cambridge, Cambridge University Press.

Williams, J. M. G., Barnhofer, T., Crane, C., Herman, D., Raes, F., Watkins, E. and Dalgleish, T. (2007) Autobiographical memory specificity and emotional disorder. *Psychological Bulletin*, 133, 122–148.

Wilson, J. (1998) *Child-focused Practice: A Collaborative Systemic Approach*. London, Karnac Books.

Wood, J. J., Piacentini, J. C., Southam-Gerow, M., Chu, B. C. and Sigman, M. (2006) Family cognitive behavioral therapy for child anxiety disorders. *Journal of the American Academy of Child and Adolescent Psychiatry*, 45, 314–321.

Part 2

Chapter 4

Experiencing refugee status after previous trauma

David Trickey

Background information and referral

Jyrgen was 5 years old when in 1998 the political situation between the Serb government and the people of Kosovo deteriorated such that there was open conflict between the Kosovo Liberation Army (KLA) and the Serb police. Jyrgen's family were Kosovo Albanians and his father joined the KLA to fight for their people's independence from Serbia. This resulted in him being away from the family home much of the time. As the situation worsened in Kosovo, Jyrgen witnessed armed Serb police raid his house searching for his father. He saw much news coverage on the television of Kosovo Albanians being killed, he heard the shelling of villages around him, and was exposed to many stories of other Kosovo Albanians being killed. Kosovo became increasingly dangerous, especially for any family thought to be connected to the KLA. When he was 6, Jyrgen's parents decided to take him and his younger brother and leave their home, their family and their friends preferring the uncertainty and unfamiliarity of another country. They were able to arrange transportation out of Kosovo in a lorry. They arrived in the UK and claimed asylum. They were housed by the local authority, received minimal benefits and were able to get their children into local schools. They were assigned a solicitor who took on their case and handled the long drawn out process of claiming asylum in the UK.

In 2002 Jyrgen was referred by his GP to a specialist trauma service for children and families, because he was refusing to sleep on his own, and was "psychologically disturbed" as a result of his experiences in Kosovo.

Assessment

The assessment appointment was attended by 9-year-old Jyrgen, his mother, his father, his 7-year-old brother and his 9-month-old sister. I worked with an interpreter who was familiar with the way of working at the clinic, and who had worked with me on various occasions before. I met with the interpreter before the assessment briefly to discuss the background and what I hoped to achieve from the first session. This also gave me the opportunity to use the interpreter as a cultural consultant to highlight any difficulties that I might face. She reminded me that Kosovo Albanians rarely share their problems. In some ways it was not wholly necessary to use an interpreter as both the boys and their mother spoke good English. However it is generally not considered good practice to expect a child or another member of the family to act as interpreter (Ehntholt and Yule, 2006). It is important within a therapeutic session for a child to feel that they can express their own point of view, without also having to be responsible for expressing the view of other family members. Furthermore, having to rely on a child to make oneself understood may feel very disempowering for adults. Working collaboratively with an interpreter meant that Jyrgen's father was more involved in the session without having to rely on his family to translate. He could make his point of view known and whilst Jyrgen and I conversed in English the interpreter was able to translate simultaneously to his father.

Jyrgen had seldom slept in his own bed since his father's absences in Kosovo, preferring to stay with his mother. He also wet the bed frequently. He was suffering almost nightly from terrifying nightmares involving various images of blood and killing. He feared for his own safety particularly at night, but also during the day. He was constantly reminded of the killings that he had been exposed to in Kosovo, and was often on the look out for threats. He recounted how on his way to the assessment interview he saw a policeman, and because it reminded him of the Serb police in Kosovo, he had become extremely scared and had insisted that the family turn around and take another route. He found it extremely difficult to be on his own at any time – not so much because he genuinely thought that he would be killed, but because he was so afraid of the intrusive images that occupied his mind if he was not able to fill it with something else. For example he would often ask his younger brother to accompany him to the toilet to avoid being on his own. He managed adequately at school because it was so busy and he was never on his own.

The family's asylum status remained uncertain and was proceeding through various appeals. They had been told by their solicitor that there was nothing more to do, and that they now had to wait for a response from the Home Office to their most recent appeal. They were under the impression that to try and find out more information might jeopardise their case.

The family's response to Jyrgen's difficulties was to try and reassure him, but he was often unconsolable. His father found it very frustrating that his oldest son was so distressed and that there appeared to be nothing that he could do to help. His mother was already receiving psychological treatment from an adult service and wanted to know if Jyrgen could receive something similar. Jyrgen was embarrassed about his difficulties and was very keen to find a solution.

As part of the assessment, Jyrgen completed a 13-item self-report questionnaire; the Children's Revised Impact of Events Scale – CRIES-13 (Perrin et al., 2005). This measure requires the child to indicate how often ("not at all", "rarely", "sometimes", or "often") they experience various post-trauma symptoms. The items can be scored and added to produce three subscale scores. The CRIES-13 has been shown to be useful in screening for Post-traumatic Stress Disorder (PTSD) (Perrin et al., 2005), with equally useful cut-off scores for either the total score, or the sum of the intrusion and the avoidance subscales. When Jyrgen's scores on the intrusions and avoidance subscales were added together, they totalled 38 (maximum possible 40, suggested PTSD cut-off 17), and when this was added to his score on the arousal subscale, the total was 59 (maximum possible 65, suggested PTSD cut-off 30).

Formulation

Different anxiety disorders may overlap to a certain extent, and I considered that with Jyrgen, it was not particularly important to differentiate between the diagnoses of PTSD, Generalised Anxiety Disorder, Separation Anxiety and Specific Phobia. Classifying Jyrgen's anxiety in such a way may have given it the appearance of being less complex than it actually was. In any case, the treatment of all of these disorders involves exposure and cognitive restructuring (King et al., 2005).

Drawing on a cognitive model of trauma reactions (Meiser-Stedman, 2002), my formulation was that Jyrgen's current difficulties were the result of the way in which he viewed the world, and the way in which certain memories and images were stored.

World-view

As a result of Jyrgen's experiences of the conflict in Kosovo and in particular his perception of the various threats to himself and his family, he had come to see the world as dangerous, people as malevolent and himself as vulnerable. Once these beliefs were in place, they altered what aspects of his environment he attended to and coloured his view of everything. This perceptual bias maintained his beliefs: the more dangerous he thought the world, the more he was on the look out for danger and so the more he noticed potential danger in the world; and the more potential danger he saw in the world, the more dangerous he believed the world to be (see Figure 4.1).

Memory

Jyrgen was very distressed by terrifying images associated with his experiences in the form of intrusive images during the day (particularly when not

Figure 4.1 Maintenance cycle of unhelpful beliefs.

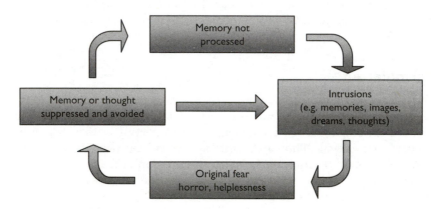

Figure 4.2 Maintenance cycle of avoidance.

occupied) and nightmares at night. Brewin's dual-representation model explains how at times of extreme stress, memories may be laid down in a different way to normal memories (Brewin et al., 1996). They remain as vivid memories formed of the sensory information (the sights, sounds, smells, tastes and touches), which are easily triggered and return to mind even when unwanted; unless and until the person is able to bring these memories to mind and process them, i.e. create a story which essentially wraps up the sensory experiences in words.

However, for Jyrgen, because the traumatic images brought with them the fear and helplessness which accompanied the event, he was desperately trying to push them from his mind, rather than thinking them through. Moreover, when people actively try to suppress or avoid a particular thought, the act of avoiding makes it more likely to come to mind (see Figure 4.2).

The unfamiliar environment of their new home in London did not provide Jyrgen with a safe and secure sanctuary in which he could process his experiences. Furthermore, the family's immigration status remained precarious. They believed that they might be deported at any time and returned to a country where they did not believe that they would be safe. The family were understandably preoccupied by this, and would often discuss it in front of Jyrgen. It was impossible for Jyrgen to think through what had happened to him in the past, when he and everyone around him was preoccupied with what might happen in the future.

Jyrgen's environment seemed to be full of extremely pertinent reminders of his traumatic past, such as school history lessons about the Second World War, games of war with his peers, and seeing police officers around London. Over time Jyrgen's anxiety became increasingly severe, and increasingly frequent. He became unable to tolerate anything that related in any way to Kosovo and his experiences. For example, the family were unable to play traditional Kosovo Albanian music because it would cause Jyrgen to become so anxious.

Treatment

Treatment continued for more than 24 months. There were periods when Jyrgen attended individual weekly sessions, times when he attended intermittently and he also attended a 5-week group intervention.

During the second session, the cognitive model of PTSD (Meiser-Stedman, 2002) was explained to the family. They were told that normally our memories work a bit like a very well-organised wardrobe (Dr Kerry Young, personal communication, January 2000), with each memory having a particular place on a particular shelf, alongside other similar items. This means that they stay neatly stored away until we need them and that we know where to find each item. But a traumatic memory is like someone throwing you a duvet full of stinging nettles and shouting "put it away quick". The duvet is painful to handle and so people shove it in the wardrobe too quickly and try to shut the doors of the wardrobe. But because it is not put away properly, the doors do not close properly, and as the person walks away, the duvet falls out and covers them. Similarly traumatic memories are painful to handle and so people try not to hang on to them so they "shove them away" rather than think them through. This means they are not stored away in the same way as other memories, so they are prone to fall out on top of us when we don't want them to, particularly when we are not busy trying to keep them at bay. Getting a friend to help carefully fold the duvet up, maybe making a bit of room in the wardrobe and placing it carefully on the shelf ensures that the duvet stays put until we want it. Similarly, sometimes with some help, it is possible to think the memory through, and store it along with other memories. This means that the memory is stored helpfully and does not fall out unexpectedly. The family all felt that this was a helpful analogy. I also told them about another boy from Kosovo that I had worked with, who compared the way that his mind worked to the waste paper bin. He put the bin on the desk and filled it to the top with screwed up pieces of paper. He explained that each screwed up piece of paper was a memory of something bad that had happened to him. He went on to tell me that when he walked to school (he made the bin "walk") the traumatic memories spill out in front of his eyes (he made some pieces of the scrunched up pieces of paper fall out) and when he lay down to go to sleep they fell out into his dreams (he lay the bin down and more pieces of paper fell out). He described therapy as taking the pieces of paper out one by one, reading them through together, and then folding them up neatly and putting them away (he folded up the pieces of paper, and placed them in the bin – so that the bits of paper were in the bottom of the bin and took up a lot less room), which meant that they did not fall out when he did not want them to, and that he had more room in his mind to think about other things.

I also elaborated a factory analogy and explained to Jyrgen individually that brains are a bit like a chocolate factory. A chocolate factory takes all the individual ingredients like the cocoa, sugar and milk and mixes them up in just the right quantities to make little packages of chocolate which are then wrapped up. On the wrapper are words which explain what is inside. This means that different chocolate bars can be sorted out and stored. Similarly our minds take different sights, sounds, smells, touches, tastes, feelings and thoughts and mix them up into little packages of memory which are then wrapped up in words. These wrappers usually stop the different sensory information of the memories spilling out when we do not actually want to open them up. In a chocolate factory if the milk is too hot, or the sugar is too sharp, then the factory will not be able to mix up the ingredients properly and may stop working. The ingredients will be left swilling around in the factory waiting to be processed. The machine might try again. But if they are still too hot or too sharp, the factory will break down again. Similarly if the things that happen to us are too scary, then our brains are unable to "process" the information into memories so the "ingredients" or the sensory information such as sights, sounds, smells, etc. are left swilling around in our brains. The events may come to mind again and again, but each time our brains may not be able to process them. The factory needs some help to cool down the milk or to be able to accept hotter ingredients. Similarly, sometimes we need some help to be able to process frightening events into normal memory packages. But until we do process the ingredients they will continue to be floating around and will keep coming back even if we do not want them to.

This explained why Jyrgen was troubled by so many frightening images, memories and nightmares. But it also explained how exposure of some description to both his past memories and current more general frightening images would help reduce his distress. Given that I was going to be encouraging Jyrgen to think through the very worst moments of his life and his greatest fears, it was important to spend sufficient time explaining the rationale to him. When Jyrgen realised that I was moving towards encouraging him to think about his fears – the very things that he spent so much of his time trying hard not to think about – he became quite agitated and simply refused. I explained that I was not expecting him to go through in great detail his worst fears right now, but just that I wondered if in time, the more he were able to think specifically about these scary things here with me in therapy when he chose to, the less he would find himself thinking about them outside of therapy when he did not want to. Although he was happy to come and see me again, he was clearly not convinced that he would be able to think through his memories.

I explained the more cognitive aspects of the formulation to Jyrgen by describing how our brains are very good at noticing things which might be dangerous because often that is what helps us to survive. Given his experiences in Kosovo it made a lot of sense that he was more aware of how dangerous the world might be than many other people, and so it was completely understandable that his brain was more "on the look out" than other people's. But he now had had so much practice at noticing things which might be dangerous, that he had become particularly good at it – in fact he was a little too good at it. I pointed out that the reason David Beckham was so good at free kicks was that he spent so much time practising it, and that if he stopped practising, he would not be so good at it.

Although according to the formulation, some form of exposure was likely to be necessary, it was clear that Jyrgen was not yet willing or able to engage in such work. As with many other traumatised children and families I suggested that I work together with Jyrgen and his family to develop the sense of stability and safety, the familial context, sufficient therapeutic rapport and Jyrgen's own psychological resources that would ultimately enable him to embark on the exposure and cognitive restructuring. This can be thought of as moving up the layers of a pyramid, with each step building on the previous one (see Figure 4.3).

Stabilisation

It was important to make Jyrgen's environment as stable and safe as possible before embarking on any trauma-focused therapy.

> It is difficult to overstate the importance of creating a safe, stable caretaking environment as prerequisite for effective treatment. Clinical services for children and adolescents with PTSD must devote adequate resources and efforts toward this fundamental goal.
>
> (Vernberg and Johnston, 2001, p. 234)

I worked with Jyrgen and his mother on developing regular routines and predictable structures to help punctuate Jyrgen's day. This would make his

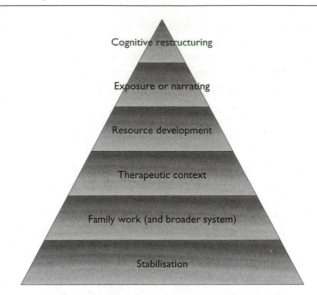

Figure 4.3 The processing pyramid.

environment more predictable and easy to anticipate, which would make it less anxiety-provoking. Such measures are different from the unhelpful safety-behaviours that some clients engage in as a way to try and cope with their anxiety. These were appropriate routines from which most children would benefit. We focused particularly on the routines and rituals leading up to bedtime. Additionally, Jyrgen was keen to work on his bed-wetting, which responded well to a straightforward behavioural intervention. At this stage, his sleep problems had not improved at all and he was continuing to need to be near to his parents in order to fall asleep. This was not unexpected as the formulation was that Jyrgen's sleep difficulties were not the result of his bedtime routine, but more due to his anxiety resulting from his trauma-related view of the world, and partly due to his anticipation of terrifying nightmares. However, at this stage he was not yet prepared to engage in the exposure work. It was not so much that he made an active choice to retain his symptoms rather than do the exposure work, but more that he could not imagine being able to bring the memories of the visions of his nightmares to mind, without being wholly overwhelmed with distress.

I was contacted by Jyrgen's family's solicitor who requested a legal report to assist in their claim for asylum. This can often be a difficult area for clinicians to become involved in. I discussed the matter with Jyrgen and his family. I was concerned that writing such a report might get in the way of the therapeutic support that I was offering Jyrgen and his family, and having spent a long time discussing the nature and scope of confidentiality I was concerned that it would muddy the waters to suddenly be sharing details with the solicitor who would then pass the report on to the Home Office. The family was very keen for me to write the report as they believed that it would assist their claim for asylum. I agreed that I would write a report, but I would discuss it with them before I sent it to the solicitor. I also assured them anything they told me in the future would be subject to the same confidentiality agreement we had negotiated at the beginning of my work with them.

This report could not be an "Expert Witness" report because an Expert Witness must be objective and their duty is to the Court. I had been working with Jyrgen and his family for some time, I was not objective and I considered that with certain very specific exceptions, my duty was to Jyrgen and his family.

At this point there was nothing further to be done regarding the family's asylum status. The uncertainty undermined their sense of safety, but the family's life was as stable as it could be given their circumstances: they lived in reasonable accommodation, were making good use of the limited financial resources that were available to them, the two boys were attending school, and there were appropriate structures and routines in place.

Family work (and broader system)

Following traumatic experiences, some families avoid talking about the experience completely for fear of re-traumatising their children, occasionally families are so preoccupied with events that they do nothing but talk them over time and time again without really processing what happened (Scheeringa and Zeanah, 2001). Working with avoidant families often involves encouraging them to make the events talkable about, without putting pressure on the children to do so. By creating the appropriate familial environment around the child, it is more likely that they will process the events spontaneously with less direct professional intervention.

Jyrgen's family was very supportive of Jyrgen and did all they could to offer him support and reassurance. However, Jyrgen's father understandably wished to gain as much information about his home country as possible and therefore frequently watched cable television programmes about Kosovo, many of which showed graphic images of fighting and death. The television was situated in the living room where most of the family spent most of their time. This meant that Jyrgen had the choice of being in his bedroom on his own, or being with his family and being exposed to frightening images which reminded him of how dangerous the world was. I asked Jyrgen's father through the interpreter if he thought that this had an effect on Jyrgen, and he answered that it was important for him to know what was going on in his country. We discussed this in more detail, and the family decided that they would censor the television to a certain extent, by only watching the more graphic reports after the children had gone to bed.

Jyrgen's family talked about their history as and when it came up, and during such conversations, they reassured their children that they were safe now. Therefore there seemed to be little further work to do with the family as a whole.

At about this time, Jyrgen's school contacted the clinic to ask for help in knowing how to cope with Jyrgen's anxiety at school. Although he was a popular and hard-working pupil, the school had become very concerned when during a normal playground game his peers had pointed imaginary guns at his head. Jyrgen had become so distressed that it had clearly frightened his friends and even some of the teachers. With the family's permission, a colleague spoke at length with the school discussing the nature of Jyrgen's anxieties, how they might manage situations and how they might help him to develop his own strategies for dealing with difficult situations.

Therapeutic context

If a therapist is going to expect a child or young person to talk about the traumatic experience in great detail, then it is important to make the place in which that will happen extremely safe. This may develop naturally over time, but sometimes, the therapist needs to invest time and energy nurturing it. Jyrgen took to therapy very readily, partly because of the endorsement of his family, and partly simply as he became familiar with the clinic, the therapist and the routine of therapy.

Resource development

Enabling a traumatised child to control their emotions and the images in their mind may help them to function better generally, but are also useful skills to take into exposure work. Someone is likely to be more willing to purposefully think about the frightening images if they know that they have skills to control images and the emotions elicited.

As it happened, the clinic ran a group intervention for traumatised refugee children. This was a manual-based intervention aimed largely at symptom management, but it incorporated elements of exposure work (Smith et al., 2000). Jyrgen attended the five sessions of the group. He said that he enjoyed the group tremendously and often asked when there would be another one. He seemed particularly to cherish the opportunity to meet other young people from Kosovo who were also struggling with various psychological problems because of their experiences. When it came to the exposure elements of the intervention, Jyrgen did not choose to work on any of his main fears, instead choosing to work on a very mild fear, with some success. There was a concurrent group for parents which was explicitly not aimed at their own traumatic symptoms, but was intended to support the parents in parenting their traumatised children and supporting the between-session elements of the intervention.

Individual sessions continued after the group. These focused on teaching Jyrgen about the nature of anxiety and helping him to develop the relaxation skills that he had begun to learn in the group. He realised that he had some control over his feelings and his images. His "safe place" consisted of a building which was like a fortress on the outside, and a very well-resourced youth club on the inside. It was guarded by very fierce well-armed soldiers with large tanks. The inside consisted of many rooms each with a number of activities. It was as if even in his "safe place" Jyrgen could only find sanctuary from his anxiety by distraction. There was one room which was a chill-out room with soft lights, bean bags and music. This room became the focus of a number of guided imagery/relaxation sessions.

Exposure and cognitive restructuring

After more than a year, Jyrgen said that he was ready to embark on some exposure work. He was terrified about it and he wanted to know that he could stop and change his mind if he wanted to at any time. Although he was reluctant to do the work, he was wholly fed up with the inconvenience of his symptoms; he wished to do something about them and thought that he needed to put his fears "through the factory". Rather than process his past experiences, he preferred to work on his fear of being alone. Together we drew up a hierarchy of spending increasing amounts of time on his own and this was worked on both during and between sessions. We continued using fairly standard CBT techniques for anxiety (Smith et al., 1999). Work progressed slowly, with some progress and some set-backs.

The family unexpectedly asked to attend one of Jyrgen's appointments and announced that they had been granted indefinite leave to remain in the UK by the Home Office. Although they had heard more than a week before they said that they still could not quite believe it. They had plans for moving to a new house, and gaining jobs, and at last feeling able to settle down. Jyrgen's anxiety continued and he was only occasionally managing to sleep in his own room without one of his parents with him, but then only if his younger brother was present.

Jyrgen arrived at one session and said that he had had a particularly distressing nightmare the previous night, and asked if he could work on that in the session. This was the first time that he had been prepared to talk in any great length about his nightmares. He described a haunting face with scars and blood which he had seen in his nightmare. In describing the face Jyrgen became visibly distressed and asked if he could open the door in case he needed to run out.

I invited Jyrgen to draw the face which he had found so frightening, and he looked at me in disbelief. I reassured him that he was safe, that his mother was downstairs, that we could stop any time he liked, that this was a face from his nightmares and not a face that could hurt him now. He told me that the face reminded him of all the killing that he had seen in Kosovo and in particular about the dead bodies that he and his family had walked past as they left. He said that it made him scared that he would be killed too. I reassured him that he was safe now, and added that by drawing it he would in some ways be taking control of the image, rather than have the image control him. Finally, I said that by drawing it, he might be able to leave the picture and the image in the consulting room rather than taking it home. Reluctantly Jyrgen drew a face. I could see why he had been so scared. His drawing got faster and faster, when he completed it, he said very briskly "can we stop now?" and started to walk down the corridor towards the waiting room. I considered whether to encourage him to return, but he had already reached the end of the corridor and was walking down the stairs to the waiting room. I caught up with him and praised him for being so brave and being able to get the picture out and on to the paper. When he was safely back with his mother, he was grinning and appeared to be pleased with the work that he had done. This was an appropriate return to a safe and secure base following a therapeutic excursion towards his fears. We continued with various sessions of exposure to his fears where we discussed and often drew the images that haunted him. In order to help him take control of the images, we also worked on various imagined machines and people that would help him to vanquish the images. Through the exposure and discussion, he was able to break the link between the image and the fear, and simply by making his thinking explicit he spontaneously challenged and changed many of his unhelpful thoughts with very little input from me.

In what unexpectedly turned out to be the last session of individual therapy, Jyrgen asked if he could show me what he had been working on between sessions. He showed me a picture of a special car which had been helping him with his worries. Each time he became worried, he would simply use the special features of his car to get rid of his anxiety. Essentially the special features of the car served as a reminder of different techniques to cope with his anxiety.

The family went on an extended trip over a school holiday so there was a break in my contact with Jyrgen. When they returned they phoned the clinic and asked for an appointment. The whole family attended and they told me that things had continued to improve over the previous few months and that they did not feel it necessary to come at present. They were keen for me to keep the case open for a while so that they could return if there were any problems. I asked for more details of the improvements, and they explained that Jyrgen was sleeping through the night in his own room (which he shared with his brother) most nights. He was not only able to tolerate traditional Albanian songs, but also enjoyed singing them and he was able to go to the toilet on his own. As part of a standard outcome measure, I asked Jyrgen to complete the Children's Revised Impact of Events Scale again. This time, his scores on the intrusions and avoidance subscales when added together totalled 6 (score at assessment 38, suggested PTSD cut-off 17), and when this was added to his score on the arousal subscale, the total was 15 (score at assessment 59, suggested PTSD cut-off 30).

Conclusions

Jyrgen eventually benefited from exposure and cognitive restructuring, during which his traumatic memories were processed and he was able to make a more helpful meaning of his past, which changed the way that he saw his future. However, initially he was not willing to embark on such work. He understood the rationale for it, but was simply not prepared to undertake it. It seemed that various factors were necessary but not sufficient to enable him to confront his most frightening thoughts: the safety and stability provided by his family's asylum status, the creation of a secure therapeutic context, the development of his psychological resources, his creativity and imagination, and his motivation. Once he had "survived" one exposure session, improvement was relatively rapid and he clearly carried on the therapy between sessions, with the assistance of his family.

References

Brewin, C. R., Dalgleish, T. and Joseph, S. (1996) A dual representation theory of posttraumatic stress disorder. *Psychological Review*, 103, 670–86.

Ehntholt, K. A. and Yule, W. (2006) Practitioner Review: Assessment and treatment of refugee children and adolescents who have experienced war-related trauma. *Journal of Child Psychology and Psychiatry*, 47, 1197.

King, N. J., Heyne, D. and Ollendick, T. H. (2005) Cognitive-behavioral treatments for anxiety and phobic disorders in children and adolescents: A review. *Behavioral Disorders*, 30, 241.

Meiser-Stedman, R. (2002) Towards a cognitive-behavioral model of PTSD in children and adolescents. *Clinical Child and Family Psychology Review*, 5, 217–32.

Perrin, S., Meiser-Stedman, R. and Smith, P. (2005) The children's revised impact of event scale (CRIES): Validity as a screening instrument for PTSD. *Behavioural and Cognitive Psychotherapy*, 33, 487.

Scheeringa, M. S. and Zeanah, C. H. (2001) A relational perspective on PTSD in early childhood. *Journal of Traumatic Stress*, 14, 799–815.

Smith, P., Dyregrov, A., Yule, W., Perrin, S., Gjestad, R. and Gupta, L. (2000) *Children and War: Teaching Recovery Techniques*. Bergen, Norway, Foundation for Children and War.

Smith, P., Perrin, S. and Yule, W. (1999) Cognitive behaviour therapy for post traumatic stress disorder. *Child Psychology and Psychiatry Review*, 4, 177.

Vernberg, E. M. and Johnston, C. (2001) Developmental considerations in the use of cognitive therapy for posttraumatic stress disorder. *Journal of Cognitive Psychotherapy*, 15, 223–37.

Chapter 5

Foster family change and transition for a looked-after child

Miriam Richardson and Andrew Edge

In order to respect the confidentiality of the children and carers we work with, this case study describes a fictional child and foster family, who have many of the characteristics of those we see on a regular basis. We gratefully acknowledge all we have learned from the children and foster carers with whom we have worked and who, along with colleagues, have contributed significantly if indirectly to this chapter.

Introduction

Jason was 11 years old when we met him and his foster mother following his referral to the Children Looked After Service, a targeted team within a specialist Child and Adolescent Mental Health Service (CAMHS). Of particular concern were Jason's hyperactive behaviour, demands for attention and violent outbursts at home and school. The carers found it difficult when his violent rages led him to attack their young grandchildren, or a younger child who was in a permanent foster placement with them. They also feared his exclusion from school. This was a 'bridging' short-term placement, until a permanent foster family could be found for him, but the stress on the family was so great that they were considering asking for him to be moved immediately.

As we explored the situations and relationships within which Jason's difficult behaviour took place we came to understand it as a communication of his fears, of overwhelming anxiety. We were also aware of considerable anxiety among the adults who shared responsibility for Jason, and from our systemic perspective we were curious about the interconnection between their anxiety and Jason's. Our therapeutic interventions consequently took place with a number of different people, hoping to encourage collaboration that would 'hold' Jason and his carers, whilst enabling him to find ways to grow and change and begin to make successful transitions.

Recognising the complexity of the Looked After Child's situation we routinely allocate two therapists to a referral like Jason's, one to offer individual work to the child and the other to work with the adults. Andrew

Edge's (AE) work with Jason was completed in 46 sessions. For a child with Jason's history, anxiety is associated with deep-seated and justifiable fears, present in his life from early infancy, and associated with an absence of adults who can be relied on to provide safety, as well as with on-going transition. Therapeutic interventions need to be multi-layered and responsive to history and circumstance.

Theoretical framework

Our therapeutic approach has its roots in systemic theory, which focuses on people in relationship with each other, the effects that we each have on those connected to us, and the effects they have on us (see for example Dallos and Draper 2000 for historical and theoretical overview). It also has roots in social construction (McNamee and Gergen 1992) and communication theory (Pearce 1994). Gregory Bateson (1972) pointed out that behaviour and communication have meaning only when we know the contexts in which they take place. The meaning we give, however, is constructed through our communication and relationships with others, starting from the moment we are born, and we understand it as both bodily and verbal communication. Contexts of culture and society, family stories and relationship all shape our 'realities' and our sense of what we should and should not do (Cronen 1994, Cronen and Lang 1994).

The focus of the curiosity and interventions of systemic therapists is interpersonal relationships and circular patterns of interaction between people. The Milan and post-Milan methods (Palazzoli et al. 1980, Cecchin 1987) stress the usefulness of hypothesising about the meanings that might be given to actions and experience. As is always the case, our own hypothesising was influenced by our beliefs and values, as well as by the beliefs, values and practices that surrounded us. Jason's behaviour might have been given different meanings, but the hypothesis of anxiety became increasingly useful as our work developed.

Fredman's (2004) work on emotion was useful in our approach to Jason's difficulties. She looks at emotion as created and shared in the relationships between people, within their culture and community.

In our practice we believe that those we work with are 'experts' in many aspects of their lives and this helps us to enter their world, experience and language (Anderson and Goolishian 1992). Our methods of working drew on systemic, narrative (White and Epston 1990) and non-directive play therapies (Axline 1969, Wilson and Ryan 2005), as well as theories of child development, the impact of abuse and trauma, and attachment (e.g. Cairns 2002). The processes of the work were informed by Shotter's writings on 'joint action' (1993) and spontaneous responsiveness to the unique moments of our interactions with each other (2005). Griffith and Elliott Griffith's

(1994) work on 'emotional postures' has been particularly relevant in working with anxiety.

Jason's early history

Jason's history was typical in its complexity to that of many of the children referred to our CAMHS Children Looked After Service. One of the threads through his life had been change and impermanence.

His mother was 21 when he was born, the second of four children all by different fathers (see Fig. 5.1). Jason, his older half sister and two younger half brothers lived – more or less – with their mother until Jason was four, but it was four years of upheaval, uncertainty, neglect and harm. His mother's own childhood had been troubled, and she suffered mental health difficulties, taking overdoses when feeling suicidal. The children had periods of separation from her when she was in hospital but information on when these significant separations had happened was not available. Their mother's partners were men who seemed to offer help and salvation, but who became physically, emotionally and sexually abusive to her and her children. As a young child Jason witnessed domestic violence, severe sexual assault on his mother, and the death in their home of a drug-addicted friend of his mother. Life was disrupted by escapes to refuges, moves from town to town. The local authority knew of sixteen such moves. After the children had been found in the care of a heroin addict they were taken into care by Social Services, who found foster families for them.

Life in the care of the Local Authority was for some time no more settled. Jason's behaviour was challenging, and between the age of 4 and 10 he had lived in six different foster homes and had attended at least five different schools. He had been with his current carers for a year when he was referred to our service by a Social Services manager, as 'High Priority'.

The foster family

The foster carers Pauline and Brian were a couple in their fifties, with a daughter at university and a married son with two young children 3 years and 18 months old. They often looked after their grandchildren. They also fostered a 7-year-old girl, Tamsin, to whom they had offered a permanent placement (see Fig. 5.1).

Caring for a boy with highly complex needs had an impact on the family. They were concerned about the effect his behaviour seemed to be having on the other children. They found his short-term exclusions from school hard to manage, and were aware that academically he was dropping further and further behind his peers. They did not feel they were making any progress with Jason.

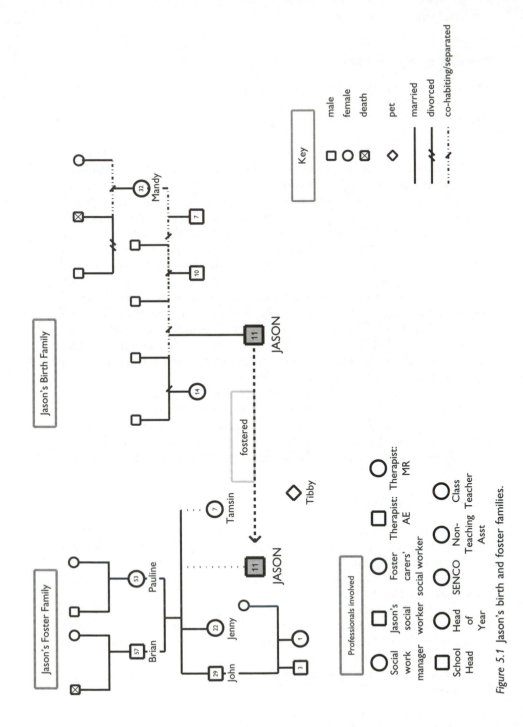

Jason's Birth Family

Jason's Foster Family

Key

male
female
death

pet

married
divorced
co-habiting/separated

Mandy

JASON

fostered

Tamsin

Tibby

JASON

Pauline

Brian

Jenny

John

Professionals involved

Social work manager

School Head

Jason's social worker

Head of Year

Foster carers' social worker

SENCO

Therapist: AE

Non-Teaching Asst

Therapist: MR

Class Teacher

Figure 5.1 Jason's birth and foster families.

The professional network

A complex network of adults is responsible for the well-being of a child in the care of a local authority (see DfES 2006, and Fig. 5.1). As well as the foster family and the social worker who supported and supervised them, Jason had his own social worker to look after his interests. The Looked After Child's social worker is key in the child's life. He or she holds their history and continuity, the connections with birth family, and legal responsibility for their future. Due to staff changes Jason had been allocated a new social worker (his sixth) who hardly knew him.

At school the Head, Head of Year, SENCO (Special Educational Needs Co-ordinator) and a non-teaching assistant were all closely involved with Jason. They had recently moved him to a different class hoping this might help him, only to find he became even more challenging. They were resorting to short-term exclusions to manage his aggressive behaviour.

As we collected information following the referral we became aware of the high level of anxiety shared not only by the foster carers but also within the rest of the professional network, as each person responded to what they believed they ought to do to meet the priorities of their profession and their agency (Cronen and Lang 1994, p 10). Their anxiety was communicated by conversations that were blaming and critical, flurries of email, physical and verbal stress. As therapists we wondered about the impact that this might be having on Jason, with the heightened sensitivity to adult anxiety that many Looked After Children experience, and the connections they make with the possibility of rejection (see Fig. 5.2).

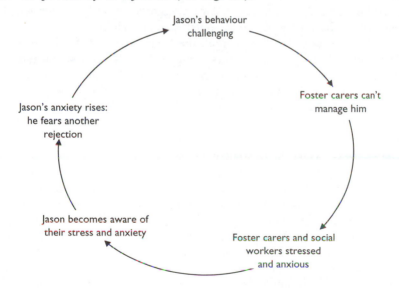

Figure 5.2 Circular connections between Jason's anxiety, his behaviour and adult stress.

The assessment process and developing hypotheses

As a first step in the assessment process we requested a meeting with the adults in Jason's life, to gain as many perspectives as we could on his difficulties. We also hoped, through a process of dialogue which valued each person's thoughts, opinions and feelings (Anderson 1999, pp 65–6), to invite this fragmented and highly anxious adult network to move together to a more reflective thoughtful position, where they might collaborate in support-ing each other to work in the best interests of Jason. (See Egan 2004, especially pp 281–2.)

Initially none of the adults could identify patterns for Jason's outbursts, but talked 'as if a switch had suddenly been turned on', describing a charming boy who was suddenly out of control. They thought he probably had ADHD. However, as their own anxiety levels dropped, and the sense of collaboration and mutual support became more tangible, their thinking became clearer and their understanding changed. The foster carer made a connection between his moody emotional outbursts (she called them 'hypos') and any change in routine. School realised that the less structured times, like break and particularly the longer lunchtime, were very hard for him to manage, as had been the change of class. They also realised that being told 'No' would lead to an outburst, and we wondered with them if Jason might experience *any* 'No' as rejection, connecting with past loss and disruption. They began to notice that if another child – or adult – ignored him, or was not clearly on his side, he would assume that they disliked and rejected him, and he would respond with aggression. They recognised that in many ways he functioned like a much younger child.

This shift in understanding marked the beginning of different responses from adults and we felt Jason was being sufficiently contained and sup-ported for individual work to begin (see Fig. 5.3). We met with him and his foster mother. ADHD had recently been ruled out by a paediatric assess-ment, and Jason's nervous, but managed behaviour during the hour we spent with him also pointed to a primarily emotional basis for his beha-viours. For children with complex histories and difficulties like Jason's, a misdiagnosis of ADHD can sometimes be given.

Pauline's biggest concerns for Jason were that he seemed unable to make friends and 'bullied' smaller children. Jason himself agreed he sometimes 'accidentally' swore, and went 'hypo' and hurt other children. At such times he felt the 'strops just burst out' and he wished he had more control over them. While wanting friends, Jason's view of the world was that because other boys did not like him, he did not like them. He thought he had lived with his carers for about six months (in fact it was a year), got on with them about 'half' the time, but felt Tamsin often competed for attention. Jason's biggest wish was for a 'permanent' foster family, though there was a

Figure 5.3 Circular connections between adults' calmness and Jason's anxiety and behaviour.

sense, as he described himself as being 'big and getting bigger', that he thought the chances were becoming increasingly unlikely.

By now we were developing hypotheses to help guide AE in the individual therapy with Jason and Miriam Richardson (MR) in the therapeutic consultations she was offering the foster carers. We were coming to link his aggressive behaviour with anxiety (see Chapter 7), his 'fight' (rather than flight or freeze) response to perceived danger. For Jason, it may also have been, from birth, the way he experienced people relating to each other when highly stressed, the way he saw boys expressing emotion at school: a learned method of coping, a communication to those around him of his anxious feelings.

We hypothesised too that earlier experiences had made it necessary for Jason to be hyper-vigilant, hyper-alert, to anything that could be seen as dangerous, especially as the adults in his life had not consistently been able to keep him safe and had often been the source of danger (Thompson 2001, p 163). His difficulty in making friends could be connected to this, so that any behaviour by another that was ambivalent, he would see as negative, hostile, and so would go on the attack.

In hypothesising we drew on theories of attachment, and research into the effects on young children of repeated trauma and neglect (Heard and Lake 1997). We considered the view that early abusive experiences create a primarily anxious view of the world, where others are perceived as unsafe. Fear or anxiety of becoming the type of person who perhaps created the greatest fears/anxieties for the child (especially if the child is the same gender as the abuser), can increase anxiety further, ironically making the child more susceptible to enacting similar violent behaviours. So the child can develop a sense of themselves as being dangerous/bad, which can be inadvertently reinforced by others' reactions, creating a circular self-fulfilling prophesy. When these episodes of increased anxiety occur in the present, feelings associated with past traumatic experiences and fears for the future can all become a muddled, terrifying, overwhelming morass for the child. Jason expressed this as violent anger and 'hyper' behaviour. Given his likely anxious experiences of himself and the world, we had a sense that Jason's greatest wish for a permanent foster family, which he bravely shared in the initial meeting, probably felt unachievable for him.

His social worker and foster carer shared this view, and as we began individual therapy with Jason and parallel therapeutic support for Pauline, we ensured that the wider professional network was kept involved through regular reviews at roughly three monthly intervals, and less formal telephone contact.

Jason's individual work with Andrew Edge

What is created within the therapeutic relationship between the therapist and the child is seen as the principal agent for change, from both the systemic psychotherapy (Shotter 1993) and non-directive play therapy (Wilson and Ryan 2005) perspectives, which primarily inform my practice. Both approaches believe trusting the child to decide the focus and goals for the work allows for more helpful and ethical outcomes. Deciding when to make tentative suggestions about potential activities and when to leave this entirely to the child is considered on a case by case basis. In this instance in the early stages, while the content of therapy sessions was determined by Jason, I took more of an active role in suggesting activities which might help him achieve his clearly articulated goals. Throughout the 46 sessions over 18 months, a variety of interconnected themes seemed present, but certain themes appeared more to the fore at different stages, so following this seemed a helpful way of structuring this account. All sessions took place in the same generic therapy room, the only play materials being a dolls' house with furniture, art materials and four boxes for figures, animals, 'monsters' and homemaking toys, which I placed in one corner.

Early stages

Making connections

A link Jason made from the outset was how others reacted to his angry behaviour. So while his highest priority was to make friends, he decided that rather than look at this he should focus on managing his 'hypos', as he believed friendships would automatically follow. We began using techniques which linked physical sensations to his unwanted behaviours (Gordon and Dawson 1996), which Jason named 'Early Warning Signs', such as feeling 'excited' before losing control or what others have described as 'anxious arousal'. Specific episodes of violence were 'tracked' (explored in detail) using anger mountains and freeze frame cartoons (Jenkins 1990). Narrative therapy techniques like 'externalising' (White 1989), where powerful feelings are personified, enabled Jason to invent his own Yu-Gi-Ho characters for anger and powerful forces to defeat them. Captain Calm marshalled the Oxygen Army inside his body to combat 'excited, stressy and scary' feelings, which Jason began to identify as the precursors to rage. Gradually Jason became able to develop increased connections and strategies from an 'observer' (Pearce 1994) or 'fly-on-the-wall' position to his own behaviour.

Making circular connections/past, present and future

Through this process Jason apparently began to understand not only the relationship between his feelings and behaviours, but also the circular relationship of how others' behaviour affected his thoughts/feelings/behaviour, and then in turn how this affected others' responses. Although initially this involved links with current events, we began tentatively to explore how his feelings and behaviours might connect with his understanding of the past and future visions of life. We practised relaxation and 'Take Five' techniques, to help Jason reconnect with the present when 'flashbacks' occurred. Understandably Jason was also muddled around where he had lived pre- and post-care, how he could be part of a birth and foster family and what might happen next, for as he told me in the sixth session, 'the future is important'.

We started addressing these areas through 'representational' timelines and genograms, together with Jason beginning to use the available toys for more 'symbolic' (Axline 1969, Wilson and Ryan 2005) exploration of issues. One of the advantages of symbolic play is an increased potential for it to connect simultaneously at different levels of meaning for the child and hopefully allow the exploration of increasingly complex relationships/ processes. It can also allow children to explore concepts and connections that are in 'advance' of their currently developed language and cognitive skills. Initially the symbolic play elements occupied only the final 5 minutes of sessions but appeared to have a greater emotional intensity than preceding work. Examples included Jason talking for the first time about his mother, who had often been violently beaten, while pushing an ambulance (perhaps in part connecting with their joint vulnerability/abuse) or sharing his worry no one would like him even if he changed, after describing the slimy Alien Baby toys as 'disgusting' (possibly a safe way of Jason communicating that his sense of self was so 'terrible' that he believed no one who knew him well would ever want to form a close relationship).

From the seventh session onwards, once Jason seemed to develop a nascent belief that he and his future could be different, the proportion of symbolic play rapidly began to increase. He initially managed this transition by suggesting we use the soldiers to act out the now decreasing angry episodes, rather than 'freeze framing' them on paper. Over the course of our work Jason continued to use toys for concretely 'representing' current dilemmas, yet increasingly much of the play seemed to relate more 'symbolically' to generalised unspecified anxieties connected with past experiences, future fears and self image.

Middle stages of therapy

Safety

Unsurprisingly given his early experiences, one of these anxieties appeared to relate to feeling unsafe in infancy. 'Disgusting' Alien Babies played on steep roofs, close to hot cookers, and were abandoned in woods. Over time though Jason decided they 'came in peace and should be cared for'. A related theme seemed more about fears for the future. Week after week my play character, of an 'Ordinary Guy' represented by a rope doll, would be attacked in his home by Jason's 'Immortal Pirate', who knew no pain, hunger or fear. Interestingly in an earlier session Jason had told me the scariest film he ever saw was *Pirates of the Caribbean*, where immortals fight to find peace and be allowed finally to die. Having tried to frighten my character, the pirate would then seek to befriend him but would often move so fast both of them would end up hurt. Like several other looked-after children I have worked with, at one point in such play Jason suddenly said how angry and upset he had been in a Harry Potter film when someone said, 'If the bitch is bad so is the pup'. I hypothesised these play sequences could relate both to current angry outbursts and Jason's fears of what he might do to himself and others as an adult, because of his family history.

While I formed many such hypotheses, which I used to guide my understanding of the work, I was careful not to offer interpretative links to past experiences, current events or future visions, believing Jason would make useful connections himself. Instead I tentatively commented on characters' thoughts and feelings or how I thought Jason was feeling in a particular moment. For me this fitted both with systemic psychotherapy, where the therapist facilitates the client in making their own useful new meanings and the 'child led' (Axline 1969, Wilson and Ryan 2005) non-directive play therapy training I began during the course of this intervention.

In the review meetings, involving Jason, his carer and MR, we began to hear of significant changes. After 16 sessions it was reported that despite having to manage another change of social worker and resumption of sibling contact, Jason was less angry, behaving more age appropriately, helping round the house and had some friends. Jason thought it important to continue therapy as he still occasionally had violent outbursts. In addition, unbeknownst to Jason, contact with his mother was about to resume, and despite his significant attachment to his current carers efforts were being made to find a permanent foster family.

Anger

In the following sessions, through to the 24-session review, the Immortal Pirate play developed apparently to explore extreme anxious anger, with the character 'feeling no pain because he's angry' but eventually being able to 'use his mind and slow motion' to manage his behaviour. A less frequently played, alternative future vision seemingly emerged in the form of Peter Pan, who, while immortal, used his powers to defeat villains and make friends. Although at times Jason would allow me to tell his carer about specific difficulties he faced, such as being bullied by a boy at swim club, the content of sessions otherwise remained confidential. Before reviews we would discuss whether therapy should continue, what themes I would be sharing and what Jason wished to share or ask. In the 24-session review Jason explained how therapy, 'Helps me think about life and what effects things have on my life'. Despite hearing Jason now had close friends, a 12-year-old's vocabulary, could manage his behaviour in different contexts and was increasingly independent, it was decided work would continue, as he was becoming increasingly distressed by the thought of not remaining permanently with his current carers.

Identity and belonging

During the course of the following sessions, Jason changed so markedly that Social Services struggled to keep his profile updated in their advertisements for permanent foster carers for him. Play was increasingly used to explore sense of self, feelings about not being wanted long-term by his carers and anxieties about whether anyone else would. Epic struggles between 'good' and 'bad' ensued, represented by Slayers and Vampires. Having shifted sides endlessly, Jason decided he was neither, inventing a Highwayman named Captain Blood, 'a bad guy who does good things'. The Captain, having saved women and children from an evil grave robbing family (similar in composition to his foster family), had a son Young Red 'who might turn out good in the end but never takes his mask off'. Eventually in session 33, having seen his father killed by the grave robber family, Young Red, 'who no one has ever seen so angry in the history of time', kills them all and removes his mask so others can 'see his anger and pain'. Working from a position that the same piece of play can simultaneously have different levels of symbolic meaning specific to the individual child, one of the ways I understood these scenarios was Jason perhaps beginning to believe that a family could want him even if they knew about his history and the powerful/complex ways it still affected him at times. In the weeks that followed the Lord Vampire tried to make Young Red his apprentice, but after terrifying Satan in hell and killing an archangel in heaven, Young Red decided to remain a Highwayman, who terrorised then saves a family, before choosing to live alone in a forest. This play possibly represented Jason exploring his fears both of becoming like those who had abused him but equally that if he unquestioningly took on the values of his foster families he might lose his sense of self, and eventually realising there might be a third way, where he could be a 'good enough' person and true to himself.

Ending sessions

Separation and reconnection

Our final four sessions took place as Jason began introductions to his out-of-county permanent foster family. Important issues seemed to be anxieties about moving, whether his new family would really want him if they knew about his different aspects of self, including the now infrequent times of anger and vulnerability. Some of the ways these powerful, interconnected and deeply personal anxieties were explored included characters falling into dark holes, hiding their feelings when others were watching, saying they did not believe in mothers and helping cubs reunite with lionesses.

Understanding difference

In the last session Jason chose to have a 'goodbye party' and did not undertake any symbolic play. Instead Jason talked, while we ate the food he had selected, about different things making different people angry and their ways of managing it. Jason explained that something which made him angry was when people said he had no parents, because even though he had not seen his dad for years and only infrequently met his mum, he still had parents. This led to a conversation about different peoples' abilities to understand others' and their own feelings. As Jason left he commented, 'Well at least *you* understand' and I replied how important it was now for Jason to feel understood, understand himself and others.

Therapeutic interventions with foster carers

While AE was undertaking this work with Jason, MR met with his foster mother. (His foster father's work prevented him from attending.) Initially we met weekly, but this became monthly as the sense of crisis passed. Working with a strong belief in the therapeutic role of sensitive and responsive foster care (Dozier et al. 2002), we followed two interconnected themes: ways in which Pauline and Brian might help Jason with his difficulties, and support for the carers themselves in all the many ways in which caring for Jason impacted on their lives and on those close to them. To keep the different threads of the work connected, AE and I had frequent conversations, as well as 3-monthly reviews with him and Jason, and regular meetings with his social worker. This also provided opportunities for us to remind ourselves of the positive changes that were taking place, as this sense of progress sometimes got lost in the day-to-day struggles.

Looking back on the work, I became aware that processes that developed between Pauline and me in our sessions resonated not only in AE's work with Jason but also in Pauline and Brian's interactions with him at home. These interconnected processes included:

- Creation of relationship within which collaborative exploration and learning could take place.
- Understanding the story of Jason's life and connections between past traumas and present experiences.
- Finding ways of talking about difficulties that enabled us to find new ways of managing them, including rehearsing new ways of going on that built resilience and resourcefulness.
- Preparation for change as a way of preventing anxiety, including planning good endings.

I worked collaboratively with Pauline to create a responsive relationship that enabled us to explore, reflect and learn together (Anderson 1999). I was inspired by her commitment to Jason, her growing determination to make the placement work, and her resourcefulness. She in turn treasured Jason's unique sparkle, and the potential she saw in him.

As her relationship with him deepened during the course of the work, she was able to help him develop his ability to reflect and learn. We interwove through these conversations about Jason and his difficulties others that invited Pauline to reconnect with her own resources, the values that had led her to foster, the people and situations where she found calm and renewal.

We recognised that Pauline was 'expert' in her knowledge of Jason. From the first session we looked at what was working well, identifying and developing Pauline and Brian's abilities that would attend to Jason's anxiety: a watchful awareness of his needs, an ability to stay calm when he was agitated, and consistency. She became increasingly attuned – spontaneously responsive (Shotter 2005) – to his communication of his needs, pre-empting his outbursts and helping him find ways of managing his moods and actions.

Developing stories and understanding

Looking together at Jason's history, we explored possible connections between past experiences and the meanings he might give to current situations. This shifted the problems from Jason as an individual to seeing them in the context of relationships and situations of different times in his life. Had he had, for example, to compete fiercely with siblings – with other children – to ensure his needs were met, while at the same time having to protect and care for them? And were these patterns persisting, if now unnecessarily? Was the 'hypo' about packing the car for a weekend away connected with distressing memories of luggage going into cars when he was being taken away from all that was familiar, another fearful rejection? The development of this understanding gave new meaning to what he did, allowing Pauline to 'externalise' his behaviour (White 1989) and to see it not as personal defiance and rejection of her. This in turn enabled her to stay calmer and be more positive and reassuring.

Finding a language to talk about difficulties, and developing resources

The process of externalising also helped us find a way of talking about difficulties that made it easier to explore them in detail, and find ways of managing them. Again, this was part of *our* conversations, part of AE's work with Jason, and also an aspect of Pauline's relationship with Jason that she believed to be important. She encouraged him to *talk* about his worries, his difficulties. (This process can be especially useful for the child whose early life has been dominated by trauma, such that their cognition, emotional understanding and language may be underdeveloped [Cairns 2002].)

Pauline talked with Jason about the likely impact of his behaviour on others, and suggested alternatives. She helped him rehearse ways of saying No, ways of talking appropriately on the phone, ways of sticking up for himself verbally rather than physically. She noticed and appreciated his growing ability to be self aware, to discuss difficulties and reflect verbally on the consequences of his actions.

Pauline and Brian encouraged his friendships, seeing it as important for the future that he could form good relationships. Unknown to them, this too connected with the work AE was doing with Jason. As he experienced more positive relationships he began to understand that other children's indifference did not necessarily mean they rejected him. His foster parents were full of praise when they heard he had managed a quarrel by not hitting the other boy, and had later said to the boy 'Let's be friends'. This was a marked difference from the violent way he had dealt with similar situations a year earlier.

Pauline and I also worked to develop practical strategies. For example, if one of the goals was to help Jason get less upset and stay on a more even keel emotionally, we talked about how the foster parents could minimise conflict, whilst holding on to things that were important to them as a family. Which battles were worth fighting, which rules were important to keep, and which might they take a more relaxed position with? Not hitting Tamsin and the grandchildren was one of the important rules. Not clearing away his dirty dishes might be less important, at least initially!

Managing change

The recognition of the connections between Jason's difficult behaviour and anxiety led Pauline to give careful consideration to any change he had to manage. An example was when they were planning an extended holiday. She realised he might become very anxious, fearing he could be 'left behind', abandoned. Her response was to involve him in the plans and the processes. They showed him on the calendar when they would go. They showed him on the internet the house they would be staying in. The sequence of events for the journey were explained in great detail, including how they and their daughter-in-law would look after the needs of Tamsin and the young grandchildren. Pauline took him with her when she took the cat to the cattery, and he was able to look round, so that he would know that Tibby would be well cared for in their absence. The outcome of this was that Jason participated appropriately and cheerfully, managing the holiday with only a few 'hypos' and a lot of fun.

A year and a half into our work a permanent foster home was identified for Jason. Changes that he had managed successfully, and that we had explored and reflected on in our sessions undoubtedly paved the way for this momentous move. Pauline and Brian spent time preparing him. Again a process of appropriate involvement of Jason (for example letting him decide where and how he would first meet his new carers) within an overall strategy managed by the adults, enabled the move to be positive. In our sessions Pauline was able to express her own fears and sense of impending loss more freely than she liked to do with her family, and we saw this as indicative of the quality of the relationship she had developed with this foster child.

The wider professional network also managed the change with care and deliberation, so that all those involved were appropriately prepared. The transition to the new family was unlike any Jason had experienced before, when moves had been connected with failure. Pauline and Jason cried together before he left, sad to be parting but full of hope for his future. These were anxieties and losses that could be appropriately expressed by his carers and by him, a different ending that marked a new beginning.

References

Anderson, H. (1999) Collaborative learning communities. In McNamee, S. and Gergen, K.J. (eds) *Relational Responsibility: Resources for Sustainable Dialogue.* Thousand Oaks, CA, Sage.

Anderson, H. and Goolishian, H. (1992) The client is the expert: a not-knowing approach to therapy. In McNamee, S. and Gergen, K. (eds) *Therapy as Social Construction.* London, Sage.

Axline, V. (1969) *Play Therapy.* New York, Ballantine Books.

Bateson, G. (1972) *Steps to an Ecology of Mind.* New York, Ballantine.

Cairns, K. (2002) *Attachment, Trauma and Resilience: Therapeutic Caring for Children.* London, British Association for Adoption and Fostering.

Cecchin, G. (1987) Hypothesizing, circularity, and neutrality revisited: an invitation to curiosity. *Family Process,* 26(4), 405–14.

Cronen, V.E. (1994) Co-ordinated management of meaning: practical theory for the complexities and contradictions of everyday life. In Siegfried, J. (ed.) *The Status of Commonsense in Psychology.* Stamford, CT, Ablex Publishing.

Cronen, V.E. and Lang, P. (1994) Language and action: Wittgenstein and Dewey in the practice of therapy and consultation. *Human Systems: The Journal of Systemic Consultation and Management,* 5, 5–43.

Dallos, R. and Draper, R. (2000) *An Introduction to Family Therapy: A Systemic Theory and Practice.* Maidenhead, Open University Press.

DfES (2006) *Care Matters: Transforming the Lives of Children and Young People in Care.* Nottingham, DfES Publications.

Dozier, M., Albus, K., Fisher, P.A. and Sepulveda, S. (2002) Interventions for foster parents: implications for developmental theory. *Development and Psychopathology,* 14, 843–60.

Egan, J. (2004) 'Joined up working' at clinical and managerial levels: you can't have one without the other. *Human Systems: The Journal of Systemic Consultation and Management,* 15(4), 273–87.

Fredman, G. (2004) *Transforming Emotion. Conversations in Counselling and Psychotherapy.* London, Whurr Publishers.

Gordon, S. and Dawson, A. (1996) *Keeping Children Safe from Abuse.* Adelaide, Essence Prevention Network.

Griffith, J.L. and Elliott Griffith, M. (1994) *The Body Speaks: Therapeutic Dialogues for Mind-Body Problems.* New York, Basic Books.

Heard, D. and Lake, B. (1997) *The Challenge of Attachment for Caregiving.* London, Routledge.

Jenkins, A. (1990) *Invitations to Responsibility.* Adelaide, Dulwich Centre Publications.

McNamee, S. and Gergen, K. (1992) (eds) *Therapy as Social Construction.* London, Sage.

Palazzoli, M.S., Boscolo, L., Cecchin, G. and Prata, G. (1980) Hypothesizing – circularity – neutrality: three guidelines for the conductor of the session. *Family Process,* 19(1), 3–12.

Pearce, W.B. (1994) *Interpersonal Communication: Making Social Worlds.* New York, HarperCollins College Publishers Inc.

Shotter, J. (1993) *Conversational Realities: Constructing Life Through Language.* London, Sage.

Shotter, J. (2005) *Hearing things in the temporal contours of people's talk: transitory understandings and action guiding anticipations.* (Paper delivered at the Taos Institute Conference on Social Construction: a Celebration of Collaborative Practices, 6–9 October, http:pubpages.unh.edu/~jds/Taos.htm, accessed 16/01/2006.

Thompson, R.A. (2001) Childhood anxiety disorders from the perspective of emotion regulation and attachment. In Vasey, M.W. and Dadds, M.R. (eds) *The Developmental Psychopathology of Anxiety.* Oxford, Oxford University Press.

White, M. (1989) The externalising of the problem and the re-authoring of lives and relationships. *Selected Papers.* Dulwich Centre Publications, 5–28.

White, M. and Epston, D. (1990) *Narrative Means to Therapeutic Ends.* New York, W.W. Norton and Co.

Wilson, K. and Ryan, V. (2005) *Play Therapy: A Non-Directive Approach for Children and Adolescents.* London, Baillière Tindall.

Chapter 6

Prevention of disabling fear and anxiety in a young child and family: a case illustration following a traumatic accident

Mandy Bryon

Introduction

Alice was four and a half when she was admitted to the general surgery specialty following an accident which required surgery to her bowel. She would stay in hospital for six months. Prior to this she had been a happy, popular little girl. She was bright and enjoyed all the pastimes expected of a child her age. Her parents had no medical concerns for their daughter and were looking forward to her leading a normal life.

Alice lived with both her natural parents and her younger brother Mark, aged two years, her mother (Caron) was aged 32 years and worked part-time and her father (James) was aged 38 years and worked full-time. Though both Caron and James's families lived abroad, they had lived in their present home for many years and had made good friends. It was intended that both children would attend the local primary school and continue to belong to a large social network.

Alice was born full term, normal delivery. She reached milestones at expected ages and made good developmental progress. She remained a healthy child and had no hospital admissions.

The purpose of this chapter is to describe in detail the process of psychological case management to illustrate the psychological symptoms inherent in being the recipient of medical and surgical intervention. It would be inaccurate to refer to this case as an instance of anxiety-management; it is more appropriate that the case is unfolded to demonstrate how anxiety manifests in children and families who face medical intervention following accidental injury. Alice and her family could not have prepared for such an event to occur – their anxiety and concerns were completely normal given the circumstances.

Medical background

The injury sustained caused a tear in Alice's rectum and sucked out her bowel. She was admitted to her local hospital where emergency surgery was performed. The suction had caused massive damage to her bowel and colon. All of her small bowel and right-sided colon was removed and the remaining bowel resected. An extensive tear in her rectum was repaired. A colostomy (hereafter referred to as stoma) was performed to avoid use of her colon and rectum. This meant that faeces would be discharged at a higher point in her bowel through an exit made in her lower abdomen and collected outside the body in a bag.

The immediate medical treatment was to ensure nutrition and hydration whilst monitoring the function of the remaining bowel. In Alice's case, the bowel was functioning adequately enough to enable very small amounts of oral fluids and nutrition to be fed directly into the blood stream via a "long-line catheter". There are few veins in the body suitable for accepting nutrition in this way so it is important to keep the site free from infection for as long as possible. The insertion of a long line must be done under general anaesthetic. Feeding in this way is called total parenteral nutrition (TPN). The amount of feed via TPN and output via her stoma must be monitored carefully.

Psychological presentation

Meeting Alice

The clinical psychologist's first contact with the family occurred one week after Alice's accident and the presenting anxiety at that time was not from Alice but from her parents. Caron and James were still in a state of distress as a result of the accident. They spoke for a long time about concerns and issues related to Alice's future, the family and everyone's mental state. While much of this discourse was confused, it may have had a cathartic benefit. The parents were asking questions but were not emotionally receptive to the answers. At this stage the questions were an expression of their distress and disbelief at what had happened to their daughter. It was possible, however, to identify several issues which could be addressed over the next sessions to help the family adapt. These were:

1   How best to tell Alice what had happened.
2   What could she remember of the accident, could she remember any pain?
3   How to talk to each other about the accident (Caron witnessed the accident, James was at work at the time).
4   How to eat in front of her (Alice would be unable to take food orally for some time, if ever).
5   How to go home; both parents felt torn between staying with Alice and a need to return to their home.

6   How to inform Alice's younger brother about the accident, Alice's treatment and assessing his understanding of the accident as he was also present at the time.

7   How to help Alice cope with painful and invasive medical procedures.

The initial plan was to meet the parents, provide opportunity for concerns to be raised, to listen and offer no medical opinion, to help them clarify their thoughts and so reduce the confusion they felt. It was essential to begin to build a relationship with the family which would inevitably be long term.

Management proposals

At the time of the referral for psychological intervention there was no date for discharge of Alice from hospital. There was opportunity for relationships to develop between Alice, her family and the medical team. In order to discover Alice's understanding of and memory of her accident, it was essential to enable her to become familiar with the presence of the psychologist. She was therefore visited every day to engage her parents in innocuous conversation at the bedside and gradually build up the amount of interaction directly with Alice. Eventually, the plan was to see Alice alone.

Sessions with Caron and James, to discuss their concerns, monitor their adaptation and help prevent any potential difficulties occurred daily initially, then several times per week as required. These sessions were held in a side room of the ward, never in front of Alice. Conversations about Alice only took place in her presence if we could be sure she would fully understand the content or if we were prepared to answer her questions.

Organising the team

The nursing structure of the ward meant that a small number of nurses would be assigned to Alice. The nurses provided much more than just medical treatment; they developed relationships with Alice and were able to notice changes of affect, and were crucial in helping her cope with painful procedures. The ward had a play specialist who has trained to use play in helping children cope with the hospital environment. The nurses and play specialist were involved in assessment of Alice's response to her accident, being in hospital and her resultant physical condition.

Weekly ward meetings of the medical team meant that multidisciplinary feedback could occur, as well as the opportunity for discussion of strategies for staff–child–parent interaction. These meetings also had a staff support function. Some members of the nursing team were shocked by Alice's accident. They struggled with the fact that a young child innocently playing could result in such trauma. The majority of cases admitted to the surgical ward were of children born with medical conditions for which surgical intervention was necessary. Though these cases were complex, they usually presented a routine formula and role for the nursing staff. Alice's situation differed from the norm and it was necessary for the emotional impact on the ward staff to be acknowledged, legitimised and discussed. The staff support function allowed staff anxiety to be aired and contained so that they could interact with Alice and her parents without communicating their concerns and worries.

Investigations and rationale

Medical communication and reaction to diagnosis

Obviously the way in which information is communicated to the family is crucial. The reactions of parents to "bad news" can affect the way they perceive the illness and the hospital staff. Good communication is associated with better doctor–patient relationships, more patient satisfaction and increased likelihood that treatment advice will be followed. The family's perception will influence the child and his/her attitude to the medical condition (Maguire and Pitceathly, 2002).

The first investigation was to discover from the doctors Alice's medical condition, treatments done, those due and what they thought they had told the parents. Subsequently, we spoke to the parents to discover their knowledge. The diagnosis came in stages following each operation and test. When the full extent of her injuries was known, prognosis was not definite. The parents had to cope with much uncertainty.

For the first few weeks Alice was mostly sedated and so communication with her was limited. There could not be a direct interview with Alice but it was important that communication occurred. Both the parents and medical staff informed Alice what was being done to her. Thus, Alice was not disregarded but given the same respect as before the accident.

Identify potential stressors

Researchers of maladjustment in sick children have found that being ill does not lead automatically to disturbance in the child or family. Instead, families are viewed as normal, using established resources to manage the illness. A family may only encounter dysfunction when faced with an event which leads to specific feelings of stress for family members. Reports from the nursing staff suggested that the family members were behaving in ways expected following a traumatic event. Both parents were constantly present, they were not interfering with medical treatment although they were interested and asked appropriate questions. They protected Alice from visitors and continued to perform as much of her care as possible in the circumstances.

Potential stressors have been identified in the literature falling broadly under the headings of environment, medical condition and the child. It was possible to investigate the presence of these in this case for intervention or prevention.

Environment

The hospital environment itself has long since been recognised as a potential source of stress. The Platt report, as far back as 1959 (HMSO, 1959), made recommendations to improve the practical care of children in hospital. Although these measures have been met, the stress of painful procedures is still associated with hospital. Parents often report additionally that the ward environment can place stress on usual family roles. The parents must hand over the care of their child to others who "know best". There is a balance to be achieved between a necessary dependence on the medical staff and the need to maintain independence in their parent–child relationship. Parents also report problems with the lack of privacy, having to expose their parenting skills to professionals, feeling that their skills are being judged.

In Alice's case, her parents did not report finding the hospital environment per se anxiety-provoking; rather the potential long-term stay was a source of stress. Initially, both parents found it difficult to leave Alice's bedside. This meant they were unable to have discussions about the accident and its repercussions. They were also unable to be with their younger child. How to leave Alice and return home for a while was a major issue.

Medical condition and uncertainty

The medical condition itself, the daily treatments required and the potential pain these involve produce stress for the child and family. A review of research on the effects of chronic illness on quality of life highlighted the frequent finding that a temporary deterioration in psychiatric status accompanies stressful stages of the illness (Garralda, 1994).

Uncertainty of prognosis and future lifestyle were problematic for the family at some stage as Alice's condition progressed and the sequelae of treatments and surgery became apparent. Initially, the results of the surgery were slow in coming. Caron and James found themselves guessing outcomes and rehearsing "bad news". Caron and James imagined that Alice had suffered such trauma that she would never recover emotionally. The uncertainty of her eventual state was the source of stress at this time.

As Alice progressed, the family developed an increasingly stable normality. This was important information for all the team working with the family, as it is easier for the professionals to move to a more optimistic, practical view than it is for the family. Staff had to be aware of the family's pace of adaptation to the condition of their child. It is now accepted that distress fluctuates over time and such behaviour should not be construed as psychopathology (Wortman and Silver, 1987).

Caron and James had some concerns regarding the painful procedures Alice would endure and to know the best way to inform Alice about her changed physical condition. Alice would need to know why she could not defecate in the normal manner and why she was being refused food. Caron and James were concerned that Alice may perceive them to be denying her food and allowing others to inflict pain and, therefore, not fulfilling their parental role. Similarly, they did not wish Alice to associate all medical staff with pain and thus become disturbed by her environment.

The child

A review of the literature on children suffering post-traumatic stress disorder (PTSD) promised some guidance on indicators of stress. There has been progress in defining and diagnosing PTSD despite initial controversy. Research has provided screening measures for use with children and adolescents (Ward-Begnoche et al, 2006; Kennardy et al, 2006) and indicators and longitudinal effects (Zatzick et al, 2006). Symptoms of note are re-experiencing the event, avoidance and hyper-arousal symptoms. These symptoms are associated with risk for ongoing difficulties. Daily observations of Alice during her admission would be alert to such phenomena.

Identifying the stress which Alice felt presented a difficult psychological assessment task. Clearly, methods would be ongoing and dependent on the relationships built with Alice by the psychologist and the rest of the team. Intervention for parental adaptation would have an indirect effect of helping Alice. There would be no need to develop coping strategies for Alice unless specifically required. None of the behaviours described as indicators of PTSD in a young child were ever observed or elicited.

The strength of family relationships

It has been consistently found that mothers bear the burden of caring for a sick child. Additionally, the mental health of mothers may suffer as a result of this burden (Quittner et al, 1992). A mother's emotional state can affect the child's ability to cope with the illness and can increase the child's report of symptoms. There is little work examining the role of the father in influencing the family's adaptation to illness. The father can be a crucial figure in reducing the mother's burden (Davies and May, 1991). Unfortunately, the fact that mothers play the major caring role often means that professionals communicate mostly with the mother and ignore the father. Thus, he may be marginalised in the care of his sick child.

In this case, as Caron had experience of the medical profession, the risk was that she would be treated as an informed professional rather than a mother. This could alter the balance of the marital relationship, with Caron having to explain Alice's medical condition to her husband, potentially being the harbinger of bad news. There was the possibility of implementing some preventative work which would enlighten the medical team to involve both parents in the teaching of Alice's medical management and reporting of progress. It was important to avoid the temptation to use medical jargon in the knowledge that Caron would understand it.

For Caron and James there were signs that a rift was developing. Caron needed to tell her husband the details of the accident. She needed to know whether he considered her to be at all to blame. James, on the other hand, could not bring himself to think of the distress his daughter may have suffered. Caron and James could articulate concerns Alice's condition would present for them as parents; they had a need to put the accident behind them in order to concentrate on the immediate future. They had different ways of approaching this task. The couple needed help to resolve their impasse (see below).

Talking and using play with Alice – first thoughts

Previously, guidance on the best way to communicate with children about their medical condition has been confusing. There are two opposing views, on the one hand a child should be shielded from the full knowledge to prevent increasing fears and anxieties (Bluebond-Langner, 1978). On the other hand, children were thought to collect information about their condition from overhearing discussions, the media, peers, etc., but to be unable to discuss these with parents and doctors. The implications were that the child could become more anxious and isolated than if they had been fully informed. Recent research has helped clarify best practice in this area. Accurate knowledge of one's own medical condition correlates with less distress, less confusion, improved relationships with the medical team, better adherence to medication and an improved emotional well-being (Veldtman et al, 2001).

In Alice's case the medical team advocated a plan to inform her of all relevant information. The rationale was that Alice would have some drastic changes in physical appearance and diet, and therefore she would need an explanation. Alice would also have long-term daily medical treatments which she would eventually manage herself, and frequent outpatient appointments. The medical team, however, would respect the wishes of the parents if they felt that Alice should be protected from full knowledge. Caron and James intended that Alice should be informed and were accepting of advice as to how and when to do this.

Treatment interventions

Communication with Alice

Research has shown that many children can give sophisticated descriptions of their own illness irrespective of age (Eiser, 1989). Children acquire knowledge from a range of sources and personal experiences and create "scripts" of events to guide their comprehension (Nelson, 1986). Thus, the information given to a child about their own illness should not be restricted according to age. Additionally, it must be acknowledged that it is not possible to control the information a child will acquire from other sources.

The plan to inform Alice about her condition was to be honest and detailed. Whilst ensuring that Alice could understand the gist, accurate medical terms were used as these would be in constant use by the professionals around her. Three approaches to formal information-giving were adopted; direct questioning and discussion, play with a doll and real equipment, and finally, jig-saw and books of body parts.

In order to be cognisant of the "script" Alice was forming of her experiences, she was frequently asked about her treatments and daily routine. This allowed assessment of accuracy of knowledge, extent of anxiety around discussion of such topics, and fostered an open line of communication for Alice to air her concerns.

The play specialist introduced a doll which Alice named. Using real equipment, where possible, Alice attached the same visible tubes and bag to the doll as she had herself, with the support and encouragement of the psychologist to assess knowledge, questions of concern and areas of anxiety. Playing "doctor" assigned Alice some control over the treatments she performed. This temporarily reversed her role as victim and Alice was observed to vent her anger by inflicting pain on the doll. This displaced her anger from the true targets (the treatments and medical staff). Additionally, there was opportunity to assess the extent of her understanding of the function of her treatment and to correct mistakes. The doll was also used to explain intended treatments. A child of Alice's age would be likely to anticipate more pain from a procedure than there actually is. The doll could prepare Alice and enable her to ask questions about a procedure before it occurred.

To inform Alice of the loss of her bowel a jig-saw of a girl which taught body parts was used. Clothing and skin were removed in layers to reveal body organs. It was possible, therefore, to remove part of the intestine to illustrate the part of Alice which was absent. Thus, the jig-saw girl was the subject of our discussion rather than Alice. This avoided any anxiety which direct examination of Alice may have caused.

Alice became very interested in discussions about body parts and function. For a short period of time, her main interest was the jig-saw and books illustrating the body. It was likely that this temporary fascination allowed Alice to vent her anxieties about her situation. It certainly gave staff and parents an opportunity to discuss an anxiety-provoking topic. Caron and James were reassured by the ease with which Alice would discuss her surgery, stoma and TPN.

Management of invasive procedures

Not surprisingly, children report that invasive procedures are the worst aspect of visiting or staying in hospital (Kuttner, 1989). The preschool child's patchy understanding of pain and its causes may add to their anxiety as they may not share an adult's ability to form a logical sequence between medical test and appropriate cure or treatment. For the young child potentially, a medical test is an event in itself seemingly being deliberately inflicted with parental consent with no just cause other than to cause pain. McGrath and McAlpine's (1993) developmental sequence of a child's understanding of pain is useful to see a child's perspective. A child of Alice's age *would* be able to give a gross indication of intensity of pain, and attach emotional terms and adjectives to it, therefore it would be important to ensure that she was helped to understand the rationale for invasive procedures.

Strategies of pain control for children are well documented. Packages of cognitive behavioural interventions for pain management with children have been found to be superior to valium, or watching cartoons prior to the procedure or general anaesthesia (Kazak et al, 1996). Appropriate techniques for a child of Alice's age would include parental presence, stroking, blowing, distraction, imaginary involvement. The context is just as important as the strategy, thus, listening to the concerns of the child, giving the child control, being unhurried, explaining the procedure, etc., are all known to be good clinical practice although they are not formally evaluated in research projects.

For Alice, such clinical practice was adopted. She was informed of procedures even when barely conscious and her expressions of concern were always responded to. Alice reported that cuddles from her parents were the best way to make her better and so they were always included when a procedure was to be administered. Specific techniques used for Alice included blowing bubbles to help relieve a cough, and "practising" the procedure on the doll supplied by the play specialist before and during the procedure (when possible) as a means of distraction.

Communication between family and friends

Intervention here was preventative. Given the amount of research which stresses the importance of maternal mental health and ease of emotional expression as factors influencing the adaptation of the whole family, it was essential to attempt to facilitate communication.

James was unable to hear details of the accident but Caron did not feel that she could carry that knowledge alone. The focus of the sessions was to highlight this dilemma so that the parents could begin to be sensitive to each other's emotional needs. They could be informed about their differences in coping styles and pace.

Caron's needs were more immediate. She needed to recount the accident for some cathartic effect and to prevent herself laying down a distorted memory, whereby she assigned herself blame.

As Alice's affect improved James, in particular, found he could begin to acknowledge the accident as he saw Alice returning to her old self. Caron and James arranged a special meeting and agreed to discuss the accident. They both described the occasion as stressful but useful. It meant that Caron and James were released from their embargo on discussion of the accident.

Caron and James requested guidance on how best to communicate with Mark, Alice's younger brother. Mark was aged two years at the time and it was more probable that he required explanation of the absence of his parents than information about his sister's accident. Following the accident Mark had been with familiar people and remained in his home environment. As Alice's condition stabilised, James made journeys home and brought Mark to the hospital to see Alice. During the course of her admission he stayed for longer periods of the day and became involved in ward activities with the play specialist. Caron and James were given preparation to explain the accident and Alice's medical condition as Mark became interested.

Research on the effects of chronic illness on healthy siblings is sparse. Indications so far are that maladjustment is seen in siblings only when the family is dysfunctional, rather than as a direct result of the illness (Foster et al, 1998). Thus, the message for the parents was to ensure that they gained continued support for the stresses caused by managing a child with a chronic illness.

Mealtime management

A major concern of Caron and James was how to manage meals since Alice was now unable to take food orally. Initially, they believed they would never be capable of eating in front of her and were concerned about the social occasions which involved food; parties, picnics, McDonald's, etc. This was a reasonable reaction to the instigation of life-long TPN treatment, resulting from their overwhelming anxiety and worry. This would dissipate as Alice recovered. It was likely that Alice would be allowed food and drink but this would be restricted. Once Alice had medical permission to begin some oral intake, both Alice and her parents were noticeably happier.

To help Alice accept her restricted diet, it was important for her to feel some choice in the matter rather than have her favourite foods denied. It was recommended that a nurse help Alice write a list of her diet, with Alice drawing happy faces at the food she liked best. After several weeks monitoring the output from the stoma, the diet was expanded to be low in fat, sugar and fibre. Thus, the restrictions were less but all meals were very small portions.

Mealtimes would become the most difficult aspect of treatment to manage at home following Alice's discharge. Alice would ask for more at every mealtime and her parents found it very trying to have to refuse her. The suggestions for management followed a behavioural approach. Namely, her parents were helped to see that Alice was not being naughty in asking for more; even though she knows she cannot have it, this is understandable behaviour. It was important, therefore, to have some clear rules and consistency about when they would and would not allow Alice to eat more than normally allowed, such as that Alice would not be allowed any extra food during weekdays but extra food would be allowed at weekends and for special occasions. Food should never be used as reward or punishment for Alice as this muddies the boundaries. Caron and James were also helped to understand that they were not in opposition to Alice, but working together with Alice to maintain her health. When Alice was allowed more, they could examine her output with her to let her see the results of eating more; thus aiding the association between eating and her health and encouraging self-responsibility.

Adaptation to a chronic illness

Immediately following the accident Caron and James demonstrated and described heightened distress. They felt constant worry and physical anxiety. As Alice's condition stabilised and some medical planning could begin, Caron and James's concerns were with the task of learning to administer the medical treatments and consider the transition to home life.

It was important for the doctors to consider the pace of the family's adaptation in their plan for discharge. The team was reminded to involve both parents in taking responsibility. A gradual teaching programme for the parents and Alice began. Once they were seen to be competent and confident then visits home could begin, initially for a matter of hours, leading to whole weekends before final discharge.

Regular sessions with the parents for psychological intervention occurred. This gave the parents opportunity to express their anxieties and for feedback to the medical team. It was possible at this time to prevent conflicts and identify sources of stress. The main aim was to help the parents implement Alice's medical treatments while maintaining a normal family life. They had to ensure attention was shared between siblings, and Alice was involved in activities expected of a child her age to avoid overprotection and Alice developing a self-perception as a sick child.

Following discharge

Alice was in hospital for a total of 6 months. The family have adapted well to managing Alice's medical treatments at home. Alice enjoys a good quality of life. She returned to her local primary school where she continues to be very popular and achieves academically. She is allowed off her TPN one night per week which enables her to spend nights away from home if desired. The family has also obtained a portable pump which supplies the feed for TPN and the family went abroad on holiday for the first time since the accident.

Alice attends the hospital approximately quarterly as an outpatient. Alice is allowed to eat slightly more, but this does affect her output and so mealtimes continue to be difficult for the family. This is the main topic of psychology sessions.

Currently, Alice is very stable on her TPN feeding. She still uses the same central line which means she has the maximum number of sites available. One of the complications of TPN is that the lines might become infected and the patient runs out of potential sites for feeding.

The next phase of invasive treatment planned for Alice is to reverse the stoma so she can defecate in the normal way. Alice will be assessed to see how viable this course will be. Although this appears a desirable option, the family and doctors fear that they may be "rocking the boat". Alice is leading an almost normal life and the possible complications a reversal may bring are unknown.

Alice will never be able to survive without TPN feeding. The only solution is a bowel transplant, a procedure which is still in its infancy.

Conclusion

An unpredictable accident with catastrophic long-term medical effects has an impact far greater than the physical management of the condition. The above chapter illustrates via a case example how the emotional effects are at times paramount for treatment priorities. Management of worry and anxiety for all family members and the front-line care staff needs to be an integral part of the treatment package for successful rehabilitation and prognosis.

References

Bluebond-Langner, M. (1978) *The Private World of Dying Children*. Princeton: Princeton University Press.

Davies, P.B. and May, J.E. (1991) Involving fathers in early intervention and family support systems: issues and strategies. *Children's Health Care*, 20: 87–92.

Eiser, C. (1989) Children's understanding of illness: a critique of the 'stage' approach. *Psychology and Health*, 3: 93–101.

Foster, C.L., Bryon, M. and Eiser, C. (1998) Correlates of wellbeing in mothers of children and adolescents with cystic fibrosis. *Child: Care Health and Development*, 24: 41–56.

Garralda, M.E. (1994) Chronic physical illness and emotional disorder in childhood: where the brain's not involved, there may still be problems. *British Journal of Psychiatry*, 164: 8–10.

HMSO (1959) The *Welfare of Children in Hospitals, the Platt report*. London: Her Majesty's Stationery Office.

Kazak, A.E., Penati, B., Boyer, B.A., Himelstein, B., Brophy, P., Waibel, M.K., Blackall, G.F., Daller, R. and Johnson, K. (1996) A randomized controlled prospective outcome study of a psychological and pharmacological intervention protocol for procedural distress in pediatric leukemia. *Journal of Pediatric Psychology*, 21: 615–631.

Kennardy, J.A., Spence, S.H. and Macleod, A.C. (2006) Screening for post-traumatic stress disorder in children after accidental injury. *Pediatrics*, 118(3): 1002–1009.

Kuttner, L. (1989) Management of young children's acute pain and anxiety during invasive medical procedures. *Pediatrician*, 16: 39–44.

Maguire, P. and Pitceathly, C. (2002) Key communication skills and how to acquire them. *British Medical Journal*, 325: 697–700.

McGrath, P.J. and McAlpine, L.M. (1993) Psychological perspectives on pediatric pain. *Journal of Pediatrics*, 122: S2–S8.

Nelson, K. (ed.) (1986) *Event Knowledge: Structure and Function in Development*. New Jersey: Lawrence Erlbaum.

Quittner, A.L., DiGirolamo, A.M., Michel, A. and Eigen, H. (1992) Parental response to cystic fibrosis: a contextual analysis of the diagnostic phase. *Journal of Pediatric Psychology*, 17: 683–704.

Veldtman, G.R., Matley, S.L., Kendall, L., Quirk, J., Gibbs, J.L., Parsons, J.M. and Hewison, J. (2001) Illness understanding in children and adolescents with heart disease. *Western Journal of Medicine*, 174: 171–174.

Ward-Begnoche, W.L., Aitken, M.E., Liggin, R., Mullins, S.H., Kassam-Adams, N., Marks, S. and Winston, F.K. (2006) Emergency ward screening for post-traumatic stress disorder among injured children. *Injury Prevention*, 12(5): 323–326.

Wortman, C.B. and Silver, R.C. (1987) Coping with irrevocable loss. In G.R. VandenBos and B.K. Bryant (eds), *Cataclysms, Crises and Catastrophes: Psychology in Action*. Washington DC: American Psychological Association.

Zatzick, D.F., Grossman, D.C., Russo, J., Pynoos, R., Berliner, L., Jurkovich, G., Sabin, J.A., Katon, W., Ghesquiere, A., McCauley, E. and Rivara, F.P. (2006) Predicting posttraumatic stress symptoms longitudinally in a representative sample of hospitalised injured adolescents. *Journal of the American Academy of Child and Adolescent Psychiatry*, 45(10): 1188–1195.

Chapter 7

Co-occurring aggressive behaviour and anxiety – at home and school: developing a formulation

Peter Appleton

Introduction

The purpose of this chapter is to discuss a case in which aggressive behaviour was the primary presenting problem, but in which anxiety and low mood were also important components of the child's difficulties (i.e. co-occurring aggression *and* internalising difficulties – see Chapter 2). The importance of developing a detailed formulation, to incorporate *both* the aggression and the internalising difficulties, is emphasised. To further complicate matters, aggressive behaviour and anxiety/low mood were evident at home *and* at school. The assessment and formulation incorporated both settings, in order to ensure that the contextual aspects of the child's difficulties were fully understood. The emphasis of the chapter is on the development of a formulation – treatment options are then briefly reviewed (Tarrier, 2006).

Liam, aged 9, was referred to a Specialist CAMHS by his GP and school for 'anger management'. He had been permanently excluded by his primary school for aggressive behaviour, and currently did not have a school place. At home he was physically and verbally aggressive with his mother (Janice) and his stepfather (Tom). Janice and Tom both struggled to manage his behaviour – Janice had attended a child behaviour management course two years previously and had found it helpful, but felt she was just beginning to understand how to help Liam. She still showed high levels of hostility and criticism to him, and was receiving medical help for depressive and anxious episodes, which she attributed to the impact of Liam's behaviour. Tom was critical of his wife's child management techniques, and was critical of his step-son's behaviour. There was a history of marital difficulties and, in a previous relationship, domestic violence. Liam had an 18-month-old half-brother, Robert (Janice and Tom's child), and a 16-year-old step-brother, Adam, who was Tom's son by a previous marriage.

Everyone involved experienced high levels of concern and anxiety about Liam's welfare.

Assessment

Liam came along to his first meeting at the CAMH service with Janice and Tom. He had not wanted to come, and clung closely to his mother throughout the first session. She explained that Liam had said that he was afraid that 'the Doctor would put him in a cage and lock him up'.

Janice and Tom had two major concerns – Liam's aggressive behaviour, and his school exclusion. The aggressive behaviour consisted of verbally and physically attacking both his parent-figures, screaming when he could not get his own way, persistently arguing, being disobedient, destroying his own things in temper, and occasionally destroying his parents' things. His mood was described as being on a hair-trigger, with sudden shifts of emotion from being 'reasonable' to being 'obnoxious'. At school he had physically attacked a teacher and several children.

We agreed to meet several times, in order to gather more information. I sought permission to contact the school. Over the next few sessions we discovered much more about Liam's difficulties, his strengths, and his family, neighbourhood, and school contexts.

Liam's rages

Home and school reported that aggressive behaviour included anger episodes which readily progressed into a state described by the school as 'rage'. Further details led to the following description: sudden-onset partial loss of behavioural control in which Liam was violent to others, especially adults, and occasionally to self, and in which recovery was slow. It was also accompanied by destruction of objects and furniture, and possessions. Rage attacks were usually provoked by a perceived interpersonal 'attack' or criticism. Adults noted that, even after allowing time for recovery of relative calmness, Liam was *unable* to describe coherently or discuss the sequence of events leading up to and including the rage episode.

Liam's rages were not planned; they happened very suddenly. They were a form of reactive aggression (rather than proactive aggression, e.g. planned bullying) involving rapid striking back when provoked (Vitaro et al., 2002). The provocation might be a peer accidentally bumping into him, or a teacher applying normal discipline.

Anxiety, low mood, and dislike of self

In addition to the anger and aggressive behaviour, Liam had current anxiety difficulties consisting of social anxiety (e.g. worried about mistakes at school, scared to take a test, extremely afraid of looking stupid in front of others, and upset when he does poorly at tasks), separation anxiety (not wanting to be apart from his mother, afraid to sleep alone, reluctance to go to school), generalised anxiety (worried about a range of things, thinking about death, worried that something bad will happen to self), and somatic anxiety (headaches, stomach aches, feeling nauseous, feeling tired) (Ferdinand et al., 2006; Ollendick and Seligman, 2006). There was some compulsive checking of bedclothes (which had to be precisely in place). Liam would only very reluctantly wear new clothes. His hair had to be combed in a particular manner. These latter requirements, if not met, would cause severe anxiety. He was 'afraid' of 'anything new', and sought reassurance and information about upcoming events or changes of routine. His sleep was disrupted: he complained of nightmares.

Anxiety was accompanied by low mood and irritability (the irritability overlapping with aggressive behaviour). Liam frequently complained that he disliked himself and his physical appearance, felt he was no good at school, and felt he was disliked by his peers (Harter, 1999). He sometimes said 'I wish I was dead'.

Strengths

School and home were emphatic that Liam could be considerate, sweet, and kind to other children. He could be protective of his toddler half-brother, looking out for him when he was at risk of falling over, and helping Mum and Dad interpret Robert's early speech. At school he had been notorious with peers for his tempers, but was not unpopular. Adults described the contrast between Liam's 'two selves' as his 'Jekyll and Hyde' personality.

He was good at sports, although he would sometimes 'over-react' to peers, or to discipline by the sports instructor.

Although many aggressive boys experience specific learning problems (Humphrey, 2006), Liam was regarded by the school as of normal ability. This was confirmed by specialist cognitive assessment.

Janice's memories of Liam's early and recent history

Janice did not remember much about Liam's early history, but in an individual session she was able to recall some of the events in her own life around the time of Liam's birth and early childhood. The relationship with Liam's father, Mick, had begun to deteriorate during the pregnancy. Janice remembered that he used to shout at her, but not hit her. He was out of work, involved in criminal activity, and used to 'vanish' for several days at a time. Shortly after Liam's birth, Janice asked Mick to leave after he started to hit her. She became depressed, and was helped by a Health Visitor who visited and 'listened'. Janice was out of touch with her own mother and father. She summed up her own childhood as 'horrible'. Although she had some good memories, these were outweighed by memories of a breakdown in her relationship with her mother, after Janice had disclosed while a teenager that her father had sexually abused her.

When Liam was a toddler, and Mick had left, Janice recalled 'a better time' for about two years, when she had come out of her depression and felt closer to Liam. They had done a lot together. She remembered him being 'clingy', but she didn't mind.

She met Tom when Liam was about 5. She felt Tom was good for her – he was older, not violent, and helped around the house. When he joined the household Liam found it difficult – Janice, on reflection, thought that his behaviour had started to be a problem at this point. He was stubborn, and less willing to do as he was asked.

I asked about Liam's contact with his father Mick. This had been occasional, but according to Janice Liam no longer wanted to see his father – Mick had visited Janice and Liam several times after he had left – on these occasions he had threatened Janice, and she had had to involve the police.

Janice talked at length about her anxiety that Liam's aggression was inherited from his father Mick.

When Liam was 7, Robert was born. Liam had been very attentive to his mother during the pregnancy – he was worried about her. At school he was less able to concentrate. Janice remembered being called into the school shortly before Robert was born. Further discussion about this period led to Janice mentioning Tom's son, Adam. He had been living with his mother, but had started to mix with a delinquent group of peers, and had been warned by the police. Janice recalled Tom being very worried about this, and she thought that Liam also became worried.

Liam's behaviour (and anxiety and low mood) gradually became worse after Robert was born.

Currently Janice was seeing her GP regularly for depression – she was on the waiting list for the GP counsellor.

Liam's previous school

Liam's previous class-teacher talked about his rages, and the unacceptable amount of time she had had to spend dealing with his behaviour. He had kicked her on many occasions. On numerous mornings he was unwilling to engage in the class, sitting by himself. She described clearly his aggressive 'over-reaction' to other children walking close to him. When he became angry he would sometimes run out of the classroom and hide in the toilets. She was puzzled that Liam could never explain why he was upset. There were no records of Liam proactively bullying other children, or indeed being bullied himself. The teacher also remembered the 'other side' of Liam – his kindness to other children, and his interest in art. The school-based Special Educational Needs Coordinator (SENCO) recalled that he had settled reasonably well into the infant classes, although reluctant to leave his mother in the morning. His concentration had been good, and his learning to read had proceeded well. There were no problems with aggression until he was about age 7. For nearly two years the school tried to deal with the aggressive behaviour, and recommended that Janice attend a parenting skills class. Eventually, after a number of complaints by other parents about the impact of Liam's behaviour on their own children, and after several temporary exclusions, he was permanently excluded.

A new school for Liam

During the assessment period another primary school agreed to admit Liam. The headteacher of the new school visited Liam and his mother at home, took him a small present, and explained that he would be welcome in the new school. The school had a positive and constructive approach to working with children with behavioural special needs. This dealt with one of Janice's main concerns, i.e. school exclusion, but not surprisingly she was worried that Liam would struggle to settle in to the new school.

Mother, stepfather and Liam together

During assessment sessions Liam was argumentative and hostile to his mother, hitting her when she described his difficult behaviour. He was physically clingy to her, sitting on the same chair.

Questions about 'good times' elicited warm and friendly interactions between Liam and his mother, who clearly were closely 'in tune' with each other in some circumstances. They were able jointly to describe a nice time they spent together.

Tom seemed partly excluded from the close relationship between Liam and his mother. He said he felt that Liam was a 'Mummy's boy'. However, Liam called Tom 'Daddy', and they occasionally did things together, although Liam preferred his Mum also to be present.

Discipline practices

Both Janice and Tom used physical punishment to deal with Liam's non-compliant behaviour (Weiss et al., 1992). They knew that it was unhelpful, but found that they had 'run out of ideas'. They acknowledged that they had threatened Liam with being taken away to prison by the police if his behaviour did not improve. Janice told Liam that she 'loved him to bits', but that he mustn't be aggressive, and that she was worried that he was 'turning into Mick'.

Seeing Liam on his own

After two family sessions, Liam willingly participated in an individual session, conversing, drawing, and completing a range of cognitive tasks. He was able to talk about each of the current family members, but said that he didn't want to talk about Mick – 'I hate him, 'cause he hurt my Mum'. He said he felt very close to his Mum, but that he also liked Tom and Robert. He was unable to discuss the rages – simply saying he didn't know what happened when he had rages. He said he was afraid that he might be like his father (i.e. aggressive), and that his mum frequently told him so. He wished people wouldn't ask him why he had rages – ''cause he didn't know'.

One of the tasks in the session included one measure of Liam's representations of attachment relationships in the family (Kerns et al., 2005). After some warm-up free drawing, which he enjoyed, I asked him to draw a picture of his family (Fury et al., 1997). He was reluctant. Eventually he drew one small figure in blue in the bottom corner of the paper. He would say only that the figure was his dad (Mick). On the basis of the scoring suggestions by Gail Fury and colleagues, it was possible to provisionally categorise Liam's representation of attachment relationships as insecure ambivalent/resistant (Fury et al., 1997). Features of the drawing also indicated a high score on the global rating scale, with problematic scores on Vitality/Creativity, Family Pride/Happiness, Vulnerability, and Emotional Distance/Isolation. The overall degree of representations of attachment insecurity – in particular the isolated figure, absence of self and/or mother, lack of colour and background detail – reflect the psychosocial difficulties Liam faced.

In a further assessment session, cognitive assessment showed no specific learning difficulties.

Formulation

Liam's aggressive behaviour began at about the age of 6 or 7, following *several* life events: Tom had joined the household; Janice had become pregnant; Tom's teenage son Adam had been in trouble with the police – a source of anxiety for both Tom and Liam. Aggressive behaviour in school had followed the birth of Robert. Each of these events had constituted a threat to Liam's close (but ambivalent) relationship with his mother.

Liam's ambivalent attachment relationship (see Chapter 1) with his mother was understandable. During early infancy, and from age 4 or 5 onwards, Janice had been less emotionally available to Liam than she would have wished. After Mick left, and after Janice recovered from her postnatal depression, Liam (aged about 2) found himself worrying about his mother. Exposure to occasional episodes of verbal violence on return visits by Mick maintained Liam's worry, and probably led to specific fears of loss of his mother. Liam's ambivalent child–mother attachment relationship was compounded by segregated self-systems (Ayoub et al., 2003), characterised by, on the one hand a competent and empathic self, and on the other hand a reactively aggressive self.

Liam's anxiety was understandable in the light of events, the nature of the attachment relationship, and the nature of his self-system. But why anger and aggressive behaviour? There were several possible origins. First, anger and rage are regarded as an understandable response to threats of separation or loss (Bowlby, 1973). Second, he had witnessed both physical and verbal violence by his own father. Third, Janice and Tom modelled aggressive behaviour by using physical methods of discipline. Fourth, aggressive behaviour had become a highly effective means for controlling his mother and stepfather.

Janice had been emotionally available enough to Liam, especially during his toddler years and early childhood development, to give him confidence in learning and talking. This allowed him, at first, to settle into school. It also gave him confidence, within part of himself, to be attentive to his infant brother.

It was *unclear* whether Liam had been behaviourally inhibited (BI) as a young child. First, high BI and ambivalent attachment are overlapping constructs (Stevenson-Hinde, 2005) and second, Janice was not able to give specific descriptions of Liam's behaviour in infancy. However, it was clear that Liam was currently showing a wide range of anxious thoughts and behaviours – Liam was hypervigilant to a wide range of threat cues.

Liam's severe and complex anxiety and depressive problems were currently being maintained by parental threats of abandonment, parental criticism, maternal emotional unavailability due to mental health problems, marital difficulties, by uncertainties about school, and by uncertainties about peer acceptance.

An accumulation of vulnerability factors, and life events, each largely unresolved over the previous two years, had led to low mood and low self-worth.

Liam's ambivalent attachment relationship to his mother prevented healthy development of a productive relationship with his stepfather.

Strengths included his empathic self, appreciated by adults and peers; his academic ability; and the opportunity of starting a new school with a known positive approach to children with behavioural and emotional special needs

Treatment indications

Mixed aggression and anxiety/low mood in middle childhood might be addressed by a combination of parent–child behaviour therapy (focused on increasing compliance and reducing the aggressive behaviour) and family-oriented CBT (focusing on reduction of anxiety and increase in self-esteem). Such an approach would be evidence-based (Ginsburg and Schlossberg, 2002; Scott, 2002), and would allow individual formulation-based attention to Liam's specific strengths (such as his verbal ability), and specific aspects of the case (e.g. additional school-based components to the intervention would be essential).

However, aspects of the *formulation* suggest that other approaches should also be reviewed with multidisciplinary colleagues, and with Liam and his family, to ascertain whether they might be part of an overall programme (Connolly and Bernstein, 2007). Five possible psychological approaches are indicated from the literature.

1   Attachment-oriented therapy with Liam and his mother together might address directly a primary focus of the formulation, i.e. the mother–child relationship and Janice's relationship with her own parents (Davila and Levy, 2006; Toth et al., 2002).
2   A narrative family systemic intervention in which Liam's 'version of events' is given due weight, might address hidden aspects of trauma associated with the historical witnessing of violence to his mother, the current harsh discipline, and the unresolved complex relationship between Liam, his father, and his stepfather (Gorell-Barnes and Dowling, 1997; Vetere and Cooper, 2005).
3   A joint systemic intervention with school and family would address a number of specific aspects of the formulation, including the potential protective process of Liam's impending attendance at a new school with a known positive culture for children with behavioural and emotional special needs (Bowlby, 1994; Dowling, 1994; Dowling and Osborne, 1994).
4   Janice might wish to take up psychotherapy to address her own complex psychological needs.
5   Psychodynamic child psychotherapy, or one of the child-based specialised creative therapies such as play therapy (Ryan, 2005) or art therapy (Gilroy, 2006), might be considered for Liam. His rages, which were of sufficient severity to lead to permanent exclusion from a primary school, his chronic dislike of self, and his inconsistent 'internal working models' of relational experience (Lyons-Ruth, 2005) could respond to a therapy which would allow him the opportunity to communicate his experience, using a variety of narrative and non-narrative means, within the secure context of psychotherapy (see Chapters 5 and 9). Although the outcome literature on child psychotherapy for aggressive behaviour suggests that it is usually not helpful, the existing literature does not address clearly the question of whether aggressive children with co-occurring anxiety and low self-worth might benefit from these therapies.

Conclusion

Liam was referred to a CAMH service for aggressive behaviour, with a request for 'anger management'. Detailed mental health assessment brought to light a range of additional co-occurring psychological difficulties, including severe anxiety, low mood, and low self-worth. These difficulties were understandable in the context of Liam's history, including developmental, family, and school factors. A formulation was developed. A combination of coordinated therapeutic approaches, based on a detailed formulation, and on careful discussion with all parties, is indicated for children with problems as complex as those of Liam (Connolly and Bernstein, 2007).

References

Ayoub, C.C., Fischer, K.W. and O'Connor, E.E. (2003) Analysing development of working models for disrupted attachments: the case of hidden family violence. *Attachment and Human Development*, 5, 97–119.

Bowlby, J. (1973) *Attachment and Loss. Volume 2. Separation: Anxiety and Anger*. London, The Hogarth Press and the Institute of Psycho-analysis.

Bowlby, J. (1994) Foreword to the First Edition. In Dowling, E. and Osborne, E. (eds) *The Family and the School: A Joint Systems Approach to Problems with Children*, 2nd edn. London, Routledge.

Connolly, S.D. and Bernstein, G.A. (2007) Practice parameter for the assessment and treatment of children and adolescents with anxiety disorders. *Journal of the American Academy of Child and Adolescent Psychiatry*, 46, 267–83.

Davila, J. and Levy, K.N. (2006) Introduction to the special section on attachment theory and psychotherapy. *Journal of Consulting and Clinical Psychology*, 74, 989–93.

Dowling, E. (1994) Theoretical framework: a joint systems approach to educational problems with children. In Dowling, E. and Osborne, E. (eds) *The Family and the School: A Joint Systems Approach to Problems with Children*, 2nd edn. London, Routledge.

Dowling, E. and Osborne, E. (1994) *The Family and the School: A Joint Systems Approach to Problems with Children*, 2nd edn. London, Routledge.

Ferdinand, R.F., Van Lang, N.D., Ormel, J. and Verhulst, F.C. (2006) No distinctions between different types of anxiety symptoms in pre-adolescents from the general population. *Journal of Anxiety Disorders*, 20, 207–21.

Fury, G., Carlson, E.A. and Sroufe, L.A. (1997) Children's representations of attachment relationships in family drawings. *Child Development*, 68, 1154–64.

Gilroy, A. (2006) *Art Therapy, Research and Evidence-based Practice*. London, Sage Publications.

Ginsburg, G.S. and Schlossberg, M.C. (2002) Family-based treatment of childhood anxiety disorders. *International Review of Psychiatry*, 14, 143–54.

Gorell-Barnes, G. and Dowling, E. (1997) Rewriting the story: children, parents and post-divorce narrative. In Papadopoulos, R.K. and Byng-Hall, J. (eds) *Multiple Voices: Narrative in Systemic Family Psychotherapy*. London, Duckworth.

Harter, S. (1999) *The Construction of the Self: A Developmental Perspective*. London, The Guilford Press.

Humphrey, A. (2006) Children behaving badly – a case of misunderstanding? *The Psychologist*, 19, 494–5.

Kerns, K., Schlegelmilch, A., Morgan, T. and Abraham, M. (2005) Assessing attachment in middle childhood. In Kerns, K. and Richardson, R. (eds) *Attachment in Middle Childhood*. London, The Guilford Press.

Lyons-Ruth, K. (2005) The two-person unconscious: intersubjective dialogue, enactive relational representation, and the emergence of new forms of relational organization. In Aron, L. and Harris, A. (eds) *Relational Psychoanalysis: Innovation and Expansion*. Hillsdale, NJ, Analytic Press/Erlbaum.

Ollendick, T.H. and Seligman, L.D. (2006) Anxiety disorders. In Gillberg, C., Harrington, R. and Steinhausen, H.C. (eds) *A Clinician's Handbook of Child and Adolescent Psychiatry*. Cambridge, Cambridge University Press.

Ryan, V. (2005) *Play Therapy: A Non-Directive Approach for Children and Adolescents*. London, Elsevier Science.

Scott, S. (2002) Parent training programmes. In Rutter, M. and Taylor, E. (eds) *Child and Adolescent Psychiatry*, 4th edn. Oxford, Blackwell Science.

Stevenson-Hinde, J. (2005) The interplay between attachment, temperament, and maternal style: a Madingley perspective. In Grossman, K.E., Grossman, K. and Waters, E. (eds) *Attachment from Infancy to Adulthood: The Major Longitudinal Studies*. London, The Guilford Press.

Tarrier, N. (2006) An introduction to case formulation and its challenges. In Tarrier, N. (ed.) *Case Formulation in Cognitive Behaviour Therapy: The Treatment of Challenging and Complex Cases*. London, Routledge.

Toth, S.L., Maughan, A., Manly, J.T., Spagnola, M. and Cicchetti, D. (2002) The relative efficacy of two interventions in altering maltreated preschool children's representational models: implications for attachment theory. *Development and Psychopathology*, 14, 877–908.

Vetere, A. and Cooper, J. (2005) Children who witness violence at home. In Vetere, A. and Dowling, E. (eds) *Narrative Therapies with Children and their Families: A Practitioner's Guide to Concepts and Approaches*. London, Routledge.

Vitaro, F., Brendgen, M. and Tremblay, R.E. (2002) Reactively and proactively aggressive children: antecedent and subsequent characteristics. *Journal of Child Psychology and Psychiatry*, 43, 495–505.

Weiss, B., Dodge, K.A., Bates, J.E. and Pettit, G.S. (1992) Some consequences of early harsh discipline: child aggression and a maladaptive social information processing style. *Child Development*, 63, 1321–35.

Chapter 8

Anxiety and Asperger's Disorder

Ayla Humphrey

Introduction

Diagnostic criteria for Asperger's Syndrome (ICD-10) or Asperger's Disorder (DSM-IV) do not mention anxiety. Deficits in reciprocal social interaction and restricted, repetitive and stereotyped patterns of behaviour are the hallmarks of this disorder as outlined in the diagnostic manuals. Yet every clinician working with children who have Asperger's Disorder knows that these children often become incapacitated by their anxiety. In fact, one world expert on autism spectrum disorders recently commented that anxiety was the primary difficulty for people with these disorders. Prevalence studies have provided evidence that individuals with autism spectrum disorders are at an increased risk of anxiety disorder. One recent study has found that 14 per cent of their sample of children with autism (IQ > 70) met diagnostic criteria for an anxiety disorder, 51 per cent for a phobia, and 37 per cent for Obsessive-Compulsive Disorder (OCD) (Leyfer et al., 2006). Kim and colleagues (2000) found prevalence rates of 13 per cent over-anxious symptomology and 8 per cent for separation anxiety. This was in contrast to a 3 per cent rate in their normal control group. These researchers also found that the rates of anxiety symptoms were not significantly different when children with Asperger's Disorder were compared to children with autism. This is important, as most studies have combined these two groups. Zandt and colleagues (2006) found that a sample of children with autism spectrum disorders had fewer compulsive and obsessive symptoms than a contrast group of children with OCD, but both groups had significantly more OCD symptoms as compared to a normal control group. If we add to these figures children who don't have a diagnosed anxiety disorder, but whose functioning is affected by anxiety, the risk is of course even greater.

How can we understand the association between Asperger's Disorder and anxiety? One explanation might be that this is a sequential co-morbidity – children with Asperger's have trouble with social interaction so when placed in socially demanding situations they become anxious. Social clumsiness and the motor clumsiness associated with Asperger's Disorder are likely to lead to bullying by peers and sometimes by adults, which will lead to a child's additional worry about being attacked. Another explanation could be that there are pleiotropic genetic effects at work – one genetic disorder with a phenotype that includes both the symptoms of anxiety as well as those of Asperger's Disorder (Bolton et al., 1998). Of course both of these mechanisms may interact with an underlying genetic disorder explaining a portion of the anxiety and the interaction between the child and the environment further exacerbating the anxiety.

If, indeed, there are multiple explanations for the association between Asperger's and anxiety, treatment efficacy may be enhanced by consideration of independent factors contributing to a child's anxiety. For example, Kim et al. (2000) found a high correlation between anxiety and mood problems and difficulties with disruptive behaviour in children with Asperger's Disorder. Ascertaining whether this correlation is causal in either direction will inform the choice of treatment for anxiety. The first case presented below represents my view that there is a bi-directional causality, but that anxiety is a powerful and primary cause of aggression in children with Asperger's Disorder and needs to be treated before aggression will diminish.

Some have argued (Zandt et al., 2006) that there is no added benefit for treatment in a secondary diagnosis. I hope to illustrate that this is not the case. First, a diagnosis of Anxiety Disorder or OCD will help to inform the child, child's family, and clinician about the possible developmental trajectory of the anxiety symptoms. Most importantly, however, these diagnoses enable clinicians to make well-informed decisions about choice of treatment. A child with Asperger's Disorder and social anxiety will require different treatment from a child with Asperger's Disorder and OCD. There is very little written about treatments for anxiety in children with Asperger's Disorder (Sofronoff et al., 2005; Reaven and Hepburn, 2003). What is written suggests that what works for children who don't have Asperger's Disorder works for children who do.

The two cases I present here describe how commonly used cognitive-behavioural strategies with some adaptions do alleviate anxiety in children with Asperger's Disorder.

Simon

Simon was diagnosed at the age of 14 years with Asperger's Disorder. The following year, the diagnosing clinician referred him for help with his anxiety and anger. Simon's parents and his teachers knew that social interaction with his school peers made him nervous. If he could, Simon would stay in the house all day long with his computer. The threat of meeting strangers was overwhelming to him. Simon could, perhaps, be compared to many a fairy-tale character – a gentle but threatening giant, bigger than his age with the flatness of facial expression that is characteristic of Asperger's Disorder. If you didn't know Simon, you would think he was perpetually cross. If you didn't know Simon, you would not know from his face or from his voice that he experienced happiness. The awkwardness in his conversational timing added to his threatening demeanour. When met with a long pause after we speak, it is instinctive to question what we have done to offend our conversational partner. Simon's pauses did not mean that he was offended. They were but a sign of the time he required to work out the intention of the speaker and then to work out how he should respond. He often said to me, "I didn't know if he was serious, or not." Simon could not read the social world around him and so the social world could not read him. There was potential for misunderstanding all around. There was, therefore, no dearth of legitimate reasons for Simon to feel angry. He was, like most children with Asperger's Disorder, a prime target for bullying from his peers. He stood out. He was also misunderstood by some of the adults in his life. He found it distressing to be in crowds, and teachers sometimes interpreted his refusal to take a seat in a crowded classroom as disobedience for which he was punished.

The distance between Simon's anxiety and his anger was short. It was seconds from his misinterpretation of the question, "how are you doing today?" to the throwing of a chair. The classic three-part *feeling-thinking-behaviour* loop had to be picked apart and time slowed down using cognitive-behavioural therapy. We worked on helping him to identify the physical signs of anger such as clenching of fists. Ironically, the rigidity of thinking characteristic of Asperger's Disorder can be used advantageously in cognitive-behavioural therapy. Maladaptive rules can be replaced with adaptive rules to which these children will strive to adhere. In Simon's case, he was studying Kung Fu. We were able to use the principles he was learning in martial arts to help him modulate his mood. Relaxation techniques thus employed the mantra "guard your centre" and the deep breathing exercises he had been using in his Kung Fu classes.

Most importantly, we worked on the cognitions which followed from Simon's pervasive belief that he was being bullied and teased and helped him to develop a flexibility in thinking which could accommodate other explanations for people's behaviour. Simon's thinking could be described as dichotomous. People were either "good" or "bad"; they were with him or against him. We worked on helping Simon to consider that people he didn't know well could be on his side. We also challenged the common cognitive error seen in individuals with problems of aggression – the misinterpretation of events as directed towards themselves rather than as undirected events or events directed at someone or something else. Lastly, we worked on Simon's difficulty recognising humour and sarcasm.

The matter of behaviour in the three-part loop was addressed by helping Simon to identify the current consequences of his aggression, as well as future potential consequences including exclusion from school and perhaps even prison. In parallel, we talked about his self-worth as a motivator for avoiding such catastrophic outcomes. Simon had a persistent thought that he was "mentally ill". He also thought that if he went away other people's problems would go away. We identified characteristics that he could value in himself including his intelligence, his musical ability and computer prowess. This was helped by asking him to bring materials in to the session such as books and computer disks. We developed a mantra that he could use to remind himself of an alternative to aggression, "talk to an adult".

The work I have described happened over the period of a year. It stopped when Simon stopped having aggressive outbursts. One year after regular sessions ended, Simon's parents brought him back to the clinic. They were worried about his anxiety – the aggression never re-emerged. Simon was closing curtains and not opening the front door, afraid that strangers would try to hurt him. I was briefly worried he might be paranoid and possibly thought disordered, but this was not the case. Simon was worried. We undertook brief work to challenge his belief that "if you don't know them you can't trust them". He told me of one experience that summarised his predicament. His parents had taken him to a fair. He told me that he was troubled by persistent self-questioning, "I am where I have never been before, shouldn't I be anxious?" Just then his mother did something to make him angry. "I was so relieved," he told me, "She made me so angry I was distracted from my worry. We went to the fair and I had a great time." I was confident that Simon had made great progress as we laughed together about how his anger, but not aggression, had served an adaptive purpose.

Asperger's Disorder and anxiety go hand-in-hand. An expectable response to not accurately interpreting and navigating the social world is to feel anxious. An anxious child with well-developed social skills can become rigid in their thinking and stereotypic in their behaviours as a function of their anxiety. Children with Asperger's Disorder often develop anxiety as a function of their rigidity and stereotyped behaviours, but they can be helped with cognitive-behavioural techniques. Indeed they may even be able to modulate their anxiety using the very features that give rise to it as a therapeutic tool.

Billy

Billy was practically bed-ridden with anxiety when he came to the clinic at the age of 10. He had been diagnosed with Asperger's Disorder when he was 7 years old and now received a further diagnosis of OCD. The risk of OCD is greater in those with Asperger's Disorder when compared to the general population (Russell et al., 2005; Bolton et al., 1998). This risk is greater still in individuals with Asperger's Disorder who have a parent diagnosed with OCD (Abramson et al., 2005), as was the case for Billy. His mother had struggled for years with OCD and had managed to successfully control her symptoms with medication and cognitive-behavioural therapy.

Billy's anxieties initially varied and included worries about electricity and haircuts. When I first saw him, he had settled on contamination anxieties. Compulsive behaviours included frequent hand washing to the point of causing skin irritation, use of excessive amounts of toilet roll after using the toilet to the point of blocking the drainage in the house, frequent changing of clothing, and avoidance of anything that he might consider messy or that reminded him of excrement. This included modelling clay, ink, paints, bird droppings, and even his mother if her hands were wet or if she had been in the same room as clay. His anxiety was so great he spent most of the time out of school, in his room and on his bed petrified to touch the floor.

Billy's high level of distress and inability to function led us to start treatment with a selective serotonin re-uptake inhibitor (SSRI). Within weeks, Billy's distress had lessened and he was able to move about more freely in the world, although he continued to have persistent worries and frequent compulsions. I chose to use the exposure-response prevention treatment protocol detailed by March and Mulle (1998). This included working out a hierarchy of obsessions. Billy was able to rank his greatest worry as touching his underpants after having used the toilet and the worry causing the least amount of anxiety was stepping on bird droppings. He was able to use the schematic tool of an "anxiety thermometer" on which he could rate the level of his anxiety by colouring the mercury up to the point at which it accurately represented his level of anxiety. Despite the fact that children with Asperger's Disorder often do have poor insight into their feeling states, they usually are able to use a numerical ranking system to quantify the degree of their anxiety. Perhaps it appeals to their love of order and in some cases, numbers. Billy was a very talented cartoonist and we were able to use this talent to draw pictures of the "Misery Man", Billy's name for the external embodiment of his worry. We also recorded an exposure tape, which Billy listened to regularly.

Billy found cognitive relaxation strategies difficult to use. He could not easily imagine a relaxing situation, but he could easily identify a relaxing activity – jumping on the trampoline. He was able to do this activity at home when he felt anxious following exposure.

Billy was able to engage in in-vivo and audio-recorded exposure exercises in the clinic and at home. He enjoyed raging against "Misery Man" until his temperature on the anxiety thermometer went down. As his compulsive washing and wiping decreased, he attempted to employ his parents to undertake behaviours that provoked his anxiety such as wiping after using the toilet. With encouragement, they were able to resist his requests to help him avoid triggers to his anxiety. Billy's parents also helped by limiting the amount of toilet roll to which he had access.

After four sessions and continued treatment with medication, Billy returned to school. Compulsive behaviours were almost non-existent by the tenth weekly session. There remained occasional exacerbation of obsessions and compulsions when there were changes in Billy's routines, an indication of how obsessive-compulsive behaviours in children with Asperger's Disorder can be provoked by situations with which they can not cope because of their developmental impairments. Like most people affected by OCD, secretive compulsions emerged from time to time – in Billy's case, not using pens during art class.

Regular sessions ended after approximately three months. In a review session held one year after the cessation of treatment, Billy's parents told us that he had few compulsions, but that they spent a lot of time correcting the remaining symptoms such as leaving the room if his brother used clay. They found this level of vigilance difficult to maintain. We suggested that they ignore symptoms that did not impede Billy's or the family's life. A further review with the family found that both Billy and his family were happily living with a bit of OCD. Treatment with SSRIs has continued and when we recently suggested that Billy begin to decrease his medication, he said "no, I can't cope". He then told us that he was brought forward to an educational authority inspector by his school SENCO as a model of how well a student in his school could progress. We agreed that he was coping very well.

Conclusions

Anxiety in children with Asperger's Disorder often present as difficulties of anger control or obsessive-compulsive behaviours. These different presentations may, indeed, reflect differing aetiologies – anxiety secondary to core characteristics of Asperger's Disorder and primary anxiety perhaps a consequence of an underlying discrete genetic influence. Indeed, recent research suggests that there may be one genetic influence giving rise to social communication difficulties and a separate genetic influence underlying repetitive and rigid behaviours. It is when these two genetic influences co-occur that we see the triad of impairments characteristic of an autism spectrum disorder (Ronald et al., 2005).

It is important when considering treatment of anxiety in children with Asperger's Disorder to differentiate between repetitive behaviours which often alleviate anxiety in children with developmental disorders and the compulsions that are associated with obsessional cognitions and anxiety. In the case of OCD, compulsions maintain, not relieve, anxiety. This differentiation can be difficult in children who do not have linguistic ability to communicate their thoughts and feeling (Baron-Cohen, 1989). However, children with high functioning autism and Asperger's Disorder are usually able to describe their worries and the accompanying cognitions.

Simon and Billy benefited from treatment techniques routinely used to treat anxiety and its associated behaviours. While the treatments were not identical both children were able to use relaxation in the form of self-directed verbalisations, activities, and in one case imagery. Both children were able to use strategies which took advantage of their strengths. Both children were able to use their interest in rules and ordering to engage in cognitive-behavioural therapy. Using the child's strength not only adds to treatment efficacy, it has the added benefit of helping to ameliorate the low self-esteem that children with Asperger's Disorder experience as a consequence of having always felt different from other people.

Children with Asperger's Disorder do reflect on how they stand out in the world and this causes them great distress, a distress which further intensifies their anxiety. Before Simon entered his secondary school, his head teacher announced that one of the incoming pupils had Asperger's Disorder and could the community be accepting. Surely, this head teacher must have been making the same error we risk as clinicians when we argue that children with Asperger's Disorder can not self-reflect and communicate about their emotions and cognitions at a level that would permit "ego-dystonic" worry and behaviours. Simon was horrified that this announcement had been made in school and he would also be stunned if I had assumed he was comfortable with his anxiety.

References

Abramson, R., Ravan, S., Wright, H., Wieduwilt, K., Wolpert, C., Donnelly, S., Pericak-Vance, M. and Curraro, M. (2005). The relationship between restrictive and repetitive behaviours in individuals with autism and obsessive compulsive symptoms in parents. *Child Psychiatry and Human Development*, 36(2): 155–165.

Baron-Cohen, S. (1989). Do autistic children have obsessions and compulsions? *British Journal of Clinical Psychology*, 28(3): 193–200.

Bolton, P.F., Pickles, A., Murphy, M. and Rutter, M. (1998). Autism, affective and other psychiatric disorders: pattern of familial aggregation. *Psychological Medicine*, 28: 385–395.

Kim, J.A., Szatmari, P., Bryson, S.E., Streiner, D.L. and Wilson, F.J. (2000). The prevalence of anxiety and mood problems among children with autism and Asperger syndrome. *Autism*, 4: 117–132.

Leyfer, O.T., Folstein, S.E., Bacalman, S., Davis, N.O., Dinh, E., Morgan, J., Tager-Flusberg, H. and Lainhart, J.E. (2006). Comorbid psychiatric disorders in children with autism: interview development and rates of disorder. *Journal of Autism and Developmental Disorders*, July 15, epub.

March, J.S. and Mulle, K. (1998). *OCD in Children and Adolescents: A Cognitive-Behavioural Treatment Manual*. New York: The Guilford Press.

Reaven, J. and Hepburn, S. (2003). Cognitive-behavioural treatment of obsessive-compulsive disorder in a child with Asperger syndrome. *Autism*, 7: 145–164.

Ronald, A., Happé, F. and Plomin, R. (2005). The genetic relationship between individual differences in social and non-social behaviours characteristic of autism. *Developmental Science*, 8(5): 444–458.

Russell, A.J., Mataix-Cols, D., Anson, M. and Murphy, D. (2005). Obsessions and compulsions in Asperger syndrome and high functioning autism. *British Journal of Psychiatry*, 186: 525–528.

Sofronoff, K., Attwood, T. and Hinton, S. (2005). A randomised controlled trial of a CBT intervention for anxiety in children with Asperger syndrome. *Journal of Child Psychology and Psychiatry*, 46(11): 1152–1160.

Zandt, F., Prior, M. and Kyrios, M. (2007). Repetitive behaviour in children with high functioning autism and obsessive compulsive disorder. *Journal of Autism and Developmental Disorders*, 37: 251–259.

Chapter 9

Complex anxiety in an adolescent with a learning disability: the girl who split off her stupidity

Helen Bell

> Mental growth is attainable and beautiful but is never effortlessly achieved.
>
> (Elmhirst, 1980, p. 166)

Introduction

The notion of the development of thinking is central to psychotherapeutic work carried out with young people with learning disabilities. In this chapter I will introduce you to a young woman, Jennie, aged 14, who at the start of therapy, presents with extreme anxiety. Jennie is helped by once weekly psychodynamic psychotherapy carried out over two years. My clinical work is influenced by psychoanalytic theories put forward by Freud, Klein and Bion. In particular, Freud (1917) suggests that it is the work of the clinician to help a person know more about themselves by making what is currently held in the unconscious available to the conscious mind. Jennie has a moderate learning disability, which for her means that she finds it difficult to make sense of what others mean by their words and actions, and it is difficult for Jennie to understand and convey her thoughts and feelings to others. Retrospectively (in that at the start of therapy this is not known but unconscious), I am able to say that what Jennie needs to 'know more about herself', is awareness about her disability. Disability inevitably means difference and difference is painful. A central task of any work with a young person with a disability is to be brave enough to speak of this disability and to speak of this in a timely and sensitive manner.

What happens between me and Jennie, our therapeutic relationship, is my main tool and it is this relationship that enables change to occur. My work draws on what has come to be known as 'object relations theory'. This theory is based on the assumption that people desire to be in relationship with other people (objects). These relationships then become incorporated in to our thoughts (as 'internal objects') and help to shape our future experiences with others and how we view ourselves. I will describe my journey with Jennie and show the development of thinking in the work, from a starting point of not being able to think about or with Jennie, to a gradual experience of providing what Bion refers to as 'a container' (1962a) where Jennie can know about herself and be known by others.

The experience of nameless dread

Jennie is referred following concerns about her 'insecurity' and extreme anxiety. Jennie's mother, Mrs Brown, describes her as 'clingy' and says that Jennie does not like her to be out of her sight. Jennie appears anxious and hyper-vigilant, as though she is constantly 'on guard' from any attack that might come upon her. Any noise heard outside the room makes Jennie jump nervously and she looks round suspiciously. In our first individual meeting together Jennie's heightened anxious state is apparent when I ask her what she thinks about coming to see me. She replies that she thinks that I am going to tell her off and hurt her. I am alarmed at Jennie's perception of the situation and, despite her fears, her apparent willingness to be left alone with me. In the subsequent sessions, Jennie continues to talk about hurting and being hurt, whether others could get hurt and who is capable of hurting whom.

From the start of meeting Jennie, I am left feeling terrified and helpless. It is as if these feelings are physically lodged in me and belong to me; in psychoanalytic terms this is an example of projective identification. Feelings that belong to Jennie are put in me (projected) and are felt so powerfully by me that I mistake these feelings (identify with them) as if they are my own. Jennie calls me 'stupid' for not understanding, and in my 'stupid state' I believe her. I have become identified with the disabled, stupid part of Jennie's personality. After our time together, I realise that I am unable to think when I am with Jennie and that she leaves me feeling stupid; it is as though I am in a fog. I learn about Jennie by experiencing firsthand what she feels; this is an example of counter transference. My own supervision is essential at this time to help me re-find my mind and in order that I can then begin to, in Segal's (1991) terms, 'mentally contain' Jennie. Helping Jennie to face her reality of difference has been a slow and painful part of the work. Bion (1962b) coined the term 'nameless dread' which for me helpfully encapsulates the emotional experience I have sought to describe in my early encounters with Jennie. Counter transference feelings of high anxiety and mindlessness are to remain with me for several months at the beginning of my work with Jennie. Jennie's powerful projections leave me unable to disentangle the meaning of her communications and instead leave me feeling mindless.

In my mind

A central tenet of psychoanalytic theory is the importance of the first relationship between a baby and its caregiver to ensure an infant's healthy emotional development. These early relationships are emotional templates from which other relationships develop and later relationships may glean something about the nature of these primitive experiences. Bion (1962a) describes this first relationship as 'containment'; the caregiver provides a 'container', a mental and emotional space, in to which an infant's thoughts and feelings (projections) are 'contained'. For example, when a baby becomes distressed, the caregiver hears the baby's cries and tries to make sense of what these might mean: 'Is she hungry?', 'Does she need her nappy changing?', 'Might she need a cuddle?' Once the caregiver satisfactorily understands the baby's distress (acts as a container) they then try to meet the baby's needs, thus the baby experiences being heard and understood (i.e. is contained).

Bion suggests that difficulties arise within this early relationship when a caregiver is repeatedly unable to accept and make sense of a baby's feelings and so gives these feelings back to the baby in an unprocessed way. So for example, a baby might be repeatedly distressed yet their caregiver is not able to think about or with the baby. This might happen when a caregiver is preoccupied by other things, for example marital disharmony or their own emotional difficulties. It is the *repeated* experience of not being heard and understood that will leave a baby vulnerable to feeling uncontained; it is possible for a caregiver to make mistakes, as will inevitably arise in all parenting.

In the same way that Bion speaks of the vital containing relationship between a caregiver and an infant, so too can the relationship between a therapist and a client be thought about in this way. I seek to work within the transference relationship, that is: 'What is happening between us that might shed light on the client's relationships with other people, both past and current?' For example, I might wonder whether Jennie is behaving with me as if I am her mother, or, I might ask: 'Am I finding myself feeling or behaving in the way her mother does when she is with Jennie?' The combination of possible relationships, both actual and imagined, is numerous and may shift rapidly and coexist. It is through examining the nature of the transference relationship that I learn more about how Jennie experiences the world and how she is experienced by others.

In the initial stage of therapy, Jennie is preoccupied as to whether or not I like her. This is a common theme I have encountered when working with young people with learning disabilities. She states that I am merely 'pretending' to like her; whilst at other times she disbelievingly exclaims that I could not possibly like her. With great seriousness Jennie says to me: 'you must tell me when you are fed up of listening to me'. Jennie's experience of others as being negative towards her (consciously and unconsciously) has over time lead her to believe, or in psychoanalytic terms internalise, these things for herself. Moreover, Jennie has experienced how others view her as persecuting and hostile, as can be seen in her telling comment during a game of 'hangman'. I comment that it is as if she wants me to guess what is in her mind. Jennie responds, 'Let the torturing begin'. Jennie has an idea that I do not want to know about her and that what I might find I would not want to know.

Another part of me

From the start of therapy, Jennie talks incessantly about the pop singer Noel Gallagher. Several months in to therapy this fascination extends to bringing in CDs of his music. I am confused as to the importance of Noel Gallagher for Jennie and then one week after Jennie becomes angry with me she begins to draw a picture of Noel Gallagher. I observe how thinking about Noel Gallagher helps her to calm down and feel better. I tell Jennie about my thoughts and she says she needs me to listen to his music so I can know how she feels. I slowly begin to understand that Jennie's persistence in talking about Noel Gallagher and listening to his music is for her the only way that I can know about her: the possibility for me to know what is on her mind by telling me directly seems to be impossible. To work with Jennie in the displacement of Noel Gallagher and his music, is a vehicle that Jennie begins to use to think about herself and to understand about her own internal experience.

At the same time in therapy, I become aware that Jennie believes that I know everything that she knows, that is, we share the same mind. A couple of clinical examples will serve to illustrate this point:

> When talking about a person's personality I ask Jennie what she might like to change about her own. She responds reproachfully, 'You should know, you've known me long enough'. I reply no, and that perhaps she believes I know how she feels and thinks. When I am stupid and do not understand she is angry with me for not knowing.

And on another occasion:

> As we walk from the waiting area to the therapy room, Jennie comments that there should be a tunnel (connecting the two separate buildings) so that people do not have to walk outside in the cold. I comment that this is a good idea. Jennie asks whether I have already thought of this and I say yes. Jennie continues, 'I was listening to Noel Gallagher on my headphones and as I took them off, Mum said aloud exactly what I had been thinking about. It was like she could read my mind'.

In Jennie's phantasy we are enmeshed as one. (Phantasy here is spelt with 'ph' to indicate that this is unconscious as opposed to a conscious fantasy.) For an individual to be able to think and for thoughts to be remembered, it is necessary for them to develop what Bick (1968; 1986) has termed 'psychic space'. Whilst Jennie views us as one, it is not possible for her to develop such necessary mental and emotional space. Bion writes that:

> The dominance of projective identification confuses the distinction between the self and the external object. This contributes to the absence of any perception of two-ness, since such an awareness depends on the recognition of a distinction between a subject and object.
>
> (Bion, 1962b, p. 113)

Over time, Jennie does begin to become aware of such a distinction between us. This happens first at an unconscious level, for example when Jennie brings lyrics to the session that describe feeling being a part of someone else rather than a separate person, and later at a more conscious level:

> Jennie comes in to the room and sits down. She looks at me as though she has never quite noticed me before and says what nice clothes I am wearing. For the first time I feel that Jennie is seeing me as someone separate to herself.

The emergence of a container

The beginnings of what Bion (1962a) has termed 'mental growth' (Symington and Symington, 1996) truly begin in the third phase of therapy. Prior to a review with Jennie's parents, Jennie plays a Noel Gallagher track entitled 'Little by Little'. In it, I feel Jennie is beginning to think about her own imperfection and how she must begin to face who she is as a young woman who is different.

I reflect on this with Jennie and this leads to a capacity to think together about her, as illustrated in the following session. In this session, Jennie speaks of 'disability' for the first time, both within herself and in Noel Gallagher:

> Jennie asks me whether I know she goes to a school for children with disabilities. I say yes I know and perhaps this means she has got a disability. Jennie replies, 'Yes, I have got epilepsy'. Jennie goes on to describe how frightening it is to have a fit, saying how she feels she has been 'run over by a steam train'. She continues, 'I do not understand why I had to be born with this thing'.

Rather than Jennie 'evading' frustration (Bion 1962a; 1962b), this is tolerated and thought about. Jennie goes on to think about disability in relation to Noel Gallagher:

> 'I suppose Noel Gallagher has disabilities'. They are: 'not being able to look after himself properly by taking drugs' and 'not having control over his temper'.

Jennie is beginning to grapple with the question of her identity and what it means to be disabled. Jennie's obsession with Noel Gallagher might be understood as her identifying with him when others disparage him because of his differences, what Jennie refers to as his 'disabilities'. Jennie is now able to explore the issue of 'sameness and difference' within a contained physical space (the safety and familiarity of a consistent therapy room) and within a contained mental space (being thought about in my mind and increasingly within her own mind). This issue is considered central to any work with a young person with disabilities (Sinason, 1992; Miller, 1998).

Shortly after this conversation, Jennie asks to go to the toilet, and on her return, I pick up the thoughts that are developing, whilst acknowledging her anxiety:

> I say, 'I wonder whether you went to the toilet because you felt nervous about what we were talking about?' Jennie responds, 'I am worried that when I am older I am not going to be good at anything and nobody will like me. But if Noel Gallagher can be successful, I suppose I can'.

Jennie is now more able to think about herself, rather than remaining solely in the displacement of Noel Gallagher. Making comparisons between herself and Noel Gallagher brings Jennie comfort. I am beginning to understand the importance of Noel Gallagher for her that she first tried to communicate to me in our second and subsequent meetings. In these early encounters, I am not able to tolerate Jennie's powerful projections for long enough and I am therefore unable to modify her fears and give them back to her in a more palatable form (Bion, 1959).

Jennie's ideas about Noel Gallagher are now more realistic and balanced. Noel Gallagher is no longer a purely good object, as had been supposed in earlier conversations. Jennie is able to consider both the good and bad parts of him, his 'disabilities' and abilities, and similarly, the good and bad parts of herself. Jennie expresses anxiety about whether or not she will be liked by others and she is also able to consider that she might be successful at something. Klein terms this shift in thinking, whereby objects are either all good or all bad (the 'paranoid-schizoid position') to an ability to have mixed feelings about an object, as a movement towards the 'depressive position' (Klein, 1935).

Shortly after this initial conversation about 'disabilities', Jennie puts on a 'performance' for me in the session. She performs a Noel Gallagher track, enacting both the moves and words of his song. I am struck by how Jennie adopts Noel Gallagher's entire persona; it is as if I am watching and listening to Noel Gallagher. I comment on this likeness to Jennie, she replies: 'I feel better being Noel Gallagher'. I wonder how she might sing and dance as Jennie. Jennie replies that she would 'be lost without Noel Gallagher'. The discomfort Jennie feels with 'being herself' and her lack of acceptance about who she is is portrayed here. Jennie's identity is intrinsically linked to Noel Gallagher's identity; she struggles to define herself as separate from him.

Out of sight out of mind

Eleven months into working with Jennie, the question of whether the therapy is to continue is put in doubt. In a meeting with Jennie's mother, Mrs Brown, Mrs Brown says she does not think the therapy is doing any good and she wants it to stop. Mrs Brown tells me that she came here for answers as to why Jennie is anxious, but instead she has felt accused and no explanations have been given. In this meeting I am unable to metabolise Mrs Brown's projections and by the end of the session, I am filled with the uselessness that Mrs Brown has projected in to me; the anxiety Mrs Brown expresses about being a good mother is now stuck in me and I am left with an overwhelming uncertainty about my own abilities. The mindlessness that I had felt in the initial stages of therapy with Jennie is reiterated here with her mother. My inability to make sense of her daughter's experiences leaves me feeling bewildered, doubting the usefulness of the work. However, in the subsequent meetings with Jennie, Jennie has brought the source of her anxieties herself; she is now the one in possession of a mind:

> Jennie says hello to the teddy in the room and comments that she loves soft animals. She tells me that her favourite animal is a teddy that she has had since she was a baby. She then reaches out her hands to me and shows me some marks. She says, 'They remind me of being a baby. My grandma said to me I was a miracle baby and everyone thought I might die. I was lucky to survive'.

Jennie continues explaining what it means to be premature:

> 'I was in an incubator to begin with and I had to be tube fed, that is why I have these scars on my hands. I will always have these'. Jennie

says she had to have an operation to separate her heart and her lungs. She points to her chest and says, 'There is a piece of metal in my lungs it is still there now and helps me to breathe'.

I am astonished and moved at Jennie's articulate, intelligent description of her early life and also puzzled that there has been no mention of her prematurity during the course of our work together. I arrange a further meeting with Jennie's mother to explore this some more. Mrs Brown says that she had told me about Jennie's premature start in life, and indeed looking back on the notes, this is stated. However, there is an unusual lack of detail in comparison to what I might usually ask; Mrs Brown's scant storytelling coupled with my own lack of curiosity are indicative that the material was too difficult to be told at this earlier time and too difficult to be heard. At this later stage Mrs Brown is able to tell me the story of her own childhood, pregnancy and Jennie's birth, and I have a mind that is more able to listen:

'When I was fourteen I was told I could never have children, that it was too dangerous because of having high blood pressure. Of course, when I got a bit older, the one thing I was told I could not have I wanted even more. When I was eleven I had been in intensive care for two months and I overheard my mum say that I had nearly died. I spent the next year terrified of dying'.

And Mrs Brown continues:

'When I was pregnant with Jennie, I was told that I would have to change the tablets I was on as my blood pressure was dangerously high. They told me that the new tablets would make the baby distressed and they would have to operate. They said they would try to save my life but the baby might die'.

As a child Mrs Brown herself encountered illness and a near-death experience. This seems to remain largely unprocessed by her and consequently, she has been unable to provide Jennie with the necessary containment that she has needed. Mrs Brown has been unable to provide a mind to metabolise Jennie's anxiety and for her to give these fears back to Jennie in a modified form that she can bear.

In addition, Mrs Brown and Jennie's premature separation happened before they were 'psychologically and physically ready' thus disrupting the gradual individuation process that is thought to take place between a mother and her baby during the second stage of pregnancy (Tracey, 2000). Following birth at full term, Tracey (2000) states that the mother holds the infant 'psychically in the womb of her mind'. Winnicott (1956) refers to the intensity of a mother's state of mind around this time as 'primary maternal preoccupation'. Winnicott (1956) suggests that primary maternal pre-occupation provides a 'protective shield' around the infant, protecting them from over-stimulation from the external and internal world. When a mother has been unable to carry their child to full term, as is the case for Mrs Brown, this shield is 'fractured' (James, 1960). Mrs Brown might have been left feeling that she was unable to protect her baby.

For Mrs Brown and Jennie, the 'state of safe being together' experienced when a baby is in the womb (Bion, 1962a; Tracey, 2000) was lost by Jennie's premature arrival. Tracey (2000) suggests that a mother of a baby whose existence is uncertain may 'dare not to know' their child, for fear of them failing to survive. The powerful experience of mindlessness evident throughout this work has its origins in Mrs Brown's own uncertain exist-ence and her inability to act as a mental container for Jennie's fears.

As well as Mrs Brown being unable to contain Jennie mentally, Mrs Brown is also unable to contain Jennie bodily (Alvarez, 2002). Instead, Jennie is reliant on artificial systems to sustain her existence (Lazar et al., 1997). Bick writes:

> The need for a containing object would seem, in the infantile unin-tegrated state, to produce a frantic search for an object . . . which can hold the attention and thereby be experienced . . . as holding the parts of the personality together. The optimal object is the nipple in the mouth, together with the holding and talking and familiar smelling mother.
>
> (Bick, 1968, p. 56)

Learning about Jennie's start in life enables me to understand more clearly Jennie's communications during our work together thus far. Hear-ing of Jennie's abrupt, premature arrival into the outside world and her fight for survival reminds me of an experience that has taken place several weeks previously and which up until this point I had been unable to process:

> Towards the end of the session Jennie asks to go to the toilet. She leaves the room and is absent for about five minutes. During her absence I forget as to why I am sat there. It is only on Jennie's return that I remember I am waiting for her.

In Jennie's absence, she completely drops out of my mind. The fear that Jennie feels at being forgotten about is re-enacted in the transference and is re-experienced by me in my counter transference response of feeling terrified and horrified at having forgotten about her very existence.

Jennie's hunger for knowledge

In the second year of therapy, Jennie's projections gradually become less persistent and destructive. Jennie is beginning to tolerate thinking about herself and what it means to feel different. She comments:

> 'I am not obsessed by Noel Gallagher like I have been, like when I used to bore you with all his songs'. I comment that I think she does not need him in the same way anymore, that she used to think about him to help her think about herself, about how she felt different and weird, but that now she could think about herself without Noel Gallagher. 'I need to fit in, you cannot sit in the corner with a sign saying: "I am lonely" all your life, you have to make an effort to fit in. I fit in maybe ten percent of the time'.

Jennie now moves to a deeper level of understanding, where she begins to explore the painful reality of having a learning disability:

> Jennie tells me she has watched the film 'The Wizard of Oz'. She says: 'My favourite character is the Scarecrow'. I reply, mistakenly, that Scarecrow has not got a heart. Jennie replies: 'No, he hasn't got a brain'.

Jennie's retort at my mistake hits me like a hard blow. I momentarily turn stupid. I am not able to think about Jennie's communication to me; that she is worried that she has something wrong with her brain. Even now, a long way in to the work, Jennie is able to project in to me powerful communications that are so overwhelming that they disable me, preventing me from thought. At this point Jennie holds on to her thought, she thinks about the meaning of her communication and she remains open to a painful state of mind. She is the one in possession of a mind (Bunenger, 1999). I ask Jennie what she likes about Scarecrow. She says:

> 'He is dumb sometimes. He has ideas but he doesn't realise he has thoughts in his head, like helping Dorothy escape from the witch's castle. My mum thinks the film is a waste of time, because they all had what they were looking for all along, but I don't think it is, because that's why the Wizard of Oz is there, to show him he has thoughts'.

Jennie's use of her objects has changed in the course of therapy parelleling a development in her capacity to think (Klein, 1930; Segal, 1957).

There has been a shift from Jennie using her objects in a concrete way (Noel Gallagher) to them being used as symbols (Scarecrow). In the same way that the Wizard of Oz helps Scarecrow make sense of himself, I serve as an 'emotional container' (Hinshelwood, 1994) for Jennie's projections.

> I ask Jennie how she might be similar to Scarecrow. 'I am stupid sometimes I suppose'. I wonder whether Jennie is thinking about what kind of brain she has. 'Pretty normal' Jennie says and she says she will try and guess my IQ. I say I don't know what my IQ is and that the average IQ is 100. Jennie says 'Wow! I bet Stephen Hawking has got a big IQ then because he is very clever. He is intelligent and disabled. I would like to know what my IQ is'.

Jennie has internalised an object that is capable of self-knowledge. The emergence of curiosity, Jennie's wish to know about herself and about her mind, is further evidence of a development in learning (Klein, 1931; Simpson, 2004). Miller (2004) writes of the low self-esteem she often finds in adolescents with a learning disability. She suggests that the adolescent might internalise what they see when they look in their parent's eyes, that is, of not having matched up to the mother's 'anticipated ideal' (O'Shaughnessy, 1999). For Jennie, at the start of the work, the presence of a 'harsh internal superego' is evident. Now, she can experience herself and think about herself, she has developed a helpful superego (Klein, 1931).

Conclusion

In my work with Jennie I have endeavoured to provide what Britton (1992, p. 104) has described as a 'bounded world (the container) where meaning can be found (the contained)'. From the senseless, mindless beginnings of therapy, sense is slowly created; what is once, in Bion's (1962a) analogy, indigestible, can now be digested. Jennie is now able to think about the beginnings of her existence and the meaning of therapy: 'Take that teddy over there. He started off life as just a piece of fabric and then someone stitched him together and made him in to a toy teddy'. Through the process of containment, Jennie is finding her own shape and character.

The importance of thinking, a fundamentally emotional process, is essential in every individual's development. For an infant with a learning disability, the task of 'knowing and being known' may be more difficult perhaps because of the mother's struggle to know the reality of her child and in turn the child's ability to face the reality of disability that they must inevitably bear (Simpson, 2004). In this chapter, I seek to convey the usefulness of using psychoanalytic concepts to understand the processes at work between a mother and an infant with a disability, by considering the nature of the relationship between the therapist and client. Through the experience of Jennie being known by me, her 'nurturing object' in therapy (Bion, 1962a), Jennie develops an internal space to be curious about her own mind and curious to know about the mind of others.

References

Alvarez, A. (2002) Failures to link: attacks or defects, disintegration or unintegration? In A. Briggs (ed.) *Surviving Space: papers on infant observation*. The Tavistock Clinic Series, Karnac.

Bick, E. (1968) The experience of the skin in early object relations. In A. Briggs (ed.) (2002) *Surviving Space: papers on infant observation*. The Tavistock Clinic Series, Karnac.

Bick, E. (1986) Further considerations on the function of the skin in early object relations. In A. Briggs (ed.) (2002) *Surviving Space: papers on infant observation*. The Tavistock Clinic Series, Karnac.

Bion, W.R. (1959) Attacks on linking. In W.R. Bion (1967) *Second Thoughts*. London, Karnac, pp. 93–109, 1984; first published (1959) *International Journal of Psychoanalysis*, 40, 308–15.

Bion, W.R. (1962a) *Learning from Experience*. London: Heinemann. Reprinted London, Karnac, 1984.

Bion, W.R. (1962b) A Theory of Thinking. In W.R. Bion (1967) *Second Thoughts*. London, Karnac, pp. 110–19, 1984; first published (1962) *International Journal of Psychoanalysis*, 43, 306–10.

Britton, R. (1992) Keeping things in mind. In R. Anderson (ed.) *Clinical Lectures on Klein and Bion*. London, Routledge.

Bunenger, J. (1999) Becky. Motive in her mindlessness: the discovery of autistic features in a learning disabled adolescent. In A. Alvarez and S. Reid (eds) *Autism and Personality: findings from the Tavistock Autism Workshop*. London, Routledge.

Elmhirst, S. (1980) Bion and Babies. *Annual of Psychoanalysis*, 8, 155–67.

Freud, S. (1917) Lines of advance in psycho-analytic therapy. In J. Strachey (ed.) *The Standard Edition of the Complete Psychological Works of Sigmund Freud*, vol 17. London, Hogarth.

Hinshelwood, R.D. (1994) *Clinical Klein*. London, Free Association Books.

James, M. (1960) Premature ego development: some observations on disturbances in the first three months of life. *International Journal of Psychoanalysis*, 41, 222–94.

Klein, M. (1930) The importance of symbol formation in the development of the ego. *International Journal of Psychoanalysis*, 11(1), 24–39.

Klein, M. (1931) A contribution to the theory of intellectual inhibition. *The International Journal of Psychoanalysis*, 12, 206–18.

Klein, M. (1935) A contribution to the psychogenesis of manic-depressive states. *International Journal of Psychoanalysis*, 16, 145–74.

Lazar, R.A., Ropke, C. and Ermann, G. (1997) *Learning To Be: on observing premature babies*. Tavistock Clinic Paper No. 211.

Miller, L. (1998) Psychotherapy with learning disabled adolescents In R. Anderson and A. Dartington (eds) *Facing It Out: clinical perspectives on adolescent disturbance*. Tavistock Clinic Series.

Miller, L. (2004) Adolescents with learning disabilities: psychic structures that are not conducive to learning. In D. Simpson and L. Miller (eds) *Unexpected Gains*. London, Karnac.

O'Shaughnessy, E. (1999) Relating to the super-ego. *International Journal of Psychoanalysis*, 80, 861–70.

Segal, H. (1957) Notes on symbol formation. *International Journal of Psychoanalysis*, 38, 391–7.

Segal, H. (1991) *Dream, Phantasy and Art*. The New Library of Psychoanalysis 12. London: Routledge.

Simpson, D. (2004) Learning disability as a refuge from knowledge. In D. Simpson and L. Miller (eds) *Unexpected Gains*. London, Karnac.

Sinason, V. (1992) *Mental Handicap and the Human Condition: new approaches from the Tavistock*. London, Free Association Press.

Symington, J. and Symington, N. (1996) *The Clinical Thinking of Wilfred Bion*. London, Routledge.

Tracey, N. (ed.) (2000) *Parents of Premature Infants: their emotional world*. London, Whurr Publishers.

Winnicott, D.W. (1956) Primary maternal preoccupation. In *Collected Papers: Through Pediatrics to Psychoanalysis*. London, Hogarth Press/Tavistock Institute of Psychoanalysis.

Chapter 10

Health anxieties within a family context

Clare White and Clare Jackson

Reason for referral

Following a visit to the GP, 13-year-old John was referred to the Child and Adolescent Mental Health (CAMH) service for help with anxiety about his health. The referral letter stated that John was showing numerous symptoms of physical illness and fears about having a terminal condition. The GP said that John's mother had a history of depression, but that there were no other family difficulties.

Assessment

John, an only child, came to the initial assessment appointment with his mother. His father did not come to the appointment due to work commitments. During the session John was very willing to talk about his problems although he appeared very anxious, particularly when talking about his fears, and kept trying to seek reassurance that he was okay. His mother would tend to calm him down by saying that everything was going to be all right.

John and his mother described John's fear of becoming ill or dying. John reported many long-standing fears about getting cancer, meningitis and MRSA, and also worries about dying violently, e.g. in a fire. As a consequence of these worries he frequently checked his body for lumps, rashes and changes, as well as seeking reassurance from his mother. Often this resulted in a trip to the family doctor, where some basic investigations such as blood tests had proved negative. John avoided hospitals, held his breath when he walked past someone who looked 'ill' and refused to eat in restaurants in case he got food poisoning.

He said he had thoughts such as 'I am going to die', 'I will have to go to hospital', and 'Other ill people are in hospital and I will catch something and die there'. John also said he imagined himself lying in a hospital bed dying.

John described having many physical symptoms of anxiety, for example, a racing heart, feeling sick, dry mouth and sweating palms. John stated that he was always anxious but his symptoms were particularly triggered by medical television programmes, magazine articles about medical conditions and lessons at school about health or illness. John reported that he 'always felt ill' and found it difficult to attend school if he felt sick, dizzy or panicky as he was scared he would become ill at school and be taken to hospital. As a result John's school attendance was poor, with many days off sick. His mother reported that she did not feel able to push John to go to school when he was distressed and anxious about his health, because she was unsure about whether he was unwell or anxious. John asked for frequent reassurance from his mother about his health and they would at times engage in lengthy discussions about different conditions and their symptoms.

The family had particularly noticed John's anxiety when his younger cousin had recently been admitted to hospital to have grommets fitted. John had been unable to visit her in hospital.

When John was at school he was average academically, but he was falling behind with his schoolwork because of the amount of time he was missing from school. He had some friends at school, but was losing touch with them because of his time off. He had few hobbies or interests and rarely went out of the house, preferring instead to sit in his room and listen to music.

Looking back to when John was younger, his mother reported he had had some difficulties going to primary school, but said that things had become more difficult since his move to secondary school. When John was 8 years old his grandmother needed an emergency operation. John had been arguing with her just prior to this and he said he blamed himself for her needing to go into hospital.

John's mother reported that he had developed normally with no concerns about any developmental milestones. When John was 10 he was referred to the CAMH service for abdominal pain. At that time, John was worried that his mother would become ill and not be able to look after him. Following the assessment and some management advice the pain improved and his mother did not want any further help.

When asked about his family, John said he lived with his parents. They had moved house about the time of John's previous referral, and he had had to change school. John remembered that it had been hard to make new friends at his new school. When we met with them, John's mother stayed at home, and his father worked long hours with frequent business trips abroad.

John's mother recalled that she had been depressed when John was 4 years old and she received help from adult mental health services. She had received intermittent help from mental health services since then, although she was currently well and not taking medication or receiving any support from services. She had been diagnosed with irritable bowel syndrome five years prior to the assessment and reported that flare-ups were triggered by stress, for example her stress about John not attending school. His mother said she was feeling baffled by John's worries: she tended to try to reason with John and allow him to avoid things when he felt distressed. His father was reported to find it hard to understand John and his anxiety, becoming angry when John refused to go to school.

Initial formulation: anxiety about illness, with safety behaviours

John presented with hypochondriacal anxiety as defined in the Diagnostic and Statistical Manual of Mental Disorder (APA, 2000). This defines hypochondriasis as the worry that one has a serious disease, based on the misinterpretation of physical symptoms.

John had become particularly sensitive (hypervigilant) to noticing television programmes, magazine articles, or people talking about illness, and these all made his anxiety worse. When anxious, John would experience numerous physical symptoms of anxiety, including feeling sick, having stomach ache, feeling hot and dizzy, shakiness, difficulty breathing and heart palpitations. When John noticed these symptoms, he assumed they meant that he was going to faint, die or develop a terminal illness. This assumption made him more anxious, which in turn increased his physical symptoms, and therefore he felt that he had to try to keep himself 'safe'.

Keeping safe involved avoiding certain situations, such as hot classrooms at school (in case they made him feel ill), seeking constant reassurance that he was healthy and developing many 'safety behaviours'. Safety behaviours are things that people do that they think keep them safe, but in fact they prevent them from seeing that they would have been safe anyway. In the short term safety behaviours appear helpful because they decrease the person's symptoms at that time. However, in the long term they help to maintain the problem by not allowing the person to realise that they would have been safe anyway, even if they had not carried out the safety behaviours. John's safety behaviours included sipping water at regular intervals and sitting near the window to keep cool (to prevent him fainting), and checking his body for lumps and rashes. Over time, John developed a strong belief that it was the avoidance and safety behaviours that kept him well, and he became increasingly reliant on them to cope with his anxiety.

In summary, as suggested by the cognitive model of hypochondriasis (e.g. Warwick and Salkovskis, 1990), a vicious cycle developed whereby John's avoidance and safety behaviours strengthened his belief that he would have become ill or died if he had not done something to prevent this. In turn, his hypervigilance led to him focusing more on his body and any normal bodily changes (for example those produced by his anxiety, such as a racing heart and feeling dizzy). These were misinterpreted as signs of serious illness, resulting in a further increase in anxiety. Salkovskis (1996) reports that the misinterpretation of innocuous bodily changes is a crucial component of hypochondriasis.

Initial treatment

The above cycle (the cognitive behavioural treatment model; CBT) was discussed with John and his mother. Diagrams and analogies were used to help John understand the maintaining role of his safety behaviours and avoidance. For example,

> There was a man standing on the street waving his arms up and down. When his friend asked him what he was doing, he replied 'Keeping the dragons away'. His friend objected 'But there aren't any dragons around here', to which the first man replied, 'See, that shows how well it works!' The person with [anxiety] may be a bit like this man – the [safety behaviours] serve to keep away non-existent dragons and also feed the belief that only [safety behaviours] will keep the dragons away. What is really needed is to learn that there are no dragons.
>
> (Westbrook and Morrison, 2003, p. 8)

John said that he found the analogies helpful and that he wanted to do something about the problem. He was relieved to find that there were other people who experienced similar fears.

Early sessions looked at why physical anxiety symptoms occur as part of the fight–flight response, how they are normal and do not lead to any significant harm.

As John appeared to relate to the CBT model, and was keen to work on reducing his anxiety symptoms, a CBT approach seemed helpful. As John was at an age when he should have been becoming more independent, he and his mother were keen for him to receive individual help, as opposed to family help, at least initially. It was agreed that his family would be kept up to date with occasional family review meetings. Therefore, a series of CBT treatment sessions were arranged. These sessions focused on thought challenging, reducing avoidance, reducing safety behaviours, and behavioural experiments to test out John's predictions.

Cognitive work

Thought challenging included identifying John's anxious thoughts, such as 'I have cancer' and asking him to rate how strongly he believed the thought (from 0 per cent belief to 100 per cent believing it). He was then encouraged to consider whether the thoughts were accurate or helpful, for example by discussing the evidence for and against the thought with questions such as what is my evidence that I do have cancer?; what is my evidence that I do not have cancer?; what would I say to a friend who was worried like this? He was then encouraged to consider all the evidence and re-rate his belief. John was surprised that his belief in the worrying thoughts actually decreased when he considered them in more detail.

Another way of looking at the worrying thoughts was through the use of probability pie charts. For example, initially John thought that if he became hot, he was unwell and would faint. He was asked to list all the possible causes of him feeling hot (e.g. it was a hot day, he had been running, he was anxious) and then on a diagram of a circle, divide it up according to the likelihood of each cause. Using this technique John was able to see that there were lots of possible reasons for him feeling hot, and that this did not necessarily mean that he was unwell.

A third technique involved using continuums, e.g. looking at whether there could be degrees of illness, rather than all illness resulting in death.

Exposure

John was encouraged to stop avoiding the situations that he found anxiety provoking (exposure), in order to see that he could cope in these situations without becoming ill. At first John was anxious about taking such risks, but he agreed to try some of his less-feared situations. For example, he agreed to stay in a hot classroom, without leaving the lesson, to see that he did not faint (which he feared would lead to him being hospitalised, catching an infection and dying).

Behavioural experiments

During the exposure work, John also agreed to stop some of the behaviours that he felt kept himself safe; for example, whilst staying in the hot classroom, John was to try not to drink his cold water, so that he could see that it was not the water that had prevented him from fainting. John found the exposure work very difficult. Whilst he remained in the hot classroom and stopped drinking water, his mother had suggested to him that sucking sweets might increase his sugar levels, thus preventing him from fainting. By doing this, whilst John stopped one safety behaviour, he substituted it with another.

Behavioural experiments were used to test John's beliefs (Bennett-Levy et al., 2004). In one experiment his belief that he would faint if he got hot and had to stay in the room was tested when John put on lots of layers of clothes and remained in a warm room to see what would happen when he became hot.

Some improvements in John's anxiety were noted over this time, e.g. his attendance at school improved, his belief that some of his symptoms were symptoms of anxiety and not serious illness increased and his avoidance of some situations reduced. There continued to be times when John's mother allowed him to stay off school, e.g. when his sister had a virus and John worried he might have it too.

Setbacks

After an initial period of improvement, the situation began to deteriorate and John reported an increase in his anxiety again. After the school summer holidays, he refused to return to school. This seemed to be related to one incident in particular. Over the school holidays John had been to stay with his aunt for a weekend. During this stay he had an argument with his aunt because he refused to eat chicken (due to a fear of salmonella food poisoning) and had to return home. In the following week his aunt was admitted to hospital for tests to determine whether her previously treated breast cancer had returned. John blamed himself for making his aunt ill by increasing the stress she was under.

John continued to engage in CBT sessions. However, around this time his mood lowered and he began to feel more anxious again. A gradual return to school was planned with close liaison between John, his parents, school and health professionals.

Reassessment

Having made progress initially, John was clearly experiencing difficulties maintaining this. It was interesting to note that John's anxiety had got worse during his time at home over the summer holidays and his symptoms had become increasingly obsessional. He would not eat any food that he had touched with his hands in case they had germs on and he would not drink from a cup in case it was dirty.

It had also been noted in the family review sessions that John's mother was particularly upset if John became distressed: she found it hard not to reassure him and would provide alternative safety behaviours to prevent John becoming anxious.

At the few sessions that John's father was able to attend, he said that he found it hard to understand John's worries and tended to leave it to his wife to deal with them.

The increase in John's anxiety and obsessional symptoms coupled with observations of how John and his mother interacted when he became anxious, raised the question of the family's role in the maintenance of John's anxiety. Discussion with John's mother highlighted that she also had similar worries about illness and death, relating both to herself and her children.

These worries led to her also having some safety behaviours and obsessional and compulsive-type symptoms, including only using one set of cutlery, washing all kitchen equipment in boiling water, spending a significant amount of time each day cleaning the house and ritualistic checking. The worries also made it hard for her to let her children go into situations that she perceived might be 'risky', e.g. at school, where she perceived that other children might have illnesses. When John stayed at home his mother was less anxious, because she could keep him safe. As a result she had some mixed feelings about him becoming more independent: whilst she wanted him to be less anxious, she liked knowing that he was safe at home.

John's mother had not talked about her worries previously as she did not perceive them to be a problem, and did not feel that they had a role in John's difficulties. Her own safety behaviours meant that she rarely felt anxious: she was so dependent on them, that they were second nature to her and she was not aware that it was the safety behaviours that prevented her from experiencing anxiety.

At about this time, John got a red mark on his arm, and his mother became extremely worried that he might have meningitis. She took him straight to the hospital and when she was sent home, she began repeatedly performing the 'glass test' to see whether the mark blanched, to continue to test for meningitis. Both John and his mother were extremely anxious at this time. Discussion of such incidents and their effect on John resulted in his mother starting to question her own role in the difficulties.

Reformulation

When this further information came to light it seemed that although the CBT model explained John's symptoms, the family context was also very important. John's anxious thoughts interacted with his mother's own worries and beliefs. For example, she would repeatedly offer reassurance to John that he was not ill, even if he had not asked, and when he did ask she would herself become anxious that he was not well. As a result, maternal and child anxiety would interact, with each interpreting physical symptoms as a sign that John was ill. This resulted in an escalation of anxiety in both John and his mother. As a consequence, John's mother found it very hard to support his treatment, because although she did not want him to be anxious, she also did not want to take the risk that he might become ill. As noted earlier, she also suggested alternative safety behaviours to John because she did not want him to become distressed. For example, when John was encouraged to stay in a hot classroom, she suggested to him that he should feel his forehead to check that he was not developing a temperature.

It was difficult to challenge some of John's anxious thoughts, because his mother had the same thoughts, so they were not perceived to be unrealistic at home. This is consistent with Carr who writes:

Where parents themselves have OCD which goes untreated, their obsessional conversation and ritualistic actions may validate the child's symptoms, and the child's behaviour may be maintained by a process of modelling.

(Carr, 1999, p. 483)

Through discussion with John's mother, it appeared that his father was finding John's difficulties increasingly frustrating. Whilst John's father was invited to family review sessions, he had not often been able to come because he had started to go away on longer business trips. He left most of the childcare to his wife and as a consequence, John's mother experienced an increased sense of responsibility for keeping her children safe, which seemed to be increasing her overall level of anxiety. It was also hard for John's mother to support John's reintegration into school, because she worried that he would become ill when he went.

Further treatment

From this reformulation, it was decided that it might be useful for John's mother to be offered some sessions focusing on her own anxiety. Following discussion with her about this reformulation, including her own role in the maintenance of John's anxiety, she asked to be re-referred to adult mental health services to look at her own anxiety. Alongside this it was agreed that she would also be offered some support as part of John's treatment. This work particularly focused on how she could support his ongoing therapy, for example by not providing reassurance (despite her own anxiety) and encouraging him to carry out his behavioural experiments. John's father was encouraged to attend these sessions to help John and to support his wife. The family was offered formal Family Therapy sessions to look at their relationships and the effect of these on the difficulties. However, they were not keen to accept these.

In parallel to this John continued with his individual sessions, using the CBT model and techniques mentioned earlier.

At the end of sessions John and one or both of his parents would be seen together, to agree joint goals for between-session homework, so that it was explicitly agreed what each would do for the next appointment.

Outcome

John's symptoms improved significantly once his mother's difficulties had been acknowledged, and they were being addressed both in her own therapy and in John's sessions. John worried less about becoming unwell, and his vigilance decreased. As John carried out more exposure and behavioural experiments, and showed less avoidance, he became less anxious; as he became less anxious, so he began to avoid fewer situations. Alongside this improvement, John's father reported feeling less frustrated and irritated by John's anxiety and more supportive of his wife.

At follow-up three months later, John had maintained this progress and he was attending school full-time. John's mother continued to find her own therapy useful. However, it was interesting to note that when John's anxiety significantly decreased, his ability to join in with peer activities increased (he started to go out with his friends most evenings). As a consequence John's mother reported that she experienced an increase in anxiety about his safety: the 'function' of John's anxiety at keeping him in safe situations was highlighted in discussion with her.

At a final follow-up session John reported increased confidence at dealing with his anxiety, and that he felt happier that he was becoming more independent. He felt that he did not need any more individual sessions. His mother continued to attend adult mental health services.

References

American Psychiatric Association (APA) (2000) *Diagnostic and Statistical Manual of Mental Disorder*, 4th edn, text revision. Washington DC: American Psychiatric Association.

Bennett-Levy, J., Butler, G., Fennell, M., Hackmann, A., Mueller, M. and Westbrook, D. (2004) *Oxford Guide to Behavioural Experiments in Cognitive Therapy*. Oxford: Oxford University Press.

Carr, A. (1999) *The Handbook of Child and Adolescent Psychology: A contextual approach*. London: Routledge.

Salkovskis, P. M. (1996) The cognitive approach to anxiety: Threat beliefs, safety seeking behaviour and the special case of health anxiety and obsessions. In P. M. Salkovskis (ed.) *Frontiers of Cognitive Therapy*, pp. 48–74. New York: The Guilford Press.

Warwick, H. M. C. and Salkovskis, P. M. (1990) Hypochondriasis. *Behaviour Research and Therapy*, 28, 105–118.

Westbrook, D. and Morrison, N. (2003) *Managing Obsessive-compulsive Disorder*. Oxford: Oxford University Press.

Chapter 11

Panic disorder in the context of family change and transition

Peter Appleton

Emily was 14 when she was referred by her GP with panic symptoms. Her symptoms began when she fainted at school, during what was then a very busy schedule of academic and sports commitments, towards the end of a summer term. In the hot atmosphere of a bus she fainted and was taken to hospital. She began to be fearful of faints, and sensibly began to reduce her commitments. However, during the summer vacation Emily began to feel tired, didn't want to eat, felt nauseous, and again felt at risk of fainting. During panic episodes she felt she was going to die. At the beginning of a new term in September, in a new school, Emily was fearful of fainting, particularly on the bus journey (otherwise, she looked forward to the challenge of the new school). Indeed during the first few weeks of school Emily felt nauseous in the morning, and felt tired and drained much of the time. These symptoms continued, together with difficulty getting off to sleep, nightmares, some lack of hunger, and some restriction of going out with friends.

Emily was experiencing formal panic attacks, involving palpitations, sweating, shortness of breath, feelings of choking, dizziness, fear of dying, hot flushes, numbness, hand-shaking, and visual aberrations (e.g. 'everything going colourful and outlined'). These occurred during the day, and at night. Emily had begun to be fearful of situations that might provoke these attacks, e.g. exercise, hot or airless rooms, and travelling on the bus. Despite these symptoms Emily had courageously continued to attend school, only taking time off when she was extremely tired.

On the Multidimensional Anxiety Scale for Children (MASC) questionnaire (March et al., 1997), Emily scored at clinically significant levels on physical/somatic anxiety, and on separation/panic, and very low on social anxiety (i.e. there was *no* primary problem of social anxiety). On the Achenbach Youth Self Report (YSR) (Verhulst and Van Der Ende, 2002), Emily scored above clinical threshold on 'internalising symptoms', with both anxiety and depressive features at this early stage of assessment.

In addition to formal panic, Emily had become very anxious. She found herself worrying in advance of many daily activities at school and home. Sleep was badly disturbed, and nightmares were not uncommon. Emily said that every night she would be 'thinking about everything, and planning my day ahead. I keep myself up by watching TV or tidying. Sometimes I'm scared to sleep'. Emily's concentration was much worse than before the panic episodes – something that worried her because she usually enjoyed school.

Emily's developmental milestones had been normal, she had enjoyed school, and was regarded as a bright and highly participative student. There had been no obvious or significant mental health problems until the recent first episode.

The only developmental risk factor that the parents could remember was her proneness to very occasional prototypic 'panic' episodes when she was younger – these were described as of very sudden onset and involving Emily 'going blue' and looking as if she might pass out. Three triggering stimuli were remembered – pain, a noisy jet passing over, and a family trip when her younger brother was temporarily 'lost'.

Emily was a bright and able student, who made a major contribution to family life; her mother described her as caring and helpful.

Family context

Emily's parents had been separated for three years. They had stayed closely in touch, and were both able to attend the first appointment for their daughter.

Emily had been living with her mother and stepfather since the separation, together with her brother (aged 11). There was a new member of the stepfamily – a busy and happy 18-month-old boy.

Emily saw her father every weekend – his new family included Emily's stepmother and two stepsisters, just a bit younger than Emily. No major problems were reported in either stepfamily.

When Emily was aged about 4 her parents separated briefly, a separation which Emily remembers as potentially 'final' from her point of view. During her middle childhood (i.e. age 5–12) both parents realised that the marriage needed to end, and when she was 11 the separation actually occurred. Emily remembers being both upset and relieved. She remembered providing 'listening support' to her father at this time.

Both Emily's parents came from families of origin with complex psychological difficulties – this left a shadow on their own experience, and led them to be hugely careful about protecting Emily and her brother from undue stress. They did everything they could to be open about family change and transition, both to the children, and to myself during the assessment period.

Emily's mother had experienced severe depression during the last few years, and had benefited both from counselling and medication. Her own mother had had depression.

Emily's father remembered that he had had some minor emotional problems as a child, but after Emily's birth he had experienced panic and somatic anxiety. He then had recurrent psychological difficulties, including further anxiety and depression. Both parents were currently psychologically well.

First formulation and early treatment

There seemed to be three central factors to take into account in constructing a formulation about Emily's difficulties: first, *family* processes, including uncertainties about potential separations/transitions when Emily was young, the family transition at age 11, family history of mental health difficulties (especially during Emily's childhood and early adolescence), but also the considerable strengths of collaboration between Emily's separated parents, and the stability of the two stepfamilies; second, the precise nature of Emily's current formal panic attacks and anxiety; and third, Emily's strengths in the areas of clear thinking and planning, abilities in school, and excellent peer relationships.

There had been some noticeable symptomatic improvement during the assessment period (three sessions over three weeks), and both parents noted particularly how Emily had *started to talk more easily* about her panic and her worries.

Several features of Emily's situation led me to suggest cognitive therapy (CBT) for the panic attacks and anxiety. First, Emily had very precise abilities in describing situations and problems during the assessment period. She was also remarkably reflective for her age, i.e. 'the capacity to understand one's own and other's behaviour in terms of underlying mental states and intentions' (Slade, 2005, p. 269). Second, there appeared, at this stage, to be no major *current* maintaining factors (i.e. for the panic/anxiety) in the family situations. Third, Emily had excellent friendships, with no maintaining factors in the peer or school context. Finally, the treatment outcome literature suggests that cognitive-behavioural interventions for anxiety (including panic) are a first line treatment (Ollendick and Seligman, 2006), although Birmahar and Ollendick note that 'the study of panic attacks and panic disorder in children and adolescence is truly in its own stage of early development' and 'randomised controlled trials with children and adolescents are lacking' (Birmaher and Ollendick, 2004, p. 326).

Emily had been pleased that during the assessment period (in which we had carefully logged detailed accounts of panic and anxiety experiences, and family history, with participation of both parents) her symptoms had slightly improved. She was highly motivated to overcome the symptoms (to the extent of continuing to attend school despite high levels of symptoms), and was keen to begin CBT. We went ahead initially with four individual sessions over a period of one month, in which we began more detailed assessment of specific panic episodes, and began 'psychoeducation' about anxiety and panic.

Several important aspects of Emily's life situation and history began to emerge during these four sessions. Her descriptions of the anxiety and panic episodes were, as before, extremely detailed and specific. But it became clear that Emily had learned to *suppress* the expression of the symptoms ('nobody knew'). In one anxiety episode, triggered by a hot room at a parents' evening at school, Emily started to worry about fainting, and her heart rate increased, but she continued to 'pretend to listen to the teacher'.

In another very severe panic and anxiety episode, triggered by worries about a flu-like illness in her 18-month-old stepbrother, she hid her emotional distress, then took responsibility for telephoning her father to explain what had happened ('I kept calm over the telephone'). She was unable to communicate to either of her parents her own very considerable alarm, which included anxiety about illness for all the family ('someone could die').

There were *two* themes that emerged from situational interpretation of panic and anxiety episodes: Emily was anxious either about implied illness in a family member (and potential loss through death), or about implied potential separation from a family member (e.g. if Mum or Dad need to move to another part of the country). In one episode, there had been a normal (on reflection) marital tiff, and instead of Emily being able to interpret this normatively she 'couldn't get it out of (her) head' that her mother and stepfather would split up, and the house would need to be sold. Of course, while this might be regarded as a catastrophic interpretation, it was based on real previous experience of marital separation, and its precursors.

Another emerging issue was Emily's increasing anxiety, within sessions, about discussing the physical symptoms of anxiety ('talking about breathing is scary'; 'I don't like to think about it'). Although this is entirely consistent with the cognitive model of panic (see Chapter 2), in which clients are known to have developed catastrophic interpretations of bodily sensations (and anxiety can be cued by discussions *about* bodily sensations), there was an additional factor present in Emily's communications to me. The additional factor seemed to be that she felt so unsafe *discussing* panic feelings that she became unable to think in her usual planful and reflective manner. She seemed silenced by the topic of somatic anxiety. The psycho-education did not lead to active discussion, because it was too painful to discuss anxiety and panic. Emily was not finding this stage of therapy useful, and was not able to 'stand back' from her anxiety about talking about anxiety. Clearly this was nothing to do with intellectual ability level. It was very important to note that she *was* motivated to courageously address these problems by continuing to attend school (exposure), and by using cognitive suppression.

By the fourth therapy session (Session 7) I was concerned that the formulation required revision, and that the type or mode of therapy might not be appropriate, at this stage.

A telephone call from Emily's mother a few days after Session 7 confirmed this position. Emily had told both her parents that she had 'felt like crying' during the last session, and had experienced high anxiety throughout the session.

A communicational second formulation and later treatment

Several aspects of the *process* of Emily's disclosure to her parents about her distress in therapy, the parental response to this, and the response by the therapist, were important in framing the second formulation (Hill et al., 2003). These therapeutic and family process factors were as important, if not more important, for progress in therapy, than was the information gathered during assessment. First, Emily had been able to discuss the anxiety she had experienced in therapy with (both) her parents; they had been able to contain this expression of anxiety, and had been able to telephone the therapist and explain calmly and clearly the nature of Emily's concern. This process replicated the healthy process occurring during *assessment*, during which the parents had felt that Emily was more able to discuss her worries *with them*, and there had been symptomatic improvement.

Second, the therapist was able to schedule an appointment for Emily and either or both parents during the same week, to support the containing work of the parents. Emily came with her father. Both the father and therapist emphasised how important it had been for Emily to communicate her distress to her parents.

Third, in this review session, we worked out together a different mode and frequency of therapy, reflecting the concerns expressed by Emily, and the emerging second formulation. Therapy would be fortnightly, rather than weekly. A parent would be present, unless Emily indicated otherwise. The mode would be less structured, and there would be no pressure to discuss matters that were, at this stage, too anxiety-provoking. Safety and security were key concepts throughout this stage of reformulation and redesign of the therapy.

Safety and security, and their opposites, had also been important emerging concepts during early therapy. These were somehow linked with silencing and suppression of emotion, and perhaps unspeakable anxieties, which may have developed during the ups and downs of family change and transition. The suppression of current expression of negative emotion might indicate a pattern of putting the goals and needs of others first, and not processing important and 'scary' emotions during early and middle childhood. How might this psychological pattern have arisen?

The literature on the impact of family transition, and on the impact of psychological difficulties in parents, suggests that children and young people can sometimes find themselves needing to act *in an adult/parent role*. Emily had already explained that she had provided emotional support to both parents at various times, and perhaps had supported her younger brother at the time of the parental separation. In addition to this very demanding role, Emily might have routinely had to bear in mind her loyalties to both parents, carrying large amounts of information, and requiring high levels of empathy. Typically some children and young people find themselves 'parent-watching', worrying about how each parent might be feeling. Children and adolescents can be tempted to give up their own wishes and plans. Emilia Dowling and Gill Gorell Barnes provide the following story about 'Jim':

> Jim had just transferred to secondary school when his parents separated. Mum wanted to move away and it was very difficult at the time to listen to Jim who desperately wanted to remain in his new school which he really liked. Jim was finding it difficult to voice his wishes, and it was necessary for one of us to speak on his behalf about the need for continuity in his education which we were then able to discuss during a family interview. The parents had not fully appreciated the strength of Jim's feelings, and even though mother was still determined to move it became possible to talk about the dilemma for the family and the consequences of the decision for each member of the family.
>
> (Dowling and Gorell Barnes, 2000, p. 93)

Current concerns about separations might of course remind young people of earlier, and more profoundly upsetting anxieties about separation and loss, occurring at a stage in development when cognitive and emotional resources were less well developed. In Chapter 1 we referred to Sharlene Wolchik and her colleagues' study of 8- to 12-year-old children who had experienced parental divorce within the previous two years (Wolchik et al., 2002). They found that a child's fear of abandonment consistently predicted anxiety and/or depression – fear of abandonment included anxieties such as: 'I worry that I will be left all alone'. It is reasonable to suppose that Emily might have experienced profound anxieties such as this, when she was younger. These might no longer be conscious, but might nevertheless influence her perception of family members' health, and of parental decisions about moving house.

A key part of the second formulation was therefore that Emily would benefit psychologically from being able to disclose and discuss worries and concerns with both her parents, and to be heard in a reflective manner (as had happened during the assessment period, and after the rupture in therapy). This would be developmentally appropriate for a teenager (especially one who was otherwise fully engaged in peer friendships and school-life), and would be in sharp contrast to the adult/parent role Emily had been taking for some considerable time. The 'restructuring' that seemed necessary would be in family communication patterns rather than in cognitions – cognitive restructuring, if appropriate, would need to wait.

The next stage of treatment began in Session 10 with Emily and her father. We discussed some successes in school, then some worries about a doctor's visit. Then half-way through the session, Emily's father gently asked his daughter if he could discuss something she had mentioned to him earlier in the week. Emily agreed. Her father explained in some detail exactly what Emily had said to him, checking repeatedly with her whether he was *correct* in his reporting. Family circumstances at home with Mum were such that they might need to move house, away from the area, and Emily would be faced with the decision about where to live (with implications for increased separations from one parent, siblings and friends, and with educational implications – a factor deeply important to Emily and her parents). In addition to this uncertainty, Emily felt that she needed to continue to provide support, repeating relationship patterns that would have to change if Emily was to come back on track with her adolescent development within the families, and address her panic and anxiety. In this turning-point session Emily was able to confirm that her father's reporting was accurate, and both Emily and her father showed understanding (reflective function) about the situation in the maternal household (Fonagy and Target, 1997; Hill et al., 2003; Slade, 2005). Importantly, Emily calmly explained that she had not felt anxious during this session, despite the topic of discussion.

In the same session Emily mentioned that she had talked with a friend about her panic attacks, and had discovered that the friend also experienced panic and anxiety. Emily felt that this discovery that she was 'not alone' was extremely important. Discovering the normality of anxiety, and gaining support via peer relationships, may sometimes be more powerful for young people than as a formal part of psychoeducation.

Two further sessions, involving Emily and each of her parents, allowed reflective discussion about Emily's own plans and goals, and a chance for each parent to think through Emily's position in each family, and what would happen if one parent had to move.

For Session 13, Emily asked to see me alone. She was expecting a house move to a different part of the country. She was feeling very anxious and 'grumpy' ('a bit confused'; 'don't know what is happening'), but did feel understood and heard. Telling someone how she felt had now become crucial, and was now possible, whereas previously she had always 'put herself last'. This house move, as it turned out, didn't happen, although both parents had to move locally over the next few months.

In the following session, with her father, Emily reported considerable symptomatic improvement (confirmed by her father), about 18 months after the original onset of panic symptoms. Panic episodes were much less frequent, and she had learned a variety of skills in managing anxiety (these skills had not been learned via conventional therapy-based psychoeducation, but rather via self-directed and friend-supported learning). Crucially, Emily was beginning to take up sports again, beginning new and interesting activities which would inevitably involve exposure to cardiovascular and respiratory sensations. Emily said she had discovered that 'terrible things don't happen' when heart rate increases (Clark, 1996). We repeated the YSR and MASC questionnaires. All measures were below clinical threshold.

Two months later Emily reported continued improvement, although some panic symptoms remained, and sleep was still poor (there was no nocturnal panic, and Emily reflected that her sleep had been poor before the first onset of panic episodes). However, her life had returned to normal, and she always felt able to discuss any worries she had.

Conclusion

Emily experienced severe panic attacks and anxiety at the age of 14. These difficulties were overcome during a period of 18 months. Emily's improvement was made possible by self-determination, responsive parents, and excellent friendships. Therapy provided a focus in which we could encourage Emily to feel confident in her own thoughts and feelings about what would be helpful, and what would not be helpful. Although Emily used CBT-related techniques in overcoming panic and anxiety (e.g. exposure, cognitive restructuring, normalising), these techniques were partly self-discovered, and actively supported by friends and family.

The process of therapy allowed Emily to experience new ways of communicating with her parents, freeing herself partly from the 'adult' role of problem-solver and empathiser in a post-divorce and stepfamily formation context. The rupture in therapeutic process (Safran and Muran, 1996) during the early stages of treatment allowed rapid revision of therapeutic modality, and reinforced the powerful protective, encouraging, and empathising role of both parents in understanding their daughter's developing voice.

References

Birmaher, B. and Ollendick, T. H. (2004) Childhood-onset Panic Disorder. In Ollendick, T. H. and March, J. S. (eds) *Phobic and Anxiety Disorders in Children and Adolescents: A Clinician's Guide to Effective Psychosocial and Pharmacological Interventions*. Oxford, Oxford University Press.

Clark, D. M. (1996) Panic disorder: from theory to therapy. In Salkovskis, P. M. (ed.) *Frontiers of Cognitive Therapy*. New York, The Guilford Press.

Dowling, E. and Gorell Barnes, G. (2000) *Working with Children and Parents through Separation and Divorce: The Changing Lives of Children*. London, MacMillan Press Ltd.

Fonagy, P. and Target, M. (1997) Attachment and reflective function: their role in self-organization. *Development and Psychopathology*, 9, 679–700.

Hill, J., Fonagy, P., Safier, E. and Sargent, J. (2003) The ecology of attachment in the family. *Family Process*, 42, 205–21.

March, J. S., Parker, J. D., Sullivan, K., Stallings, P. and Conners, C. K. (1997) The Multidimensional Anxiety Scale for Children (MASC): factor structure, reliability, and validity. *Journal of the American Academy of Child and Adolescent Psychiatry*, 36, 554–65.

Ollendick, T. H. and Seligman, L. D. (2006) Anxiety disorders. In Gillberg, C., Harrington, R. and Steinhausen, H. C. (eds) *A Clinician's Handbook of Child and Adolescent Psychiatry*. Cambridge, Cambridge University Press.

Safran, J. D. and Muran, J. C. (1996) The resolution of ruptures in the therapeutic alliance. *Journal of Consulting and Clinical Psychology*, 64, 447–58.

Slade, A. (2005) Parental reflective functioning: an introduction. *Attachment and Human Development*, 7, 269–81.

Verhulst, F. C. and Van Der Ende, J. (2002) Rating scales. In Rutter, M. and Taylor, E. (eds) *Child and Adolescent Psychiatry*, 4th edn. Oxford, Blackwell Science.

Wolchik, S. A., Tein, J. Y., Sandler, I. N. and Doyle, K. W. (2002) Fear of abandonment as a mediator of the relations between divorce stressors and mother–child relationship quality and children's adjustment problems. *Journal of Abnormal Child Psychology*, 30, 401–18.

Chapter 12

Gaining autonomy and independence, following earlier experiences of maltreatment and peer victimisation

Peter Appleton

Harry, aged 15, had come home early from school, looking forward to half-term. He set about cleaning his room. By 6 pm he felt unusually tired and went to sleep. He awoke next morning feeling unwell, but made himself go round to see a friend. After a short while he found himself wanting to go home. Back home he felt physically unwell and extremely anxious. He couldn't eat. Over several days the symptoms became worse. Gradually he started to feel depressed and suicidal. Friends told him to go to his GP. During a further week off school Harry started having panic attacks, with severe breathing difficulties, during which he thought he would die. He lost weight. He began to experience terrifying feelings of depersonalisation and derealisation (e.g. feeling as though he was standing next to himself, and feeling that other people and the world around him were not real). After further visits to the GP, Harry was seen by specialists at the local hospital who could find no physical basis for Harry's symptoms.

Somehow, Harry gradually went back to school. But after a further 9 months he went back to the GP and hospital, who recommended that he see a clinical psychologist. Although the extreme symptoms had diminished, he was still very anxious, and he was due to start college the following September. Now was the time to get control of the anxiety.

I first met Harry, now aged 16½, shortly after he had started college. He was experiencing high levels of somatic anxiety, moderate social anxiety, and had been unable to leave his home town since the original anxiety episode just over a year ago. He found himself worrying hypochondriacally about his physical symptoms, and he was very self-conscious in social situations and performance situations. The anxiety impaired his concentration and sleep, and he felt unable to sit still for long. Feelings of depersonalisation and derealisation still occurred.

On the Multidimensional Anxiety Scale for Children (MASC) questionnaire (March et al., 1997), Harry scored at clinically significant levels on physical/somatic anxiety, on separation/panic, and on social anxiety. On the Achenbach Youth Self Report (YSR) (Verhulst and Van Der Ende, 2002), Harry scored above clinical threshold on 'internalising symptoms', with anxious/depressed, withdrawn/depressed, and somatic complaints featuring at this early stage of assessment. On the YSR Harry also scored above-threshold on scales measuring social interaction problems, and attention/concentration difficulties.

Harry had thought a lot about the original anxiety episode and felt that there were two possible precipitating circumstances. A week or so before the episode Harry had met up with some friends and experimented with some cannabis for the first time. He remembers that he felt very odd and went to sleep on a park bench. When he woke he was shaking, felt high somatic anxiety, and the world felt unreal. He ran home and sat with his father, although he didn't tell him why. The feelings of unrealness were to return after the first anxiety episode.

The second factor was the gradual recognition of how difficult it was to adopt a gay identity. Harry had felt that he was gay since the age of 9 or 10, but it was only just before the anxiety episode that he had begun fully to contemplate telling family and friends. In fact, friends had started to ask, and this had placed him on the defensive ('like someone punching me in the face'). He felt ashamed, and felt he had not accepted himself. He had no gay friends, and felt ambivalent about homosexual life. Harry was also concerned that I would be disapproving and would dislike him because of his sexual orientation.

Looking back to when he was younger Harry identified a number of experiences that might have made him vulnerable to problematic anxiety, and in addition he was aware of family members who were prone to anxiety and other mental health problems. After domestic violence his parents had separated when he was 5 years old. There had been a dispute about who he should live with – a court recommended that he go to his father. His father had provided security, but had also been physically aggressive to Harry on a number of occasions when he was still young. Harry and his mother had gradually rebuilt a relationship, and there was now regular contact. Harry continued to live in his father's house, but he now had his own space and lived independently.

Although Harry lived independently, he viewed his father's presence in the house as a deeply important safety factor in his life, especially since the anxiety episode. Home was being near his father. Travel outside his home town was dangerous partly because he was away from his father. Yet, Harry also found holidays spent at home anxiety-provoking. His *ambivalence* about home reflected several factors.

- The attachment relationship with his father had included elements of both protectiveness and maltreatment – ambivalent attachment is known to be associated with lower confidence in exploration and independence (see Chapter 1).
- Home had been a safe place away from bullying at school.

- Harry remembered spending long periods in his bedroom when he was younger – feeling 'alone and isolated'.
- Harry's uncertainty and anxiety about declaring his homosexual identity to family and friends was perhaps particularly focused on what his father's response might have been.
- The anxiety episode had brought an additional level of safety-seeking to Harry's thinking and behaviour.
- Harry's life-stage of independence- and autonomy-seeking enabled him to consider some of the benefits of experiences away from home.

At school Harry had been exposed to bullying over many years, up to and including the last few years of secondary school, when he was taunted for appearing to be gay.

There was a history of mental health problems on both sides of the family – Harry's father remembered experiencing severe anxiety at the same age as Harry, and relatives of his mother had received psychiatric treatment for other mental health problems.

Although Harry had experienced a number of risk/vulnerability factors, he showed considerable strengths during psychological treatment. The major factor was that he had actively sought help at the same time as carefully choosing a further education course which would take him towards a chosen career goal. Both the way in which he used therapy, and the commitment he showed to his post-school education made it possible to address directly his personal and psychological difficulties. The course was by its nature deeply challenging to the anxieties Harry had about social and performance situations. The high background level of worry and somatic anxiety also made day-to-day life on the course extremely difficult during the early stages. And travel outside the immediate area was an integral part of the course – another challenge. Each of these difficult aspects was of course an intensive opportunity to deal directly with the anxiety – a naturally occurring, and personally chosen, 'exposure programme'. Importantly, bullying was over – college provided an accepting, non-homophobic, and enjoyable life with other young adults with similar interests. An additional strength was Harry's continued group of friends outside college. Finally, as therapy proceeded, Harry's optimism emerged as a key element of treatment success.

Psychological treatment took place during 26 one-hour sessions, lasting 12 months, with cognitive-behavioural homework conducted between sessions. Harry chose to use a cognitive-behavioural approach, after reviewing information available on the Internet about different types of therapy. He found the open, negotiated, client-driven, and collaborative nature of the therapy highly conducive to his personal goals. Harry found it possible to attend not only to current goals (which formed the primary emphasis of the therapy), but also to extremely upsetting autobiographical memories from earlier in his life. These memories tended to emerge during sessions in which we were reviewing current episodes of particularly active and psychologically demanding change. Harry was beginning to see a 'new self', and was able to describe previous traumatic family and school experiences as in a different time and place ('the past is the past').

In the early stages of therapy, we agreed a formulation based on the current concerns and goals, precipitating factors, vulnerability factors, and strengths, as described above. This shared formulation, in which Harry and I had a collaborative and open understanding of the unique and complex path leading up to Harry's anxiety, and the path towards new goals, was a vital step on the ladder of change.

The next step was to deepen Harry's understanding of how anxiety works. He read material I gave to him, but the key process seemed to be active checking out by Harry about his understanding of the powerful, varied, and persistent mechanisms of anxiety. After quickly grasping the nature of physical anxiety, and vigilance for 'threat' (social and physical), he began to gain an understanding of 'worry'. Initially he felt that worry (e.g. about upcoming events, or bodily symptoms, or what others are thinking) did provide him with preparation, guarantees of safety, and a form of control of his life. Then, on reflection, he noted the negative aspects of worry, and in particular the sense in which worry controlled him (rather than the other way round). We began to discuss living with uncertainty. Harry became a skilled observer of anxiety processes, and their alternatives.

This stage in therapy, of detailed observation and understanding of anxiety ('psychoeducation'), based on an individual formulation, paved the way for cognitive restructuring. 'Restructuring' sounds almost as if the therapist, or the client, is an engineer. A better metaphor would be that of the client as architect. The architect, in his or her own house, imagines a redesigned home, with the help of another architect, who has the benefit of standing outside. The *collaborative* nature of the process continues to be crucial.

One important idea is that the client realises that their 'automatic' interpretations of social or physical events are only one of several possible ways of reacting to those events. Harry had understood at an early stage that anxiety makes one overestimate threat, and catastrophise. We looked at this in relation to one of his core areas of anxiety – performance on stage. Harry's thoughts included: forgetting lines; and an upsetting event occurring just before going on stage, but being required to go ahead. His visual images included passing out on stage due to a panic attack, and forgetting lines (known, helpfully for panic sufferers, as 'corpsing'). Harry's feelings included feeling sick as he imagined these thoughts and images. In session Harry was able immediately to review (restructure) these thoughts and feelings, pointing out that anxiety and worry 'create problems' and may promote panic. He was then able to remember a successful event in school in which he forgot his lines (noting also that this happens to everyone, and is understandable) and chose to improvise. He also noted that normal anxiety happens during the first few lines, and gradually abates.

Another core area of anxiety for Harry was travel outside his home town, an integral part of his course. Harry, in imagining a coach journey with his peers, expected that he would experience a panic attack (estimated as 65 to 70 per cent likely). He imagined jumping out of his seat to try and get out of the coach, others responding critically, then falling to the floor and passing out. Part of the imagery at this point included being left on his own, a cognition which triggered autobiographical memories of events occurring when he was a young boy. We spent a little time reviewing the autobiographical memories, and then Harry returned to the present imaginary scenario on the coach, noting feelings of frustration, anger, and upset.

It was difficult for Harry to imagine alternative viewpoints concerning travel at this stage in therapy, but he did feel ready to tackle directly the cognitions associated with performance. He also felt ready to deal with the plethora of anxiety symptoms that arose at all times of the day, but especially at night, when he was trying to go to sleep. To use his words, Harry said 'Bring it on, I will cope'.

In sessions that were primarily focused on performance anxiety, Harry also updated me on travel cognitions. The previous session in which he had located upsetting autobiographical memories had been helpful, in his view, in acknowledging these connections. However, he had found himself unable to go on one important trip – at the point of getting on the coach he had felt that he was 'lining up for the death penalty', and imagined himself passing out on the coach. Meanwhile, performance anxiety was much less problematic, following active cognitive restructuring. He had felt less anxious than expected, and reported: 'I actually enjoyed it' and 'I love proving the anxiety wrong'. He was now seeking performance opportunities.

In Session 14 further specific autobiographical memories were triggered of physical maltreatment by one of his parents (at age 8 or 9), the involvement of Social Services, and less access to one parent. Harry *also* recalled periods of felt safety and security with both his (separated) parents. He found himself talking about safety, and its role in his current difficulties, particularly the severe anxiety about leaving his home town. We reviewed the six factors contributing to Harry's ambivalence about home, and conflict about 'leaving home' (see pp. 161–2). A seventh, and equally important factor came to light during this stage of therapy: Harry felt that his parents had rarely taken him outside their home town, and had been 'overprotective'. Harry therefore had had little experience of travel. School trips were rarely taken, perhaps because of the risk of bullying.

His primary overview about his memories of previous maltreatment, was: 'The past is the past, though' and 'I can forgive'. In what may have been a turning-point session, Harry expressed strong readiness to deal directly with the anxiety about travel.

Safety behaviours were the key to understanding anxiety about travel, and because Harry had accessed core personal cognitions about safety (and had declared his motivation to leave the past behind), he was now ready to challenge his own safety behaviours.

We planned an intensive programme of trips (outside his home town) by bus, train, and car for the summer months, largely to be done with family and friends, but with an eventual goal of going independently to a major city by train. These goals were intrinsically linked to the next year of his course, in which he would need to be able routinely to travel, and also independently to attend auditions for a future further training.

In parallel to the work on performance anxiety and anxiety about travel (and autobiographical work), we attended to physical relaxation. Muscular tension had been a feature of Harry's presenting anxiety difficulties. Harry found that progressive muscular relaxation was not only helpful in itself, but also made him aware (as part of psychoeducation and cognitive restructuring) of where in his body the greatest muscular tension was to be found.

Before the intensive period of travel exposure, we repeated the measures of anxiety and psychological functioning, to check out measurable change, and to identify areas of remaining concern. On the Achenbach YSR all previously above-threshold scores were now just below clinical threshold. On the MASC physical anxiety and social/performance anxiety had reduced considerably, but separation/panic had slightly *increased*, confirming that travel away from home was the key remaining area to address.

Before the summer vacation began Harry took the opportunity of travelling with his mother by car to a nearby town. As might be expected from the MASC data, he experienced considerable anticipatory anxiety, but when in the car he carefully 'processed' where they were travelling (i.e. not using tunnel vision – not 'let's get this over with'), and enjoyed the visit. This motivated him to continue planning the summer trips in detail, with friends. He planned to stay over at a friend's house out of town, and used a session to review his severe anxieties (and rehearsals of safety behaviours) about being away from home overnight – needing to know exits from the house, needing to know the time of the first train in the morning. Anxiety about expected breathing difficulties and passing out were discussed, as were worries about becoming ill, and access to the nearby hospital. Harry's heart-and-mind understanding of the meanings of these thoughts, developed during the previous 8 months, enabled him to regard them as unhelpful (but understandable) cognitions, driven by anxiety.

During this period, Harry started talking about optimism, and how he felt that he was becoming his own person, unique, and able to find a way through the difficulties, and becoming more independent as a young adult. At the same time he had begun to go to a gay bar.

Meanwhile, intensive work on performance anxiety had paid off. At the end of the first year at college, musical performances had gone well.

Although he was experiencing some significant anxiety (including breathing difficulties), and images of going home, before performances, he was able to think clearly about the upcoming performance, and enjoy being with friends. 'Panicking but happy!' Anxiety during musical performance was no longer viewed as a significant problem.

The summer vacation (sessions 20–24) allowed Harry to focus primarily on travel exposure, while also engaging in a busy summer musical theatre performance project (thus maintaining progress in social and performance experience). Travel outside the home town was by bus, train, and car. Some journeys were planned – others were spontaneous. These were with a variety of friends, and family. While he was mostly accompanied, towards the end of the vacation Harry took the train to London by himself. Harry used sessions to review detailed and specific aspects of the travel experience. A key aspect of this was Harry's sense that he was less worried *about* the anxiety that did occur, both before and during journeys. He felt 'one step ahead'. And on some journeys there was no anxiety.

He also found himself talking in detail about his strong sense of new-found independence. Harry frequently compared his previous self with the 'new self': the new self included plans for the future which would involve moving away from his home town. He felt less anxious about his gay identity. The bullying he had experienced in school was 'in the past', and 'the chapter had closed'. Feeling accepted by peers in college had allowed Harry to feel more at ease with his emerging self.

He was confident that the second year of college would be more enjoyable than the first year. Two final sessions, during the new term, allowed us to review progress, and ensure the ending of therapy was constructive for Harry. The first week in college turned out to be extremely demanding, busy, and stressful. In session Harry was able to reflect on his new capacity to ride the storm of such a week, however difficult. A key part of his experience was a renewed enjoyment of day-to-day life, feeling 'mellow', noticing the absence of 'paranoia' when with friends. Harry felt stronger, and with more 'life skills'. He felt a powerful 'sense of control' – interestingly we had not used this phrase in therapy – so strong that he felt he could overcome any threat. Finally he experienced a 'buzz' at overcoming the anxiety.

References

March, J. S., Parker, J. D., Sullivan, K., Stallings, P. and Conners, C. K. (1997) The Multidimensional Anxiety Scale for Children (MASC): factor structure, reliability, and validity. *Journal of the American Academy of Child and Adolescent Psychiatry*, 36, 554–65.

Verhulst, F. C. and Van Der Ende, J. (2002) Rating scales. In M. Rutter and E. Taylor (eds) *Child and Adolescent Psychiatry*, 4th edn. Oxford, Blackwell Science.

Part 3

Chapter 13

Conclusion

Peter Appleton

This book has focused on complex child and adolescent anxiety in developmental and social context. Part 1 provided a developmental framework for thinking about anxiety in context, outlined the current categories of anxiety disorder (emphasising their frequent co-occurrence with each other, and with other disorders), and discussed ways of helping children experiencing problematic anxiety.

Part 2 looked, via case studies, at nine real-life contexts (see Table 13.1 to cross-reference children's pseudonyms with chapter numbers).

In concluding, I want to draw attention to two themes evident throughout the book:

- the relevance of a developmental framework (see Chapter 1 and Box 1.1);
- the importance of addressing the many meanings of 'safety' and 'security' when working with children's anxieties and fears – in particular the relevance of David Trickey's pyramid model of PTSD treatment (see Chapter 4 and Fig. 4.3) to more general formulation with anxious children and adolescents.

The relevance of a developmental framework

Many of the children in our case studies had complex histories and present circumstances – and complex anxiety. Individual assessment, formulation and treatment took these factors carefully into account. For none of the children could it be said that there was a single cause of the presenting anxiety. Jason's anxiety, for instance, became understandable once one understood his multiple moves of residence before the age of four, his witnessing of domestic violence, his six different foster homes and five different schools between age 4 and 10, and his profound uncertainty about his planned move to a permanent foster placement. Billy, with a diagnosis of Asperger's Disorder, experienced not only the anxiety of social interactions, but also co-occurring Obsessive-Compulsive Disorder. Multimodal

Table 13.1 Pseudonyms, by chapter number, context and age

Chapter number	Context	Pseudonym of child/young person	Age
4	Experiencing refugee status after trauma	Jyrgen	9
5	Change of foster family for a looked-after child	Jason	11
6	Prevention of anxiety after traumatic accident	Alice	4
7	Anxiety and behavioural difficulties	Liam	8
8	Anxiety and Asperger's Disorder	Simon	14
		Billy	10
9	Anxiety and learning disability	Jennie	14
10	OCD and parental mental health problems	John	13
11	Health anxiety and family context	Emily	14
12	Gaining autonomy in late adolescence	Harry	16

therapies (i.e. multiple therapies to address several aspects of difficulties [Connolly and Bernstein, 2007]) were helpful for both Jason and Billy – Jason benefited from play therapy and family/systemic therapy, Billy was helped by medication and specialised cognitive-behaviour therapy.

The wider social or institutional context of the child's difficulties was evident in several cases: Jyrgen from an asylum-seeking family, Alice in hospital after a traumatic accident, and Liam out of school after permanent exclusion from a primary school. In order to understand the nature of the child's anxiety, therapists had to attend carefully to the family's cultural, linguistic and social context. For Alice, prevention of problematic anxiety demanded careful attention to the institutional context of a hospital. For Jyrgen and his family, the role of the interpreter as cultural consultant to the therapist was important (Falicov, 1995).

Risk and resilience factors featured in the case study formulations. Resilience processes became crucially important during therapy, sometimes emerging more clearly after many weeks of therapy. During therapy Harry gradually identified optimism as a key part of his personality – motivating him to work positively with high levels of anxiety and multiple risks in his history. Resilience was evoked for Jason in his relationships with his foster-parents. Simon and Billy benefited from treatment approaches which took advantage of their strengths (e.g. interest in rules and ordering).

A detailed understanding of attachment history, in the context of wider family relationships, was central to the formulations for Jason, Liam, Jennie, Emily and Harry.

Relationships with peers featured in many of the cases. Jason and Liam were aggressive with peers; Simon was bullied. Good relationships with peers were important for Emily; new opportunities to forge good peer relationships were central to Harry's developmental pathway – after several years of being bullied.

The child's sense of his or her developing self was central to the formulation, or to the evolving content of therapy, for many of the young people – from the youngest, Alice, who was helped to accommodate to a traumatically changed physical self, to the eldest, Harry, whose self-goals defined the timing and direction of therapy.

Each case study is a snapshot in time. Many of the children, parents and carers were able to use therapy to reflect on autobiographical pathways 'so far'. And, of course, to envision the future.

The importance of safety and security

Anxiety, as we saw in Part 1, is concerned with safety and security, as well as detection of specific threats (Rachman, 2004). Insecure or disorganised attachment relationships act as risk factors for anxiety disorders (and secure attachments to specific caregivers act as protective factors). Trauma or abuse may lead a child to feel extensively unsafe, searching and scanning for safety. And behavioural inhibition or anxious apprehension leads a child to seek clues to safety, as well as danger.

David Trickey's layered pyramid model (see Fig. 4.3) is helpful in thinking about the establishment of increased safety in a child's life, and in therapy, as essential conditions (or pre-conditions) for psychological treatment of complex anxiety.

Stabilisation

Early work with Jyrgen focused on helping the family establish daily and predictable routines, and on clarifying confidentiality arrangements. There was close attention to the family's accommodation, schooling, finance and asylum status. For Jason, an initially tenuous stabilisation occurred through his understanding of plans for a permanent foster care placement – stabilisation work continued throughout the therapy. Alice's medical condition required stabilisation, together with predictable routines in the hospital, and availability of her parents around her. Liam, during the assessment phase, was offered a place in a school which welcomed children with behavioural special needs. Harry, in late adolescence, had provided a contribution to his own stabilisation by registering on a further education course consistent with his goals for a career, and the overcoming of his problematic anxiety.

Family work (and broader system)

The importance of family involvement at all stages of work with children and teenagers with anxiety difficulties has been clearly emphasised in the literature (Barrett, 2001). The specific contribution of the pyramid model is to draw our attention to the role of family work as a precursor to therapeutic work with the child, where necessary. For Jyrgen, carefully negotiated work with his father led to a reduction in Jyrgen's exposure to televised images of war. In addition, consultation and advice were provided to the school. Jason's foster family, and the professional network, received highly focused systemic help as a prelude to child therapy. Alice's family were a key focus of the detailed early stages of preparation for help for Alice. Liam's new school constructively joined the system of help for him during the assessment phase. In most of the other cases active family involvement was integral and important at various phases of assessment and treatment.

Work with John illustrated clearly the role of within-situation safety behaviours in maintaining health anxieties (see Chapter 1, and see Harvey et al., 2004, p. 254). Family work was essential in unravelling the social learning processes, and then providing a revised formulation.

Therapeutic context

Many child mental health practitioners consider the therapeutic relationship to be the most important determinant of treatment success (Green, 2006; Kazdin et al., 1990). Alan Carr states: 'All other features of the consultation process should be subordinate to the working alliance, since without it clients drop out of assessment and therapy or fail to make progress' (Carr, 1999, p. 113). It is therefore for good reason that the therapeutic context is a major building block in the pyramid model of treatment of children's PTSD (see Chapter 4). It was also an explicit factor in several of the other case studies in Part 2.

For instance, Harry was initially unsure whether his therapist might be critical of his gay identity, and Jennie was concerned to know whether her therapist liked her. Work had to proceed in a paced manner, in order for the young person to build trust. The young person's sense of trust in the therapist can break down at any point in the course of therapy – so-called 'ruptures' in the therapeutic alliance.

Ruptures occurred mid-way through therapy for Emily and Jennie. In Emily's case the rupture helped her and her family to revisit and review the methods and goals of therapy. Ruptures can occur 'when therapists unwittingly participate in maladaptive interpersonal cycles, that resemble those characteristic of patients' other interactions, thus confirming their patients' dysfunctional interpersonal schemas' (Safran and Muran, 1996, p. 447). Awareness of these processes is taken to a high level by psychoanalytically trained practitioners, who use the therapeutic relationship, not just as a crucial building block, but as the primary engine of change. Work with Jennie provides a clear example of this type of work (see also Jason's individual work, albeit not in a psychoanalytic therapeutic context).

Jennie's sense of safety or security had been severely compromised during infancy. This experience was enacted within the containing and safe context of therapy, allowing Jennie to express and communicate her extreme anxiety. The safety of the therapeutic context allowed her to 'think' and find meaning.

Each of the therapists endeavoured to be attuned to the young person's experience – providing security by recognising the feeling state of the child or adolescent.

Resource development

In the pyramid model, 'resource development' refers to help directed towards the child's psychological capacity to manage symptoms, feelings and mental images (see Chapter 4). It includes elements of psychoeducation and relaxation. For Jyrgen this was a detailed and important phase, including group work, preparing him for the exposure phase of therapy.

Billy's use of an anxiety thermometer and his elaboration of his cartoon-drawing skill, were important and motivating preparatory resource development activities which made exposure work possible.

Work with Simon and Billy was made possible by an understanding of the complex impact of Asperger's Disorder on social anxiety processes – leading specifically to resource development activities.

Resource development became a major part of the early intervention for Alice, providing information about her condition, and aspects of treatment, via a doll and jig-saws, which helped motivate her to communicate anxieties and questions through developmentally appropriate means.

Exposure and cognitive restructuring in the context of other levels of security-building

In the pyramid model, exposure and cognitive restructuring – critical steps in psychological treatment of PTSD – are *made possible* by the building up of skills, and communication of experience, during the earlier phases of security-building stabilisation, family and wider system involvement, attention to the therapeutic relationship and psychological resource development.

It is implicit in the model that a child may revisit 'earlier' phases. In fact, reluctance to engage in exposure and cognitive restructuring might alert the therapist to the possibility that further work is necessary 'lower down the pyramid'. For instance, when Emily was unable to consider thinking about and describing her panic experience, it alerted the therapist to consider both stabilisation and family processes. A similar perturbation occurred for John, alerting the therapists to revisit family process.

For Jason, Alice and Jennie, active work at several of the other levels (of the pyramid) had to continue throughout therapy, in order to make it possible for the young person to feel safe enough to address core anxieties, and/or to explore new grounds for self-development and self-reliance.

In conclusion, David Trickey's pyramid model (see Fig. 4.3) does appear to be helpful in formulating increased safety in a child's life, and in therapy, as essential conditions for psychological treatment of a range of different complex anxiety difficulties.

Finally

In each of the vignettes outlined at the beginning of Chapter 1, and in most of the case study chapters, anxiety, fear and other psychological difficulties existed as part of a complex background and time-line of previous, current and possible future contextual factors. These contextual factors clearly needed to be borne in mind when trying to understand the nature of the young person's anxiety, and when planning treatment, or when planning a preventive strategy.

References

Barrett, P. (2001) Current issues in the treatment of childhood anxiety. In M. W. Vasey and M. R. Dadds (eds) *The Developmental Psychopathology of Anxiety*. Oxford, Oxford University Press.

Carr, A. (1999) *The Handbook of Child and Adolescent Clinical Psychology: A Contextual Approach*. London, Routledge.

Connolly, S. D. and Bernstein, G. A. (2007) Practice parameter for the assessment and treatment of children and adolescents with anxiety disorders. *Journal of the American Academy of Child and Adolescent Psychiatry*, 46, 267–83.

Falicov, C. J. (1995) Training to think culturally: a multidimensional comparative framework. *Family Process*, 34, 373–88.

Green, J. (2006) Annotation: the therapeutic alliance – a significant but neglected variable in child mental health treatment studies. *Journal of Child Psychology and Psychiatry*, 47, 425–35.

Harvey, A. G., Watkins, E., Mansell, W. and Shafran, R. (2004) *Cognitive-behavioural Processes across the Psychological Disorders: A Transdiagnostic Approach to Research and Treatment*. Oxford, Oxford University Press.

Kazdin, A. E., Siegal, T. C. and Bass, D. (1990) Drawing upon clinical practice to inform research in child and adolescent psychotherapy: a survey of practitioners. *Professional Psychology: Research and Practice*, 21, 189–98.

Rachman, S. (2004) *Anxiety*. Hove, Psychology Press.

Safran, J. D. and Muran, J. C. (1996) The resolution of ruptures in the therapeutic alliance. *Journal of Consulting and Clinical Psychology*, 64, 447–58.

Index